Scottish
Traditional Recipes
A Heritage of Food & Cooking

Scottish
Traditional Recipes
A Heritage of Food & Cooking

Capture the tastes and traditions with over 150 easy-to-follow recipes
and 700 stunning photographs, including step-by-step instructions

Carol Wilson and Christopher Trotter

Photography by Craig Robertson

LOMOND

Notes

Bracketed terms are intended for
American readers.

For all recipes, quantities are given in
both metric and imperial measures and,
where appropriate, measures are also
given in standard cups and spoons.
Follow one set, but not a mixture,
because they are not interchangeable.

Standard spoon and cup measures
are level.
1 tsp = 5ml, 1 tbsp = 15ml,
1 cup = 250ml/8fl oz

Australian standard tablespoons are 20ml.
Australian readers should use 3 tsp in
place of 1 tbsp for measuring small
quantities of gelatine, flour, salt etc.

Medium (US large) eggs are used
unless otherwise stated.

Nutritional information

The nutritional analysis given for each
recipe is calculated per portion (i.e. serving or item), unless otherwise stated. If
the recipe gives a range, such as Serves
4–6, then the nutritional analysis will be
for the smaller portion size, i.e. 6 serv-
ings. Measurements for sodium do not
include salt added to taste.

This edition is published by Lomond Books
36 West Shore Road
Granton
Edinburgh EH5 1QD

Produced by Anness Publishing Ltd
Hermes House is an imprint of Anness Publishing Ltd
Hermes House, 88–89 Blackfriars Road, London SE1 8HA
tel. 020 7401 2077; fax 020 7633 9499
info@anness.com

© Anness Publishing Ltd 2006

A CIP catalogue record for this book is available from
the British Library.

Publisher: Joanna Lorenz
Editorial director: Judith Simons
Senior editor: Jennifer Mussett
Photographer: Craig Robertson
Home economist: Emma MacIntosh
Stylist: Helen Trent
Designer: Nigel Partridge
Illustrator: David Cook
Editorial reader: Rosie Fairhead
Production manager: Stephen Lang

10 9 8 7 6 5 4 3 2 1

Contents

The flavours of Scotland   **6**

The first settlers   8

The clan system   10

Foreign influences   12

Life in the Highlands   14

Life on the Islands   18

Life in the Lowlands   22

The Scotch whisky distilleries   24

The smokehouses   26

The king of fish – salmon   28

Feasts and festivals   30

Quality foods for the future   34

The Scottish kitchen   **36**

Fresh fish   38

Smoked fish   40

Fresh shellfish   42

Game's rich flavours   44

Scotland's quality meats   48

Dairy and cheese   50

From hedgerow and orchard   52

Wild mushrooms   54

Vegetables from the kitchen garden   56

Oats and barley   58

Bannocks and bread   60

A wealth of cakes   62

Scotch whisky   64

Breakfasts   **66**

Soups   **80**

First courses   **92**

Fish and shellfish   **110**

Meat and venison   **138**

Poultry and game   **162**

Side dishes   **180**

Desserts   **196**

Breads and baking   **216**

Preserves, relishes and sauces   **230**

Drinks   **242**

Index and Publisher's Acknowledgements   252

The flavours of Scotland

Scotland's magnificent culinary heritage has a long and illustrious history. The heather-clad moors and dense forests that covered much of the land ensured a plentiful supply of game; the seas, rivers and lochs teemed with fish; beef, dairy cattle and sheep thrived in pastures; wild fruits, berries and aromatic herbs were gathered from fields and hedgerows; while the cold, wet climate proved ideal for oats and barley.

Below *Scotland is often carved up into three distinct areas: the rugged Highlands that dominate the northern half of the country, the bustling towns and cities of the Lowlands, and the remote, dramatic Islands that lie to the north and west.*

The flavours of Scottish cuisine to this day reflect the rugged, hardy landscape. The wild mushrooms and berries complement the rich game meats, such as venison, wild boar and grouse. The smokehouses add a sumptuous taste to salmon, trout and haddock, and have resulted in local delicacies, such as Arbroath smokies and kippers.

Scottish cuisine has undergone a major progression during the past few decades, integrating new ingredients and concepts into the traditional fare. There has been an explosion of excellent restaurants offering superb dishes using local ingredients. Cottage and artisan industries have produced a wealth of speciality foods, such as jams, cheeses and breads.

A turbulent history

Scottish cuisine has been shaped not only by geography and climate but also by various social, cultural and political events. Its development was closely interwoven with the country's turbulent history – the threads producing a rich tapestry of flavours and traditions.

Over the centuries foreign invaders and settlers, particularly those from Scandinavia, had a powerful influence on Scotland's developing cuisine. The earliest impact was from the Vikings, whose lasting contribution was to teach the Scots how to make use of the rich wealth of the seas. Trade with overseas markets through Scotland's busy ports introduced new ingredients such as spices, sugar, dried fruits and wines to the Scottish kitchen. Politics too had a major role: the Auld Alliance with France, intended to curb the dynastic ambitions of English monarchs, had a great and lasting effect on the national gastronomy. All these influences brought new foods, cooking methods, ideas and skills, which over time became part of Scottish culture. Exposure to such influences occurred throughout the country's history to result in a rich and colourful cuisine based on high-quality Scottish produce.

A harsh landscape

Scotland is well known for its dramatic mountains, lochs and beautiful scenery. The geographical differences have also had a major role in shaping Scotland's cuisine and have resulted in different regional specialities according to the particular landscape and climate. The austere, rugged grandeur of the Highlands is the natural habitat of game birds, deer, rabbits and hares. The lush fertile land of the rolling countryside of the Borders and Lowlands supports beef and dairy cattle, sheep and goats while fruit and

Right Fishing boats bring in excellent shellfish for restaurants, seen here in Tobermory on the Isle of Mull.

berries thrive in the rich soils of Tayside and Fife. The islands, lochs and rivers are home to a flourishing fishing industry which exports fish and shellfish all over the world.

Traditional favourites

The Scots have always made the most of their natural resources and magnificent produce and are careful to preserve their time-honoured heritage dishes. Aberdeen Angus beef, Highland game, Tayside berries, salmon and other fish and shellfish and of course Scotch whisky are recognized as the finest in the world.

The old traditional favourites remain popular: haggis is still widely made and is often served with "neeps and tatties" (turnips and potatoes). In addition to national foods, every region has its own unique specialities, such as Forfar

Below The art of quality whisky making has made Scotland one of the world's leading producers.

Bridies, Selkirk bannocks, Arbroath Smokies, Loch Fyne kippers, Orkney, Islay and Galloway cheeses, Dundee cake, Moffat toffee, Edinburgh rock and a host of other delicious and much-loved delicacies that have been enjoyed for generations.

New speciality foods

A new generation of innovative and talented chefs has led something of a revolution in Scotland's restaurants, creating imaginative menus using Scottish produce, featuring many new and exciting signature dishes. Old favourites are given a modern twist and appear on many menus alongside traditional dishes. Restaurants in Edinburgh and Glasgow in particular blend Mediterranean with contemporary Scottish cuisine, and modern establishments serve dishes that fuse Middle Eastern and Far Eastern dishes with natural Scottish ingredients and flavours.

Food producers have also developed over the last decades, focusing on speciality quality foods, such as smoked salmon and whisky marmalades. Organic and free-range produce is increasing in popularity, with many farmers' markets springing up to promote cottage industries.

The first settlers

The early Neolithic settlers inhabited the land from around 4000–3000BC, coming from France and the Iberian peninsula. They cultivated cereals and used grinding stones to make flour. They fished and hunted for food, collected shellfish from the beaches, and also kept sheep, cattle and goats.

From 2500–700BC the Beaker People from Northern and Central Europe settled, bringing bronze tools and cooking pots and thereby starting Scotland's Bronze Age, altering the cooking and eating habits of the population. Their bonding into various tribes eventually formed a group known as the Picts (painted people), named by the Romans after their body paintings.

The Celts from Ireland

The Iron-Age Scot Celts came over from Ireland around 750BC. They came from today's Northern Ireland, where land shortages forced them to cross the Irish Sea to seek further pastures. The Celtic society was broken up into a caste system made up of warriors and Druids (the magicians, brehons, bards and seers), whose mystic beliefs were grounded in natural law. The Druids

Above *The Neolithic settlement of Skara Brae in Orkney, where evidence of cooking and household arrangements can be seen.*

performed rituals to assure the success of the hunt and the fertility of the tribe, the beasts and the land.

The Scots, as these Celts from Northern Ireland were called, brought with them the plough, horse-drawn wheeled carts and musical instruments. They lived in settlements, reared cattle

and sheep, and grew crops, most commonly oats, kale, cabbage and other hardy vegetables. Many used oats in soups and stews, and made oatcakes, which were originally cooked on hot stones and later on iron griddles (from the Gaelic *greadeal* meaning "hot stones").

The Celts left no written records but we know from ancient Roman and Greek writings that they ate little bread but great quantities of fish, meat and dairy produce. They farmed the land and grew oats, barley and vegetables such as peas, beans and cabbage, and also enjoyed wild herbs and fruits such as apples, pears, cherries and berries. They kept pigs, cattle, sheep and goats and depended on their livestock for food much more than they did their crops. Fossil records of mussel and oyster shells show that seafood was also part of their diet. The Celts roasted their food and also stewed meat and fish in pots suspended over a fire. Preservation of food was important and

Left *A replica Iron-Age crannog stands on Kenmore Loch. A large family or clan would have been able to live here in times of danger, surviving on stores of dried and smoked foods.*

meat and fish were salted to keep during the long winter months. Wild honey was collected and used to sweeten food and also to make mead.

The Viking raids

The 9th century was characterized by numerous Viking invasions, and Scotland became a melting pot of languages, cultures and foods. The Hebrides, Orkney and Shetland were ruled by Norway for a number of centuries, with the Hebrides passing over to the Scottish crown in 1266 and Orkney and Shetland in 1472. The Norse influence remained strong and is still in evidence today, with the traditional celebrations of Yule (Christmas) and Up-Helly-Aa.

The Vikings introduced Scandinavian methods of cooking, along with the salting, smoking and curing of fish and mutton. Many foods, following their Norse origins, are dried or salted and smoked – *vivda* is wind-dried mutton,

Right *The Up-Helly-Aa viking festival at Lerwick on Shetland is a poignant link to the island's Nordic past.*

dried without salt, and is served in very thin slices, and *reested* mutton (salted and smoked) is still sold by butchers in Shetland. Cabbage appears in many dishes in the Islands, as it does in Scandinavian recipes, and is eaten with pickled pork. Herring is salted, smoked and pickled and served with onions, as it is prepared in Scandinavia.

The Scots' fondness for fish, particularly in the Northern Isles, can

partly be attributed to the Vikings, and their influence has not only survived in fish dishes but is also evident in other recipes, such as *fricadellans* (meatballs) from the Scandinavian *frikadeller*. Liver *muggies* (fish stomachs stuffed with seasoned fish livers) are derived from the Old Norse *magi*.

The Viking tradition of eating out of wooden bowls and plates with a sharp pointed knife was also adopted. Spoons were made from wood, horn or animal bone and were frequently carved with intricate patterns and the heads of fabulous beasts. Similarly, lavishly decorated horns were used to serve drinks and soups.

The Vikings were great drinkers, and brought with them a number of flavoursome concoctions. *Whipkull*, an ancient festive drink of eggs and sugar whisked over heat, is identical to the Norwegian *eggedosis*, the national festive dessert served with crisp biscuits. It is also similar to an Icelandic soup.

The clan system

Key to Scottish cuisine is the illustrious history of the clans and clan culture. The system is believed to have been founded by a group of Scots who settled on the west coast of Scotland in the 6th century. The word clan is directly drawn from the Gaelic word *clann*, meaning children. The clans were made up of both "native men" (with a direct blood relationship with their chief and with each other) and "broken men" from other clans, who sought the protection of the clan. Many clan names begin with "Mac", which means "son of".

The clan chieftain shared his home with relatives and clanspeople, who were employed by him in return for their keep. The rule of the chief over his lands was virtually autonomous, but there were frequent feuds between the clans and battles were common. Stronger, larger clans predominated, with Clan Donald reputed to be the most powerful.

Tartan became an important symbol of clan kinship amongst the Highlanders and each clan developed its own tartan

Below Whisky was originally made by clans, and the quality and flavour was symbolic of the clan's status.

Above Highland cows were reared by the clans for beef and dairy products.

for identification and to depict the prestige of the clan. It was worn at feasts and clan celebrations.

It was a matter of pride and honour for the clan chief to offer his very best food and drink to visitors. Reports from travellers in the 18th century praised the generous hospitality they received from the clans in the Highlands. A breakfast of porridge (oatmeal) was typically accompanied by fresh cream, eggs, cheese, bannocks and oatcakes and was washed down with milk, buttermilk, ale or whisky. A special

drink for honoured guests was Auld Man's Milk – eggs, milk, honey and whisky beaten together.

Sir Walter Scott described the 14th-century funeral feast of a Highland chief in *The Fair Maid of Perth* (1828): "... Pits wrought in the hillside and lined with heated stones, served for stewing immense quantities of beef, mutton and venison; wooden spits supported sheep and goats, which were roasted entire; others were cut into joints and seethed in cauldrons made of the animals' own skins, sewed hastily together and filled with water; while huge quantities of pike, trout, salmon and char were broiled with more ceremony on glowing embers."

Clan repression

During the 18th century, the English government was determined to curtail the power of the Highland chiefs and prevent uprisings. They built roads in the previously inaccessible Highlands, and cleared much of the land (along with the Highland families) to make way for sheep farming and gaming

estates. The draconian Act of Proscription (1747) made it illegal to wear Highland dress (except in the military), and banned the use of clan names, celebrations and music.

The Highland Clearances had great repercussions for the Highlanders. Their self-sufficiency, which had relied on wild game and produce from cows, sheep, goats and hens, disappeared and they were left destitute. Many were evicted without their possessions, not even cooking utensils, as they surveyed their burning homes and lands. A few sympathetic English landlords distributed food to the stricken Highlanders, but it wasn't enough and thousands emigrated to the New World in search of a better life. The emptiness of the Highlands today is a lasting reminder of those terrible times.

The clans and other Scots attempted to bring the Stewart kings back to the throne; these episodes became known as the Jacobite Rebellions. In 1746, the "Young Pretender" or Bonnie Prince

Right Bagpipes, tartan and traditional clan celebrations can now be found throughout Scotland.

Charlie was defeated at the Battle of Culloden. The clan lands were confiscated, and Jacobite supporters were imprisoned – including Rob Roy MacGregor. Bonnie Prince Charlie escaped and was helped to Skye by Flora Macdonald, who disguised Charlie as her maid for the crossing.

Revival of the clans

Tartan made a welcome return in 1782 when the Highland regiments, such as the Black Watch, were permitted to wear a regimental tartan. The Highlanders became keen to re-establish (or in some cases re-invent) their family tartans and celebrate their clan culture. Queen Victoria, who loved all things Scottish, encouraged the use of tartan and interest spread. Today, especially with the energy that has

come from the new Scottish Parliament, the clans are celebrated, and many traditions, foods and festivals enjoyed throughout the country.

Below The Highland Games re-create the clan competitiveness through games such as the tug o' war.

Foreign influences

Scottish cooking has absorbed many fascinating culinary influences throughout history, as a result of foreign invaders, settlers and traders. New ingredients, recipes and cooking methods have been introduced, all of which have had a huge impact on the Scottish kitchen and the way that food is enjoyed.

The Auld Alliance

One of the biggest influences on the Scottish kitchen was the Auld Alliance. From 1295 Scotland and France united against English invaders in an alliance that lasted 233 years. James V married the French Mary of Guise, mother of Mary Queen of Scots. The latter lived at the French court and married the future Francis II of France. The widowed Mary of Guise ruled Scotland until her daughter returned in 1561 after the death of her husband. Recipes of the time owed much to the French, who came over during the Auld Alliance. The French influence remains today in many words in common use: *ashet* – a large serving dish from the French *assiette*; *hotch potch* – vegetable soup from the

Above *The French influence is seen in many grand estates, such as in Bowhill House in the Borders, built in 1795.*

French *hochepot*; and a rich bread pudding that dates back to the 13th century called *pampurdy*, a corruption of *pain perdue*, which means smothered bread.

It was during the Auld Alliance that dessert was introduced for the first time. After the main meal the table was disserved (cleared), fruits and

The origin of Drambuie

When Bonnie Prince Charlie was in hiding after Culloden, he was taken from Skye to the mainland by a man named MacKinnon. As a reward, the prince gave him the recipe for his own liqueur, created for him when he was at the French court. It was called, in Gaelic, *An Dram Buidheach* (the drink that satisfies). The MacKinnon clan made some each year, solely for their own use. In the 1870s, John Ross, the owner of the Broadford Inn on Skye, persuaded the MacKinnons to make large quantities of the liqueur so he could sell it. In 1893 John Ross's son, James, patented the name Drambuie as a trademark.

sweetmeats were eaten in another room. It was another 50 years before this custom was adopted in England.

Many dishes in French and Scottish cooking became closely related. In Scottish towns professional bakers, known as baxters (the original meaning

Left *French monks left their mark in the 13th-century Beauly Priory.*

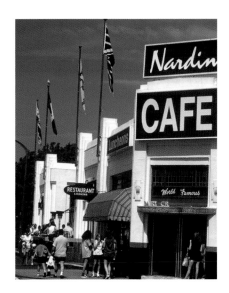

Above *An Italian ice cream parlour built in Art-Deco style in Largs on the coast of Ayrshire.*

of the word baxter was a female cook), used French methods and recipes. The bakers were patronized by the wealthy who could afford the best ingredients such as wheat flour and sugar. It was said that only French and Viennese bakers surpassed those of Edinburgh.

Later still, after the French Revolution in 1789 when many French chefs fled to Scotland, it became fashionable for wealthy Scots and the nobility to boast of employing a French chef and thus encouraging French cuisine.

The Dutch influence

Trade with Holland in the 16th and 17th centuries led to the introduction of Dutch recipes, which were integrated into the Scottish kitchen. These took advantage of the dried fruits and spices that had arrived on the ships of the Dutch East India Company. In Scotland a plain, yeasted bun is known as a cookie and the name probably comes from the Dutch *koek*, or cake. Aberdeen *crullas* are delicious sweet fried cakes and their name possibly comes from the Dutch *krullen* (to curl).

Italian cuisine

In the 19th century many Italian immigrants arrived in search of a better life and brought their culinary traditions to Scotland. Most opened restaurants and cafés. They soon realized that most Scottish people had only basic cooking facilities and worked long hours. This led some Italians to sell ready-made foods such as hot peas and, later, fish and chips, unwittingly creating the thriving take-away culture that is such a feature of Scottish cities today. Other immigrants sold home-made ice cream and it was these immigrants who introduced ice cream as a street food, selling it from gaily painted carts and crying out "*Gelati, ecco un poco!*" which is why they became known as "hokey pokey men" and the ice cream they sold was called "hokey pokey". Some sold both – hot food in winter and ice cream in summer. Their hard work paid off and by the 1920s many could afford to abandon their small shops in poorer areas and open luxurious establishments in fashionable areas such as Sauchiehall Street in Glasgow. These establishments

increased in popularity and quickly expanded into cafés with full meals on the menu. Similar cafés were opened by Italians throughout Scotland and records show that, in 1904, the number of cafés in Glasgow alone had doubled from the previous year. The cafés became popular meeting places, especially for the young, particularly as they were among the few places that opened on Sundays.

Today many of Scotland's Italian restaurants retain their impressive reputation for quality and tradition, with many coming under the umbrella of Ciao Italia, founded in 1982. This organisation is responsible for maintaining and building on the values of Italian cuisine abroad.

Scots-Italians continue to run award-winning shops and restaurants. Their role in influencing Scottish eating styles continues today. Ice cream and fish and chips, known as a "fish supper", are an indispensable part of Scottish food and eateries.

Below *Italian meets Scottish: second- and third-generation Italians have opened restaurants in Edinburgh.*

Life in the Highlands

Even before the suppression of the clans and the Clearances, life in the Highlands was bleak. The clans dominated the hardy lands, making the most of wild game and dairy products from their herds of Highland cattle.

Broths and soups were the staple dishes, providing the main meal of the day for many. They would simmer in a cauldron set over a peat fire throughout the day, with wild herbs (especially young, tender nettle leaves) added for flavour. The Highlanders ate little in the way of green vegetables, preferring boiled nettles instead, which are a natural blood purifier and contain useful amounts of iron and vitamins A and C. A few vegetables, such as kail (or kale), onions and leeks, were cultivated in the kailyard (a piece of land next to the house set aside as a sort of kitchen garden), and most of these ended up in the soup pot.

Berries and wild fruits were eaten with cream or soft cheese. Before sugar was widely available, honey was the main sweetener and boys were sent out to collect wild honey. Heather honey is

Above *The rivers and lochs have always provided an abundance of foods, notably salmon.*

a Scottish speciality and is a rich reddish-brown colour, with a dense texture and distinctive flavour. This is one of nature's last truly wild and unadulturated foods.

Every summer the cattle were moved to the mountain pastures and the women and children went with them to live in basic huts known as shielings. The women made butter and cheese from the milk of cows, sheep and goats. Butter was salted so that it would keep for use over the winter. Another traditional way of preserving butter was to bury it in a peat bog, and examples of bog butter are sometimes found today, including a 2,000-year-old specimen that is now in the Museum of Scotland in Edinburgh.

Occasionally domesticated animals were slaughtered for fresh meat. This was enjoyed in celebration feasts or was sometimes salted to preserve it for the harsh winter months. The main meats were mutton or beef as the Highlanders held pork in disdain. Food was frequently given to the clan chief in lieu of rent.

Left *Survival in the Highlands relied upon wild deer to provide venison as a delicious and nutritious food source.*

The Clearances and the crofters

The Highlands changed radically following the dramatic defeat at Culloden in 1746. Where once the clans had dominated the wilderness, power passed into the hands of lairds placed by the king to control the wayward Highlanders. Highland culture, language and even dress were suppressed for years to come and the old traditional Highland way of life disappeared,

never to return. Poverty and hardship led to the emigration of thousands of Scots during the time that became known as the Clearances, many boarding ships bound for America.

The Agricultural Revolution during the latter part of the 18th century and into the 19th century led to a change in the landscape. The great forests that covered the Highlands were cleared away within a space of 20 years.

The gradual development of

Above The picturesque fishing village of Plockton was once a Gaelic-speaking community surviving on traditional fishing and crofting.

agriculture and the destruction of woods and forests led to the near extinction of many wild animals previously hunted for food. The wild boar, elk and bears that had roamed the forests in the early period eventually died out as their natural habitat was destroyed. Deer, that had previously inhabited the forests, moved up into the hills and adapted their original diet of young tree shoots to heather.

Sheep replaced people, as land was combined into huge farming estates for the king's favourites. These landowning gentry allowed the peasants to work smallholdings, a practice known as the crofting system.

Left Crofting cottages still exist today, with the stone house at the top of a strip of land used to supply oats, vegetables and dairy produce.

Above A replica interior of a crofter's cottage, with the fire for cooking in the centre of the room.

The crofters lived in small stone houses with roofs of wood and thatch. Farm animals, such as poultry, lived in one end of the building and the family at the other. A peat fire burned continuously in the middle of the room, where food was cooked in an iron pot suspended from the ceiling. There were no windows, but a hole in the roof allowed the smoke to escape. They were often referred to as blackhouses as the interiors were black with smoke.

The crofters' diet consisted mainly of cheese, butter, herbs, seasonal fruits and vegetables, porridge, oatcakes and barley bannocks. A bowl of steaming hot porridge (oatmeal) served with thick cold fresh cream provided a sustaining and nourishing breakfast. A pot of broth often thickened with oatmeal and flavoured with wild herbs simmered all day over the fire for the evening meal, accompanied by soft barley bannocks cooked on a bakestone or girdle (griddle). A piece of mutton or venison provided a welcome addition to the pot. Filling staples were potatoes and oatmeal boiled in water (*brochan*) and meals were accompanied by milk,

buttermilk, ale or whisky. In the summer wild berries and fruits were enjoyed with cream and honey.

There are around 17,000 crofts today and most of them now have modern amenities. Crofting has undergone a revival and has seen the re-emergence of traditional cottage industries.

The Gaming Estates

Hunting was a popular sport with the nobility in the 18th and 19th centuries, many of whom travelled up from England. Large gaming estates began to

appear, the later ones becoming more flamboyant and luxurious. Every laird, as lords were known in Scotland, owned dovecotes for pigeons, and huge flocks of wild pigeons also thrived in Scotland. They provided fresh meat in winter.

Increasingly tight laws were put in place to prevent the locals from hunting and fishing, yet poaching increased as they considered that wild animals and fish could not be regarded as property – they belonged to no one and were there for the taking.

Deer and boar were hunted on horseback with dogs. A more formal hunt was the drive, where beaters drove the game to within the hunters' range. In the murky peat bogs the *tinchel* method developed. Walls of stone or brush were built on either side of a glen, and men on foot drove the deer from the hills into the enclosure.

Every part of the deer was used; even the antlers which provided deerhorn jelly. Venison was usually roasted and tougher cuts were stewed or used to fill pasties. Venison collops, a very old dish, was made with thick steaks from the

Below Elaborate hunting lodges still host gaming parties with traditional hunting and banquets.

boned haunch. Deer haggis used the heart and liver and the liver was also eaten on its own. Deer tripe (*pocha buidh* or yellow bag) was another speciality. Deer puddings were made from deer suet mixed with oatmeal and onions put into cleaned deerskins and boiled. Venison was usually served with a claret sauce or gravy.

In the late 18th century hunting methods changed radically when improved firearms removed the need for dogs. Many landowners rented out land for deer stalking. These "shooting lets" were advertised in newspapers and the thrill of hunting proved popular, despite the fact that there was no accommodation and often no roads. By the mid-19th century hunting was a fashionable pastime. Queen Victoria and Prince Albert endorsed the new vogue for hunting when they bought Balmoral, giving Albert land on which to hunt and fish while the Queen sketched and took the bracing Scottish air. Queen Victoria was very fond of game dishes, especially pheasant and woodcock stuffed with truffles, foie gras and herbs.

Hunting and fishing today

Today syndicates own many of the large estates and rent out the shooting rights. Game birds are bred to be shot for sport and for the table. Game, fish and wildfowl are protected and can only be hunted at certain times of the year, to allow stocks to be replenished.

Grouse shoots are especially popular and attract people from all over the world. The Glorious Twelfth is the start of the grouse-shooting season on 12 August, ending on 10 December. Feasts are enjoyed with tables filled with lavishly decorated game meats.

Consumption of farmed venison is increasing as more people recognize the benefits of eating this low-fat, tasty meat. Wild venison may sometimes

come from old, tougher animals, or may not have been hung for sufficient time and so have little flavour. Farmed venison on the other hand has consistency of flavour and texture and needs no marinating. Many venison farms encourage visitors.

Scotland's salmon and trout rivers such as the Tay, the Dee, the Spey and the Tweed are well-stocked and offer unrivalled pleasure for keen anglers.

Tourism and Highland activities

There has been a surge in tourism over the last few decades, and this sector today accounts for many businesses in the Highlands. Many

Above *Hunting continues to be popular in Scotland, although today it is heavily regulated to protect species and the local ecosystem.*

excellent restaurants, hotels, guesthouses, visitor centres, ancestral homes and castles have opened. Mountaineering, sailing, walking, skiing (in winter) and sporting estates attract keen sportsmen from around the globe.

There is plenty for the food-loving tourist – you can watch traditional sweets (candies) being made, or visit an oat mill, shortbread bakery or whisky distillery and of course the region's restaurants, pubs and hotels offer a selection of tasty local specialities.

Life on the Islands

The remote Scottish Islands are a world of breathtaking scenery. However, any view of a coastal cottage or village with a backdrop of towering mountains brings home the sheer isolation and struggle for existence here. Amongst the extraordinarily beautiful and dramatic lochs and massive mountains, livings are made from patches of fertile soil and the fruitful lochs and seas.

The Northern Isles (called Nordereys by the Norsemen), Orkney and Shetland, have had ties with Scandinavia since Viking times, whereas the Western Isles are mainly Celt-influenced. Piracy and smuggling were a part of life, with the latter providing a good income. Influences from shipwrecked and smuggled goods from abroad took hold. Fair Isle in Shetland gave its name to the multi-coloured knitting designs which were probably copied from the clothing worn by those shipwrecked in the 1588 Spanish Armada catastrophe.

The Western Isles off the north-west coast of Scotland include the Inner and Outer Hebrides. The Inner Hebrides are closer to the mainland and include Skye, Jura and Islay, and the sub-group of the Small Isles, such as Eigg and

Rhum. The more remote Outer Hebrides include Lewis and Harris.

Fish and shellfish have always been the staple diet on all the islands, eaten alone or made into nourishing soups, stews and pies. Seaweed collected from the shores is often cooked and eaten as a vegetable, as well as being used as fertilizer, and the ashes from burnt seaweed were once used instead of salt to preserve cheese.

Above As for most islands, fishing is the main source of income on the Isle of Lewis in the Outer Hebrides.

The culture of both groups of islands is distinct from that of the mainland and their remoteness has served to preserve their unique traditions.

The Shetland Isles and Orkney

The Vikings made the Northern Islands of Shetland and Orkney their home, and the islands still celebrate their Norse way of life. Gaelic was never commonly used, and many places still have Norse names. Christmas is known by its Norwegian name of Yule, the ancient feast of the winter solstice.

The Shetland Isles, a group of over 100 islands, were once part of the Danish kingdom. The culture, traditions and dialect still have a strong Scandinavian flavour. The peat-covered hills contrast with the green arable land of Orkney. Sheep are raised in Shetland,

Left Cows produce fine dairy foods and now support a thriving ice cream industry on Orkney.

Above *The familiar sight of a fishing boat entering the harbour of the busy fishing town of Lerwick on the remote Shetland Isles.*

but there is little agriculture; it is fishing that is most important to the islands' economy.

The most important industry has always been the deep-sea fishing for ling and cod. This was known as the *haaf*, carried out from May to August. It was a dangerous and arduous occupation, and many boats were tragically lost. By the 18th century dried ling had become a major export.

Shetlanders, like Scandinavians, are very fond of fermented fish and make use of the heads, roes and livers of white fish discarded from the salting process. Fish livers were also melted down and the oil was used in lamps.

Oats and barley are grown along with some vegetables. Livestock provides meat, milk, cheese and butter. A local wind-dried meat, such as pork, mutton or beef, is known as *vivda*. Salted and spiced minced (ground) beef is *sassermaet* and is used patties called *bröenies*.

Orkney comprises more than 70 islands (only 17 are inhabited). Its name is believed to come from the Icelandic *Orkneyjar*, or Seal Islands. Orkney has more farmland than Shetland, with oats and barley as the main crops. Potatoes are cultivated in the peaty soil and damp climate. Kale flourishes and used to be preserved in barrels with fat and oatmeal. The dairy industry produces famous cheeses, cream and, more recently, ice cream. Cheeses used to be buried in oatmeal to keep them fresh, although it was more usual to eat

cheese young and fresh. Cattle are also farmed for beef. High-quality organic salmon are farmed in vast sea pens off Orkney and have paler, less fatty flesh than ordinary farmed salmon.

Early daily fare in the Orkneys included a morning piece of half a bannock made from bere. Traditional oatmeal gingerbread is Orkney *broonie* – the name derives from the Norse *bruni*, meaning a thick bannock. Sour skons made with buttermilk are popular, sometimes flavoured with caraway seeds.

The Western Isles

On the farthest edge of Europe lie the Western Isles, many of them mountainous and infertile. In winter the weather is harsh with strong Atlantic winds and heavy rain, although snow is rare. The summer is generally warm and

it stays light until about midnight. Gaelic culture is dominant in the islands, and they remain the only place in Scotland where the language is spoken on a daily basis.

Religion is largely Free Presbyterianism and Sunday is strictly kept as the Sabbath, with no work taking place. Some of the other islands are mainly Roman Catholic, as their remoteness shielded them from the Scottish Reformation. A strongly held religion helped many communities survive the hardships experienced on the remote islands.

Whilst many of the Hebrides, such as Skye, have become successful tourist centres, others, such as the remote St Kilda, are now uninhabited.

The Inner Hebrides

These comprise the great swathe of islands lying off the western coast of Scotland – east of the Outer Hebrides, Skye southwards to the Kintyre peninsula. Each is very different in appearance and atmosphere, with its own distinct culture.

One of the most accessible of the islands is Mull, with its idyllic fishing port Tobermory drawing in tourists – now the mainstay of the economy. Fishing, especially for lobsters, is still a good source of income for the islanders. Close by is tiny Iona, one of the most important religious sites in Europe, and still a Roman Catholic pilgrimage site. Nearby, the dramatic uninhabited island of Staffa, looms out of the sea like a great cathedral of natural basalt columns. It was the inspiration for Mendelssohn's *Hebrides Overture*. Seals, whales and porpoise follow the fishing boats as they head out.

The beautiful Isle of Skye attracts tourists from all over the world to see the incredible landscapes and enjoy the local festivals. It was dominated by the Celts until the 8th century, then ruled

Left Coopers repair casks ready for use: the islands of the Inner Hebrides are famed for their fine single malt and blended whiskies.

by the Norsemen until it passed to the Scottish crown in 1226. Both Celtic and Norse traditions are strong and about half the population speaks Gaelic.

Sheep, wool, cattle and fishing are the chief sources of income, together with a growing tourist industry. Foods include locally made cheeses and seafood, including scallops, lobster, oysters, langoustines, cod, haddock, mackerel, and wild salmon and trout. Talisker, one of the world's great malt whiskies, is produced here and the brewery makes superb ales using only natural ingredients.

The Isle of Islay is famed for its whisky distilleries, producing some of the best whiskies in the world. Many of the distilleries date back to the 17th and 18th centuries, competing with each other to improve quality and flavour over the years.

Below European lobsters, as found in the seas around Scotland, are highly prized. Lobster fishing is a good source of income for the islanders on Mull.

The Outer Hebrides

A long strand of islands and islets, the Outer Hebrides lie west of the mainland. Relentlessly battered by fierce Atlantic winds, they pose a bleak and hostile environment for human life, with heather, bog and few trees. The landscape is dominated by rock and there are freshwater and sea lochs. Shellfish abound and live seafood is exported worldwide. The finest lobsters go to the best restaurants in Edinburgh, London and Paris. Shops and restaurants on the islands sell a stunning variety of fish and shellfish, both fresh and smoked.

Sheep and beef cattle are kept. The crofters used to grow potatoes and a few other vegetables on the hillsides, fertilizing the meagre soil with seaweed, but today fruit, vegetables and grains are brought across from the mainland.

The most famous products of the islands are the tweeds. Harris Tweed is world-renowned and is an important industry. Although there are now larger manufacturers, many weavers still work from home or small workshops.

Other high-quality traditional products are also made here, such as the fine smoked salmon from the Isle of Lewis, as well as some excellent local cheeses and preserves.

St Kilda is the most remote and hostile group of Scottish Islands. St Kilda was inhabited until 1930, the islanders scraping a living mostly from fish, shellfish and sea birds such as puffins, fulmar and Solan goose (or gannet) and their eggs. The sea birds also provided feathers for eiderdowns, and oil that was used for lamps.

Solan goose was a speciality, eaten fresh or preserved. The plucked and cleaned birds were lightly salted then hung in small peat huts called *stypes*,

with open ends so the birds dried in the cold dry winds. These wind-blown or blawn birds were sometimes stored in beehive-shaped earth cells called *cleits*. The cooked bird was known in Gaelic as a *guga* and was reputed to have a delicate flavour, not at all fishy or strong.

In the mid-19th century steamships provided more contact with the outside world. During World War I a garrison was stationed on the main island, but when the regular deliveries of mail and food stopped after the war the islanders felt very isolated. Food shortages ensued and this, together with the emigration of many young islanders, eventually led to a request for evacuation to the mainland, where they had to adjust their eating habits, occupations and entire lifestyles.

***Below** The shores provide plenty of foods for foraging, such as cockles and mussels and the tasty seaweeds.*

Life in the Lowlands

The lush pastures of the Lowlands stand in contrast with the rugged Highlands. They produce much of the dairy products, fruit, vegetables and grains that are consumed in Scotland.

Fishing and farming were the main sources of food in the Lowlands for thousands of years. Sheep were kept mainly for wool and milk, and pigs provided bacon and pork. Cows were kept for beef and dairy produce. Lowlanders grew grains and vegetables in their kailyards, usually bere (a type of barley), oats, beans, peas and kale – Scotland's national green vegetable. In the 18th century, the kail bell was rung at two o'clock to signal the main meal of the day.

Below *The city of Edinburgh was one of the most developed cities in Europe by the 18th century, with plentiful food provided by the surrounding lowlands.*

Bannocks were usually made with barley, often mixed with peasemeal, oats and rye, when they were known as *meslin* (mixed) bannocks. Rich Scotch ale was the preferred drink.

Fishing in sea, river and loch

Around the coast fishing was a major source of income. Ancient picturesque fishing villages such as St Monans, Anstruther and Pittenweem (the latter holds an annual fish festival) were once thriving seaports and still sell sparklingly fresh fish and shellfish. Musselburgh, a few miles from Edinburgh, was the site of an important Roman camp and its name comes from the famous mussel bed. Mussels are still enjoyed there today.

Salmon smoking and pickling were important industries in Scotland as early as the 13th century. The River Tay in Fife is renowned as one of the best salmon rivers in Britain. Glasgow was known as a salmon fishing village and the River Clyde was once a famous salmon river. The fishing rights were eagerly sought and were mentioned in charters of the 12th century. By the 18th century, enormous catches of salmon meant that it was cheap. Farm workers even stipulated in their contracts that salmon was to be served only three times a week. Today there are no salmon in the Clyde due to overfishing and pollution.

Sugar and sweets

By the 18th century, Glasgow had become the largest importer of sugar in Britain. Glaswegians became fond of making sweets and the famous Scots sweet tooth developed. The women who made and sold toffee were known as Sweetie Wives.

Above *Toffees and fudges are a speciality in Glasgow, Britain's largest sugar port.*

Every town developed its own unique sweets. The now world-famous, pastel-coloured, powdery Edinburgh rock was discovered by accident by a young sweetmaker called Sandy Ferguson, also known as "Sweetie Sandy", who went on to produce it in a grand scale. *Soor plooms* from Galashiels are round green sweets with an acid tang, believed to commemorate the day when a gang of English marauders was overcome after being caught unawares as they feasted on unripe plums. Jethart snails are dark peppermint-flavoured toffees, introduced by a French prisoner from the Napoleonic Wars. *Gundy* is an old-fashioned toffee, originally made and sold by a Mrs Flockhart in Potter Row in Edinburgh. Gold-striped Moffat Toffee is still made today in the town after which it is named and has an unusual sherbet tang. Treacle candy was a farmhouse sweet, made using the molasses kept on farms for mixing with the cattle mash.

In rural areas it was the custom for lads and lassies to meet in the evening in someone's house for sweet-making. Everyone had great fun, and the evening would usually end with dancing and merriment.

Above *Shortbreads and sweet biscuits are often topped with local berries, such as strawberries and raspberries.*

A wealth of food and drink

At the beginning of the 18th century there were approximately one million people living in Scotland and 90 per cent of these lived in small settlements and communities. Developments in agriculture and improved transport resulted in the emergence of heavy industries in towns and cities, with the result that Scotland became one of the most industrialized countries in Europe.

A decline in manufacturing in the latter part of the 20th century has led to the emphasis shifting back to food. The staple industries of the Lowlands are now fishing and farming. The fertile farmland of the Lowlands supports grain crops as well as beef and dairy cattle. The cool summers and long hours of daylight result not only in Britain's finest sweet luscious raspberries, but also gooseberries, blackcurrants, strawberries, tayberries and blackberries, which are all grown commercially in the region.

The seaside coastal towns and ports are home to busy fish markets and smokeries. The fishing ports of Macduff, Fraserburgh and Peterhead (Europe's largest fishing port) share a rich history. Buckie proudly displays its fishing heritage in a new visitor centre.

Lowland whiskies such as Auchentoshan Littlemill, Rosebank and Bladnoch are softer than those of the Highlands and Islands and can be a more gentle introduction to drinking malt whisky.

Below *The rich pastures in the central valleys provide excellent cheeses and other dairy products.*

The Scotch whisky distilleries

Ask people what they associate most with Scotland and you'll probably get a variety of answers – tartan, golf and Robbie Burns would certainly all be mentioned. But the most common answer is likely to be whisky.

Acknowledged as Scotland's national drink, whisky – in the Gaelic, *uisge beatha* (pronounced oosh-ga bah-hah), meaning water of life – has been produced here for centuries as a way of using up rain-soaked barley after a wet harvest. The whisky industry has now grown into one of the country's biggest earners, bringing in hundreds of millions of pounds annually.

During the 17th century the popularity of whisky grew steadily and many distilleries sprang up to meet increasing demand. However the finest whiskies were those distilled by the Highland chiefs for their own households, although these gradually died out with the clans.

The British Government imposed a tax on malt whisky in 1713, to the outrage of Scotland. So began the era of illicit stills and smuggling. Raids by excise men and their attempts to close down the illegal stills failed and the defiant Highlanders continued to distil whisky in huge quantities. This was smuggled into the Lowlands and England by a variety of ingenious methods, and outwitting the excise men became a way of life. One of the greatest smugglers was Helen Cumming, the wife of John who founded the Cardhu distillery in Morayshire.

Eventually Alexander, Duke of Gordon, persuaded the British Government to see the folly of its ways and in 1823 an act was passed permitting licensed distilling. Small private stills were still illegal so the practice of whisky-making in the home ceased almost completely. However this encouraged the production of whisky on a large scale and distilleries were set up in areas where the natural conditions were favourable. George Smith – a previously illicit distiller and smuggler – opened the first licensed distillery on Speyside.

Above *The popularity of whisky gained momentum through the 19th century and spread to England.*

The processes

Single malt whisky is made from malted barley in pot stills. Barley is soaked for two days then spread out on the malting floor for about ten days to germinate, when the starch converts to sugar. Then it is spread out on the perforated kiln floor, with a peat furnace beneath, to halt the germination process. Once dried the malt is ground into grist then mixed with hot water in a mash tun. The resulting sugary liquid, wort, is drawn off and the solids are used for cattle feed. The wort is cooled and poured into washbacks, yeast is added and fermentation begins. After two days wash, a weak form of alcohol, develops. It is from this that the spirit is produced.

Malt whisky is distilled twice, or perhaps three times. This involves a process of heating and cooling, evaporation and condensation. The

Left *A worker turns the grain on the floor of a malting house to encourage germination.*

first distillate, the low wines, is distilled again. After this it is a matter of the expert eye of the stillman to make sure everything goes to plan. Then water is added and the spirit is sealed in casks and stored for at least three years. Single malt whisky is left much longer for its complex character to develop. When they have reached the end of their useful lives – filled three or four times – the casks are broken up and used for smoking salmon.

In 1830 the manufacture of whisky was revolutionized by the invention of the patent still. This could produce alcohol much more cheaply than the old pot still. The Highland distillers were outraged and argued that the new product was "Scotch'd Spirit" and most definitely not whisky. The patent still did not rely on the correct climate, peat and water, and used malted and unmalted barley mashed to produce a "grain" whisky unlike malt whisky.

Below Copper pot stills have been used in Scotland since the 1500s.

Above The casks are carefully constructed from oak, imparting the wood flavour to the whisky.

Some distillers began experimenting with blends of both malt and grain whisky and from 1860 the Excise permitted the blending of whiskies from different distilleries. Skilful blending created distinctive brands, which were uniform and unchanging in character, and by the mid-19th century, patent still distillers such as Tommy Dewar were established. Sales of both types of whisky soared in Scotland and by the end of the 19th century the English had been won over too.

Whisky-making today

Scotland continues to produce outstanding malt, grain and blended whiskies. Many of the best-known quality distilleries are still owned by the family or clan that began making the whisky centuries before. Very often these distilleries compete with one another, especially those in the same region, continually pushing up the standards and improving the flavours of their products. The traditional methods are retained as much as possible, while taking advantage of the new techniques and machinery.

The distilleries have benefited from new markets. These have come from the surge in international exports and also from many Scottish food and drink manufacturers who now add whisky to many high-quality products to enhance the flavour.

The smokehouses

Smoked foods have been enjoyed since antiquity, and smoking, particularly of fish, has been practised throughout Scotland since the Iron Age. Foods were salted, and then hung in huts and caves where smoke from the cooking fires pervaded the fish or meat. It was discovered that the tarry substances in wood-smoke killed bacteria and formed an impervious layer on the surface of the food, which preserved it. The smoke also penetrated the food imparting the characteristic rich, smoky flavour. Foods were heavily smoked and salted to preserve them for the lean winter months. Smoking was also used to preserve fish that needed to be transported to the mainland or abroad.

Fresh fish such as haddock were heavily salted, then smoked for up to three weeks. Salmon was also smoked, but the end result was hard and salty – very different from the tender, mild product we know today. The famous Arbroath smokies are haddock that

Below Smoking haddock is still very much a cottage industry in Arbroath, with a designated area of the town set aside to protect the old industry.

have been dry-salted, tied in pairs then hot smoked to a rich copper colour, leaving the insides creamy white. They are still made in a number of family-run smokehouses around Arbroath harbour.

Smokehouses were built in coastal areas, where fish were smoked as they came ashore. Early smokehouses were simple wood or brick buildings fitted with beams, across which lengths of wood were balanced for hanging the fish. Fishwives gutted, split, cleaned and salted the fish and laid the fires in the smokehouses. They also smoked their own fish over peat in their home chimneys – a practice which was common throughout Scotland until the mid-19th century.

Scotland's oldest smoking house still stands on River Ugie in Peterhead. Built in 1585 for the Fifth Earl of Marischal to store his fish and game, the tiny building still has the original 16th-century scarf joints on the ceiling beams. Locally caught wild salmon and trout are still smoked here, along with top-quality farmed salmon from Orkney.

Fish was not the only food to be smoked. Women in the Highlands and Islands smoked home-made sausages in

Above High-quality smoked salmon is filleted by hand before smoking.

their chimneys. Geese were also sometimes cured and smoked. Joints of beef and mutton hams (legs of mutton cured and smoked in the same way as hams) were much sought after in the 18th century, enjoying a large export market to the New World and the West Indies. Smoking continued in much the same way until 1939, when the Torry Research Station in Aberdeen developed the Torry kiln. This was a new controlled smoking kiln, which produced a uniform product of a high quality. The process was achieved using a forced draught, which improved the drying and smoking. The fish were exposed to moderate temperatures (prime for bacterial growth) for a shorter period. The result was that more fish could be processed in a shorter time and to a higher quality.

The smoking process

The smoking process involves first curing by dry-salting, brining or marinating (according to the producer), then air-drying the food before smoking. The cure is a major factor in

Above *Whole fish, such as herring, are delicious smoked, making popular breakfast dishes.*

Above *Thinly sliced smoked salmon is soft and tender, with a delicate and subtle smoky flavour.*

Above *Smoked venison and other types of meat and game are becoming increasingly popular.*

the flavour of the food and many producers have their own particular curing recipes, which may include herbs, spices, brown sugar, whisky and molasses. The choice of wood greatly contributes to the taste of the finished product. Oak and beech are very popular as they impart a delicate nutty taste, and sometimes a small amount of aromatic wood such as juniper is added towards the end of smoking for an extra-special flavour.

Today food is smoked more for its flavour than for preservation. Although commercial smokehouses have large, specially constructed kilns, Scotland retains many traditional small-scale smokehouses using time-honoured methods of filleting, salting and smoking – a skilled craft that is difficult to achieve in large-scale smokehouses. The excellent quality and flavour of foods smoked by traditional methods speak for themselves.

Smoked salmon from Scotland is internationally renowned for its quality, texture and flavour. Other meats, such as hams, bacon, venison and poultry, are popular smoked foods today, as is cheese. Enterprising Scottish specialist smokers now even produce smoked alligator, kangaroo and ostrich.

Below *Organic salmon and mussel farms at Loch Fyne produce high-quality smoked and cured goods.*

The king of fish – salmon

The wild salmon is a magnificent creature. The skin of its sleek, muscular body shimmers silver, while its deep pink-red flesh is rich and full of flavour. The flavour and texture of wild Scottish salmon (*Salmo salar*) surpasses that of all other varieties, and it is eagerly sought after by gourmets. Keen anglers from all over the world will happily pay vast sums for the privilege of fishing for this superb fish.

Salmon in the wild

Salmon make the exhausting journey from the North Atlantic Ocean back to the river of their birth to breed. This is the best time to catch them, as their flavour and texture are at their finest – they have eaten heavily from the rich feeding grounds of the ocean before setting out on their long trip. Their flesh is imbued with rich flavour and becomes firm, succulent and plump – the long swim develops the muscles and flesh to produce a powerful, rippling body. After spawning, most of the salmon die, but some survive and go back to the sea to return to the river another year. The oldest recorded salmon had reached the grand old age of 13 years and had spawned four times before finally being caught on Loch Maree in Wester Ross.

The rise and fall of the salmon

Salmon was once so plentiful that it was despised by the upper classes. As a cheap, everyday filler, salmon was eaten

Above *Atlantic salmon has deep pink flesh with a superb flavour.*

fresh, dried, smoked and pickled. Tweed kettle – salmon gently simmered in white wine with shallots, herbs and mushrooms – was a very popular dish sold in Edinburgh cook shops in the 19th century, and could be said to be an early example of a takeaway meal.

Sadly, the wild salmon population is in decline, as overfishing and disease have gradually taken their toll. Fewer and fewer salmon are returning to the rivers to spawn. Salmon are especially vulnerable to pollution and clean oxygenated water is essential for them to spawn. The restricted waters of the few remaining salmon rivers remain unpolluted and so provide good breeding conditions.

Wild salmon fishing

Fishing the rivers for wild salmon is now strictly controlled and you must purchase a licence for a specific part of a river beforehand. Keen anglers from around the world come to the Scottish Highlands throughout the year to enjoy fishing the traditional way and plenty of

Left *Salmon-fishing rivers are now highly restricted, especially during the spawning season.*

Above Hand-sliced high-quality smoked salmon has become a speciality on the Islands.

excellent food too. The River Tweed is one of the best salmon rivers in Europe, with a long season and a good supply of excellent salmon.

Salmon farming

Since the late 1960s, salmon farms have sprung up throughout the Highlands and Islands, many of them owned and run by Scandinavians who developed the technique throughout the previous decades. Farmed salmon has the advantage of being available all year round, and it is plentiful and cheaper than the wild version. It can now be found in every major store and supermarket around Scotland.

Much controversy rages over the subject of salmon farming. Critics say that the flavour and texture of farmed salmon is much inferior to that of the wild fish, and it is true that the taste of wild salmon is completely different from that of farmed. Farmed salmon also has a softer, slightly flabbier texture than its wild relative, perhaps because of its relatively easy life, being fed, spawned and reared in carefully controlled conditions.

Farming also causes environmental problems as it pollutes the lochs and coastal areas. Some producers have taken measures to ensure that their farms are environmentally friendly, and often organic too. A few high-quality farms have been developed to address both the environmental problems and to enhance the taste of the fish.

Smoked salmon

A flavoursome luxury, Scottish smoked salmon has become well known throughout the world for its quality and excellent taste. Many producers make speciality high-quality smoked salmon, smoked in aromatic woods for fine flavours and a delicately textured fish.

Curing and smoking salmon are skills which take years to master and which are performed by dedicated craftsmen and women. The flavour and colour of the smoked salmon will vary according to the cure, the type of fuel used and the type of smoking. The art is to blend these three elements well. The traditional process is to skin and fillet the fish first, then rest it in salt, before washing off the salt and placing the fish in a smoking oven for up to 48 hours. The fish is then thinly sliced by hand.

Smoked salmon makes its mark as a first course, traditionally served with wholemeal bread, lemon juice and ground black pepper. Recently it has become a popular appetizer, served on drop scones or Scotch pancakes with cream cheese or yogurt. The Scottish breakfast menu would not be complete without scrambled eggs and smoked salmon, and it is also used in main courses to add flavour to fish dishes.

Below Salmon is traditionally smoked in large ovens lined with sliding shelves.

Feasts and festivals

Festivities, celebrations and parties are key to Scottish culture. There are the raucous Scottish reels accompanied by Gaelic music played on the accordion, bagpipes and fiddle. There are Highland Games, Burns Night and Hogmanay. Perhaps the best-known events in Scotland are the Edinburgh International Festival and the Edinburgh Festival Fringe, which together showcase music, theatre and dance.

Below *Fireworks light the Edinburgh streets at midnight at the Hogmanay New Year's Eve festivities.*

Hogmanay

New Year's Eve in Scotland is Hogmanay. Festivities involve street parties, fireworks and costumes, especially in Edinburgh where the city centre is closed to normal traffic for the duration. The origins of the word Hogmanay are unknown. It may derive from the Norse *Hoggunott* or night of slaughter when animals were killed for a midwinter feast, or from *aguillanneuf*, the old French street cry for gifts on the eve of New Year. The traditional New Year song is "Auld Lang Syne"; the

version sung today was reworked and made popular by Robert Burns, the famous Scottish poet.

A great many traditions surround Hogmanay, many related to food. The "first foot" in the house after midnight must be a dark-haired male, carrying symbolic coal, black bun or shortbread. Black bun is a very rich, dark fruitcake encased in pastry, usually accompanied by a wee dram. Clootie dumpling (clootie is the cloth in which the pudding is boiled) is a fruit pudding with a coin concealed inside. Traditionally, the person who got the coin was given the newborn lambs in the spring.

In Edinburgh and other parts of Scotland the traditional Hogmanay beverage until well into the 19th century was *het pint*, a potent blend of hot spiced ale, eggs and whisky. A couple of hours before midnight, great gleaming copper kettles of *het pint* were carried through the streets. Cupbearers pressed everyone into having a "noggin".

In Kirkwall, Orkney, a New Year Ba' Game takes place in the street on 1 January. Much merriment and excitement accompanies the game where the Uppies and the Doonies fight for a cork-filled leather ball.

Burns Night

Scottish communities throughout the world commemorate the birth, on 25 January 1759, of the poet Robert Burns with the traditional Burns Supper. The intimate and magical night is heavily ritualized. Before the meal begins Burns' Selkirk Grace is recited:

> *Some hae meat and canna eat*
> *And some wad eat, that want it,*
> *But we hae meat, and we can eat,*
> *Sae let the Lord be thankit.*

A piper enters, followed by the chef carrying the haggis. A waiter follows

Above *A chef and piper bring in the haggis at a Burns Night supper.*

behind carrying a bottle of whisky. They walk around the guests, ending at the top table, where the chairman takes the whisky and pours out two large glasses. The haggis is put on the table and the whiskies are given to the piper and to the chef. Then the haggis is "addressed" with the Burns' poem "Address to a Haggis" (1786), which begins:

Fair fa' your honest, sonsie face,
Great chieftain o' the puddin'-race!

A dirk (dagger) is plunged into the haggis and a St Andrew's cross is cut on the top. It is served with bashed neeps and champit tatties – mashed turnips and creamed potatoes. After the meal is over there are whisky toasts to "The Immortal Memory" of Burns. The evening continues with Burns songs and ends with "Auld Lang Syne" and three cheers for absent friends.

The Edinburgh Festival

The plethora of cultural activities held over six weeks each year in the summer are collectively known as the Edinburgh International Festival. The largest arts festival in the world, the Edinburgh Festival has a splendid programme of events that includes art exhibitions, café concerts, talks, lectures and workshops plus live performances by internationally renowned artists. It attracts thousands of visitors from all over the world.

Food and drink are an essential part of the festival with farmers' markets offering local foods, lively food debates with top Scottish food writers and chefs, food-themed films, opportunities to sample beers from Scottish breweries, plus wine tastings from Scottish wine merchants and a chance to discover the origins of whisky with a wee dram or two on offer! There is plenty to eat and drink too as Edinburgh's finest cafés and restaurants offer a wide choice of food and drinks.

The Highland Games

Bursting with clan rivalry, the Highland Games have their roots in ancient Celtic traditions and originated with the clan meetings organized by the chiefs. The most important games are the Edinburgh Highland Games in August, and in September the Braemar Gathering and Highland Games, and the Aberdeen and Aboyne Highland Games.

Formalization and annual gatherings began around 1820 as part of the revival of tartan and Highland culture and in 1848 the Braemar Gathering was attended by Queen Victoria. The competitions were much as they are today, with traditional stone and

Below *The Edinburgh streets are crowded with performers, stalls and food fairs during the Festival.*

Right The Highland Games include a traditional dance competition with brightly coloured tartans.

hammer throwing, tossing the caber, piping and dancing, along with running and jumping events.

Food and whisky are abundant, with plenty of spit roasts and local pies. Raspberries and strawberries abound, served with fresh cream and shortbreads.

Harvest celebrations

In the Celtic year, *Lammas* heralded the start of the harvest and it was an annual fair day in most parts of Scotland until the 20th century. The gathering-in of a successful *hairst* (harvest) has been celebrated since ancient times, and the climax was the harvest feast or *kirn*, also known as the *muckle supper* (big supper).

Ale-crowdie (also called meal-and-ale) always featured at the harvest feast in Aberdeen and north-east Scotland, so much so that it gave its name to the festival. It was always made with the first of the grain, to commemorate the renewal of the food supply. The meal

was put in a large bowl or small wooden tub and ale was poured over until it was of drinking consistency – if it was too thin it was an omen that next year's crops would be poor. The drink was sweetened with treacle, laced with whisky and left to stand. Charms were concealed in the bowl and everyone present took a spoonful.

In the Highlands the new grain was made into a bannock known as *moilean moire*. In Orkney a fruited bannock was given as a reward to the man who carried the last load of sheaves into the stack yard. He was then given a head start and chased by the other men and only allowed to eat it when he had out-distanced his pursuers.

Cranachan or cream crowdie (from the Gaelic *cruaidh*, meaning thick and firm), a luscious combination of toasted oatmeal, cream, honey and whisky, was also essential at harvest celebrations.

Hallowe'en

The coming of Christianity replaced the old pagan feasts with religious festivals. Samhain or Samhuinn, the most important Celtic festival marking the start of winter, became the Eve of All Hallows (the night before All Saints' Day) or Hallowe'en on 31 October. It was a mysterious time when it was

Left Traditional Scottish music is played at many celebrations, with fiddles, guitars and accordians.

Above *Evening celebrations often involve a ceilidh with Scottish reeling.*

believed that ghosts, fairies, demons and witches wandered the earth. Bonfires were lit to ward off evil spirits, masks were worn to avoid being recognized by the spirits, and lucky charms protected against evil. Hallowe'en "guizing" and the wearing of masks and costumes is a remnant of those beliefs.

Hollowed-out turnips with a candle inside were placed on gateposts to frighten evil spirits – the origin of pumpkin lanterns today. The custom of eating special cakes probably derives from the practice of baking spiced cakes to herald the winter. Gingerbreads and biscuits were especially popular in Scotland.

Fortune-telling and magic were other traditional customs of Hallowe'en. A fortune-telling pudding (usually a large bowl of cranachan) contained small charms. Each charm had a specific meaning: a coin meant wealth, a ring foretold marriage and a thimble indicated no marriage.

Yule and Christmas festivities

Christmas festivities were banned by the Church in 1649 at the Reformation. The annual holiday was abolished and church ministers checked on their parishioners to make sure no festive foods or celebrations were in evidence. Proper festivities did not resume until the mid-18th century, and still today the New Year is the more important holiday of the midwinter period in Scotland.

Whipkull or *whipcol*, a mixture of beaten egg yolks and sugar, was served in a special bowl to the Shetland *Udallers* (lairds) at the great Yule breakfasts. Sometimes cream was added and later still a good measure of rum or whisky. Rich, crisp shortbread is the traditional accompaniment.

Atholl brose is another popular Christmas drink enjoyed on the days running up to Christmas Day. It is made from whisky, strained honey, oatmeal and sweet cream slowly beaten together in the right order and proportion. Its creation is credited to the Duke of Atholl when, during a Highland Rebellion in 1745, he foiled his enemy by filling the well from which they drank with the heady mixture. The intoxicated men were then easily defeated and the drink became more widely known.

Up-Helly-Aa

Torches, fireworks and bonfires light the night sky in this midwinter fire festival in Lerwick on Shetland. It is rooted in an ancient Viking festival, marking the end of Yule, and the 5,000 onlookers and participants dress as Vikings.

A full-sized replica of a Viking longboat is paraded through Lerwick by the Chief Guizer, who represents Sigurd Hlodvisson – Sigurd the Stout, Earl of Orkney, who died in 1014 on the battlefield at Clontarf, Ireland. In the early evening 850 torches are lit. The guizers throw them into the ship to set it ablaze. As they do so they sing "Up-Helly-Aa". Rockets and guns are fired from ships, and the longboat burns spectacularly. Fortified with whisky, the crowds sing the anthem, "The Norseman's Home".

Below *The midwinter fire festival of Up-Helly-Aa includes the burning of a Viking longboat.*

Quality foods for the future

Scottish foods have become celebrated around the world, from the excellent smoked salmon and other smoked goods to the highly prized beef and meats. Many classic Scottish recipes have survived virtually unchanged through the centuries, and their history offers a fascinating glimpse of the past. However, Scotland's food and cooking is not content to rest on its laurels, but continues to evolve and develop thanks to dedicated artisan food and drink producers, manufacturers and innovative chefs who skilfully incorporate new ingredients, along with modern ideas and cooking methods.

One of the main catalysts for change has been the explosion in tourism that has taken place in Scotland throughout the last few decades. Thousands flock to see the spectacular scenery and to enjoy the walking, hiking, skiing and other outdoor activities, such as sailing, white-water rafting and golf.

Below Scotland's cuisine has been transformed into a celebration of the natural flavours of fresh local produce.

To meet the new demand of discriminating tourists, cafés, restaurants and hotels around the country have transformed everyday fare into internationally acclaimed cuisine. Much of the food is based on traditional Scottish, but with a twist. It may be fused and blended with modern and global preparations, cooking and serving techniques, for example haggis prepared with apples in a puff pastry pie and served with a jus of local berries. Many chefs create their own versions of Scottish specialities, such as the popular variations on the "fish supper" theme.

The new tourism has attracted top chefs to the country, including many Scottish chefs returning from training abroad. Restaurants are rated by the quality of their cuisine and compete with each other to raise standards.

Scotland is now considered a luxury holiday destination, with excellent eating opportunities. Europe's first six-star hotel is to be created in a Highland castle over the coming years, paving the way for further excellence.

Above Mussels are grown on ropes at an organic farm on Loch Fyne for a reliable and good-quality harvest.

Fish and shellfish

There has been a huge growth in the quantity and quality of fish and shellfish products. This range of excellent foods on ready supply has been recognized as a quintessentially Scottish speciality and a plethora of traditional and modern producers have risen to the challenge.

The product ranges have become more diverse and include all sorts of smoked and prepared fish and shellfish, including new smoking flavours to produce delicate smoked salmon. The quality has increased enormously and advanced techniques, skills and a competitive market have resulted in superb fish and seafood.

The amount that is produced has also grown through the surge in new farming methods. Although some farms produce superb foods, watch out for some poor-quality farmed fish that can lack flavour and texture. Organic and environmentally considerate farms, such as the one at Loch Fyne, offer excellent fish and shellfish without harming the lochs and coastlines.

Above A fair and food market at the head of Loch Fyne celebrates the boom in new foods throughout Scotland.

Quality products for export

The Scottish food and drink export market has been growing rapidly over the last few decades. These exports are not only from large-scale producers but from smaller enterprises, often family-run, using local specialist ingredients.

Appreciation of the quality and refinement of Scotch whisky has spread around the globe. It is now one of the UK's top five exports and is exported to about 200 different markets.

Traditional dishes such as smoked salmon, shortbread and haggis have achieved international renown and high-quality products are exported for those living abroad. Several tons of haggis are exported for Burns Night suppers on 25 January. Haggis is very popular in France where it is now served in top Parisian restaurants. Shortbread, Scotland's national biscuit, is also much in demand and is exported all over the world. Baxters of Speyside export their delicious traditionally made marmalades, including the ever-popular Malt Whisky Marmalade.

New foods, new markets

Modern food enterprises have also proved successful – deer farming, the seaweed-fed sheep of the Shetlands, ice creams from the Orkney Isles and a host of new cheeses. There has also been a revival of ancient recipes, such as fruit and flower wines from Orkney, silver birch wine, heather ale, and spruce and pine ales from Viking days, making excellent gifts and souvenirs.

In every city, town and village throughout Scotland, you'll find both traditional and modern examples of Scottish products. The Bridge of Allan, a tiny village near Stirling, boasts one of the best food shops in Scotland, selling top-quality Scottish food and drink from both small specialist producers and larger manufacturers.

New markets continue to open up – organic foods, such as organic heather-fed lamb, are now popular. A new generation of chefs has devised imaginative and exciting ways to use Scottish produce to create modern recipes. Pubs and restaurants offer a wealth of different cuisines using local produce.

This is an exciting time for Scottish food and drink. Thanks to the efforts of the producers who constantly strive to ensure that it is recognized as the best in the world, it looks likely that the future of Scottish food is assured for generations to come.

Below Specialist cheeses are made for local dishes and for export, such as these from the Sgriob-Ruadh Dairy near Tobermory on the Isle of Mull.

The Scottish kitchen

The Scots take great pride in their cuisine, and hospitality has always been a tradition. They prefer to use local produce, and are fortunate in the plentiful supplies of meat, game, fish and shellfish, fruit and vegetables, dairy and cereal crops that Scotland provides. Over the centuries the Scots have adopted and adapted influences from abroad and as a result cooking in Scotland is eclectic, and is still developing to this day.

Fresh fish

Scotland is home to an ancient fishing tradition, its busy fishing ports ranging all along the coastline and the Islands. The natural harbours along the east coast have produced a thriving fishing industry. On the west coast, fishing gradually developed after people lost their lands and sought sustenance from the sea. On the Islands, fishing was a way of life. A plentiful supply of fish, especially smoked and cured fish, has always been the country's traditional heritage ever since the days when slow travel made the preservation of fish an economic necessity.

Preserving fish from the earliest times was achieved by wind drying (*blawn*) or sun drying (*rizzared* or *tiled*), pickling or smoking, according to the type of fish. Oily fish, such as herring and mackerel, were more problematic and it wasn't until the 14th century that a way to preserve oily fish was devised by a

Above *Salmon steaks contain the bone and so are ideal for poaching, grilling (broiling) or adding to fish soups.*

Dutch man called William Beukelsz. The fish had to be freshly caught, gutted and rinsed, then packed tightly in barrels, layered with coarse salt to exclude air.

Entire families were involved in the business of fishing. Children collected and prepared bait and boys went to sea with their fathers when they were 14 years old. Fishing communities were closely knit and boys married girls from

Above *Salmon fillets are the preferred cut for restaurants as they contain no bones and less fat and can be accompanied by fine sauces.*

their own or a nearby fishing village. The men went to sea, an arduous occupation at the best of times, but made even more exhausting and dangerous by the occasional storms, fogs and freezing-cold weather. The women baited the lines, gutted, cleaned and cured or smoked the fish and also sold the catch – often walking some distance to the nearest town with heavy *creels* (baskets) on their backs.

All types of fish were sold by fishwives, who went from door to door in rural areas. An old Edinburgh street cry was: "Haddies, caller haddies, fresh an' loupin' in the creel", advertising live haddock flapping in their baskets.

Types of fish

The fish enjoyed today are different from those eaten in the past. Sadly, some fish are less common now. On the other hand, fish farming has led to a greater availability of some fish, such as rainbow trout.

Salmon is the fish most often associated with Scotland. There are traditionally two main types of salmon, the Atlantic salmon from the sea and the wild salmon from the rivers. In addition there is now farmed salmon of

Left *Pittenweem in East Neuk remains an active fishing port, with a fish market at 8am every morning held in sheds on the harbourside.*

various qualities. These all have different flavours, colours and textures, with wild salmon being the finest.

Herring used to be plentiful and cheap, taking pride of place in Scottish fish cooking. The "silver darlings", as they were known, swam in huge shoals in Scottish seas, but once caught they had to be eaten as fresh as possible as they deteriorated quickly.

Plump and succulent with a rich flavour, they were cooked in various ways. A favourite dish throughout Scotland was Tatties and Herring, where the fish were steamed over the almost-cooked potatoes. Enormous quantities of salt-pickled herring were exported in barrels to Scandinavia and Russia (where they were a staple of the diet) in the 19th century.

Tasty, nutritious and easy to digest, herrings can be coated with rolled oats and fried in oil for a few minutes or simply grilled (broiled). They can be bought fresh or smoked and also pickled in spiced brine from delicatessen counters in supermarkets.

Mackerel is still caught abundantly around the coast, especially by small fishermen or locals fishing over the weekend. The mackerel are eaten as fresh as possible, usually simply pan-fried or grilled (broiled).

Haddock is now the most popular white fish in Scotland, often found in fish and chip shops. In the past it was preserved by salt-curing, and this was mentioned in the Household Book of James VI in the 16th century. It is used to make the ever-popular fish and chips, known as a "fish supper" in Scotland. Haddock is also delicious baked or steamed as well as coated in breadcrumbs or batter and fried. Many experienced fishmongers believe that very fresh fish is not always the best choice, and that it should be left for a while before cutting – the actual time depends on the type of fish. This is best left to the expert.

Cod is now an expensive fish, a result of overfishing in the Atlantic. It remains popular, often as a result of the many recipes and traditions surrounding it.

Sea bass is a flavourful fish with a fine soft texture, a favourite of the fish restaurants. Most is farmed these days as it is increasingly rare in the wild.

Above
Sea trout is a rare delicacy enjoyed in Scotland's top restaurants.

Monkfish used to be thrown back off the fishing boats, but are now prized fish both in the home and on the restaurant menu. The meaty tails are served with simple sauces.

Trout Rainbow trout is now enjoyed much more widely owing to new farms that have sprung up in the lochs and around the coastlines. Both fresh and smoked trout is exported abroad.

Sea trout and river (brown) trout are harder to come by these days and are rarely seen except on the occasional restaurant menu or, of course, if you catch one yourself.

Above Mackerel are found in abundance around the coasts, and can often be bought fresh at the harbour.

Above Herring are especially popular on Shetland and the Orkneys owing to the Scandinavian influence.

Above Rainbow trout (top) are now farmed, while the river (brown) trout (bottom) can only be caught wild.

Smoked fish

In the days before refrigeration and fast transport, a major concern was the preservation of fish. They were smoked in home chimneys, over peat fires or in specially built sheds over halved whisky barrels. Today fish are generally smoked for flavour. Haddock, mackerel, sprats and herring are smoked over oak, beech, hickory, cherry wood, Douglas fir or whisky barrel chippings, which all produce a magnificent flavour. Every curer has his own unique brining recipe and secret flavourings.

Early Scandinavian settlers brought with them their tradition of hot-smoking fish, and it has continued to the present day. In the early 18th century the people of the tiny village of Auchmithie took their skills to the growing port of Arbroath, just north of Dundee and it became a centre for smoking. The salty, smoky, mellow aromas still waft enticingly through the town. Originally the fishwives arranged the fish on rods and smoked them over discarded whisky barrels, which produced a darker colour than those of today. The name "Arbroath smokie" is protected and can now only be used to describe haddock smoked in the traditional manner (dating back to the late 1800s) within an 8km/5-mile radius of Arbroath.

Smoked haddock

Smoking haddock was a particular skill of the village of Findon (pronounced Finnan), south of Aberdeen, and it was from this village that the cure took its name. Pale golden Finnan haddock is renowned throughout the world and has a superb delicate flavour.

The original cures produced a hard, heavily smoked fish, but modern cures have improved the flavour and texture enormously. There are hot-smoked and cold-smoked cures, with several regional variations.

Pales or Glasgow pales have a shorter brining and smoking time than Finnan haddock. Some are very lightly smoked and thus have only a slight smoky flavour and just a hint of colour. They are usually made from smaller fish. Smoked fillet, sometimes known as Aberdeen fillet, is a single fillet from a large haddock. The skin is left on to hold the fish together during the curing process. Golden Cutlet is made from a fillet of haddock or whiting with the skin removed. It is only lightly brined and smoked so has less flavour than any other cure.

The garish yellow dyed smoked haddock are best avoided. You'll find authentic Finnan haddock at good

Above *Quality fish and shellfish for smoking is farmed in Loch Fyne.*

fishmongers. It is delicious simmered gently in milk or water and served with a poached egg on top. Smoked haddock is an essential ingredient of Cullen skink, a creamy fish and potato soup. Hot-smoked haddock or Arbroath smokies are also known by their original names, *tied tailies* or *pinwiddies*, and are succulently moist with a wonderful flavour. Whole haddock are split open and the head and guts removed before they are tied in pairs by their tails, then lightly brined and smoked over oak or beech wood until cooked.

Above *Smoked haddock is a favourite for breakfast dishes, including smoked haddock topped with poached eggs.*

Above *Arbroath smokies are hot-smoked haddock that are left whole and always sold in pairs.*

Above *Smoked halibut has a translucent white flesh and lovely delicate flavour.*

Above
*Kippers are
smoked over
an oak fire for
4–18 hours.*

Kippers and smoked herrings

Freshly caught herrings were originally dried over smoking seaweed and sprinkled with saltwater to preserve them. Kippers are plump herring that have been split, cleaned and soaked in brine for a few minutes then hot smoked. Scottish fishwives travelled to the villages of Craster (known as the kipper capital of England) and Seahouses in England in the 19th

century to gut the herring ready for smoking. They lived in dilapidated buildings, known as kip houses, which were only suitable for sleeping in – hence the British slang term "having a kip". Those from Loch Fyne are smoked over oak chips (often from whisky barrels) and are particularly good. They can be grilled (broiled), baked or simmered in boiling water. An old way of cooking them was to place the kippers in a jug of boiling hot water and leave them for 4–5 minutes, by which time they were cooked.

Bloaters are whole herring that have been cured and lightly smoked, but not split or gutted. The name may come from the Old Norse *blautr*, or from the fact that the fish are plumper than dry-cured fish. They have a delicate smoky flavour and remain silver in colour. They were popular in the 19th century.

Other smoked fish

Almost every type of fish in Scotland has a tradition of being smoked, with lesser or greater success. Smoked salmon is without doubt the best-known type.

Above *Smoked
mackerel makes a
tasty pâté.*

Smoked trout is a favourite for making delicious patés and mousses and fine first courses, often served with dill or horseradish sauce. The best is first brined and then gutted and smoked over birch with a little peat for a smokier flavour. High-quality smoked trout is now prepared in a similar way to smoked salmon.
Smoked mackerel has a rich flavour and a succulent velvety-smooth texture. It can be eaten cold with a salad and makes a delicious pâté.
Smoked halibut has a translucent white flesh and a delicate smoky flavour. It is smoked and thinly sliced in a similar way to smoked salmon.

Above *Smoked trout fillets make an excellent first course.*

Right *Sea trout is relatively rare now, so smoked sea trout is a real treat.*

Fresh shellfish

The Scots have always made the most of their superb shellfish and have devised many creative recipes for them. The vast Scottish waters provide rich feeding grounds and yield some of the world's best shellfish.

Crustaceans

These curious-looking creatures with 10 legs make for some delicious dishes. Available around the coast, they are often exported to restaurants around Europe.

Lobster is regarded as one of the tastiest shellfish and has a rich, intense flavour. Originally eaten by the poor, it became a gourmet food in the 19th century. They are thought to be at their best in August. Lobster is usually boiled but can also be grilled (broiled). The dark blue-green shell becomes scarlet when cooked. Lobsters and crabs were originally fished by coaxing them from the rocks with a stick. In the 1750s creel fishing was introduced, using special pots fitted with bait. By the end of the 18th century catches, particularly in Orkney, were enormous.

Above
Langoustines are now a
speciality of many top restaurants.

Langoustines are also known as Dublin Bay prawns (jumbo shrimp), Norway lobsters or crayfish. They were largely regarded as a nuisance by fishermen until the 1960s when increased foreign travel began to create a demand for them. As scampi they became a gourmet food, exported all over the world and a fixture on restaurant menus. Pale orange-pink with white striped claws, they are sold fresh or pre-boiled and may be eaten hot or cold. If fresh, boil in salted water for 3–4 minutes and serve in the shell. Pull off the head and claws, cut through the cartilage underneath and open out. Remove the whole tail and take out the spinal cord. Crack the claws and remove the tasty meat.

Crabs, or *partans* as they are called in Scotland, are caught in creels and are sold live or pre-boiled. There are two main types: the common brown crab or the rarer shore variety. Their reddish-brown shells are tinged with purple and the claws are black. The flavour of the white meat is more delicate than lobster and connoisseurs regard Scottish crabs as superior to English crabs. The cooked meat is removed from the shell and claws and should be eaten as fresh as possible. *Partan bree*, a creamy crab soup, is a famous Scottish dish.

Above The brown or common crab is easy to come by along the coast. It makes an excellent dressed crab.

Left Oyster beds on Loch Fyne provide the market with succulent, well-flavoured farmed oysters.

Above *Razor clams must be cleaned thoroughly before cooking. They are collected from the island beaches.*

Above *Clams were a dietary mainstay in the past. They were collected from beaches and coastlines.*

Above *Native oysters are slow-growers and are considered the finest oysters. They are also the most expensive.*

Molluscs

Many of these small shelled creatures can simply be collected from the beaches or coastlines around Scotland, making them an excellent free food source for locals. Cockles (small clams), clams and razor clams fall easily into this category, although they are more difficult to find these days for sale.

Oysters were once so plentiful that they were a staple of the poor and were included in many dishes to eke out the ingredients. They were eaten alone, used as a stuffing for fish or meat and made into sauces. Native oyster beds were overfished, became polluted and, by the middle of the 20th century, were almost wiped out. Oyster farming in the unpolluted waters of sea lochs on the west coast and around the Islands has brought about a revival. The Pacific oyster is often used for farming and is more elongated than the native oyster. To open an oyster, hold it in one hand, well wrapped in a dish towel. Push the point of an oyster knife into the oyster's hinge and apply pressure, and retain the liquor. You could ask your fishmonger to do this. Serve on a plate of crushed ice with lemon wedges, brown bread and a sprinkling of cayenne pepper.

Scallops There are two types of scallops in Scotland – the Great scallop and the Queen scallop. The creamy white flesh is firm with a mild flavour and is enclosed in a shell that can measure up to 15cm/6in long. The orange coral is edible and has a rich flavour and smooth texture. Scallops need only a few minutes' cooking. It is important not to overcook them as the meat will become tough and rubbery, losing its sweet taste.

Scallops are also available still in their closed shells, when they are at their optimum freshness. To prepare them, scrub the shells well and place them curved side down in a low oven for a few minutes. Open the shells with a knife and wash under cold running water, then remove the grey-brown frill and the black intestine. Soak the flesh in iced water for several hours before using so the flesh becomes firm. Prick the coral with a needle before cooking to prevent it bursting. Serve the scallops in their shells.

Mussels make a wonderful main dish or first course. Musselburgh, near Edinburgh, was so named because of the large mussel bed at the mouth of the River Esk. It became a great mussel-eating centre.

Mussels (*Mytilus eduilis*) are commercially farmed, mainly along the west coast. They have less flavour and paler flesh than the wild, deep orange-fleshed mussels. Larger horse mussels (*Modiolus modiolus*) are known as *clabbie dubhs* in Scotland (from the Gaelic *clab-dubh*, meaning large black mouth) and have a robust flavour. Mussels must have tightly closed shells; discard any that remain open when tapped (and any that stay closed once cooked) as this indicates that they are not live. Scrub the shells to remove any barnacles, remove the beards then wash in several changes of cold water. Steam or boil in white wine or water, or add to fish stews.

Below *Great or king scallops have a lovely sweet taste and delicate texture.*

Game's rich flavours

Scotland's wild open country has long been home to a large variety of game, which has always had a place on Scottish meal tables, particularly in the Highlands and on the Islands. Game dealers and butchers sell game according to season, and the quality and flavour of Scottish game is unrivalled anywhere in the world.

Almost all game must be hung to develop flavour and tenderize the flesh. Birds are hung by the neck, unplucked, in a cool place. Deer are *gralloched* (gutted) and skinned before hanging. The length of time they are hung for depends on the type of game, where they are hung and the weather; game goes off quickly when it is thundery, for example.

Game is frequently cooked with the foods it lived on when alive. For example, rabbit is partnered with wild thyme and grouse with rowanberries or tiny raspberries. Any leftovers are made into soups and broths.

Venison

Scottish venison is considered to be the best in the world and is one of the glories of Scottish cuisine. Red deer live in the wild hills and are the most common. The shooting season for stags is from 1 July to 20 October and for hinds from 21 October to 15 February. Stag meat has the fuller flavour of the two. Roe deer live in forests; the season for bucks is from 1 May to 20 October and for does from 21 October to 28 or 29 February. Fallow deer inhabit forests and parks and the season for bucks is from 1 August to 30 April and for does from 21 October to 15 February.

Farmed venison is less expensive than wild and the meat is more tender, with a delicate, less gamey flavour. Some deer farmers have developed a trade in venison sausages and pies. Wild venison is usually marinated in alcohol and oil to tenderize the flesh and keep it moist as it cooks. All venison is lean and low in cholesterol.

Above *The most common deer species in Scotland are the red deer and the roe deer. The male red deer are called stags and the females hinds. The roe deer are known as bucks and does.*

The age of the animal and the hanging time greatly affect the flavour and texture of the meat. Some deer are hung for only a few days, while others are hung for two weeks, by which time they have developed a high, strong gamey flavour.

The meat is dark red and close-grained with firm white fat. Most venison cuts should be cooked quickly and allowed to rest before serving, except shoulder and shin, which are better braised. The haunch, saddle or leg are best for roasting or for slicing into medallions. Chops from the ribs can be fried or grilled (broiled). A strong-flavoured meat, venison needs to be matched with robust flavours such as spices, rowanberries, juniper berries and red wine. The flank is best casseroled or minced (ground) and the neck is used in soups. The kidneys are usually fried. The liver is a great delicacy and can be fried or used (with the heart and flank) to make venison haggis.

Above *Venison cuts that benefit from long, slow cooking include neck (left), shoulder and shin. They make tasty stews and soups and are commonly used in pies.*

Left *Red deer haunch is a prime cut, ideal for roasting or making into steaks. It is now popular as a celebration spit roast, surrounded by roast vegetables and berries.*

Above *Rabbits are now farmed (top), although the wild rabbits (middle) are leaner and tastier. The saddle and leg joints (bottom) are the most frequently used.*

Wild boar

A few enterprising Scottish farmers are producing wild boar – a very recent development that is proving popular with consumers. Unlike pork, wild boar is a red meat with a very tasty, slightly gamey flavour. It is similar to, but not as strong as, venison, and the taste becomes more pronounced as the animal ages. The meat is noted for its leanness and flavour and is sold fresh or processed into bacon and sausages. Prized cuts are the saddle and haunches, both of which can also be smoked to produce wild boar ham. Other cuts include loin, shoulder, loin chops, leg steaks and fillet (tenderloin).

Hare and rabbit

A favourite catch in the Highlands, hare is hung for seven to ten days and the blood is reserved to enrich and thicken the gravy. Hares are at their best from October to January.

A well-hung hare would go into *bawd bree*, a traditional soup-stew that dates from the 16th century. *Bawd* is the old Scots word for hare and *bree* means the juice or liquid in which food is cooked. Jugged hare, often served at harvest feasts, was made by packing a jointed hare into a large stone jar or jug with its blood, plus seasonings and spices. The jar was placed in a large pan of boiling water for about three hours until cooked.

Rabbits are best eaten fresh, (although they can be hung) and wild rabbit has a stronger flavour. The meat tends to be dry so it should be well basted or cooked with liquid. Lowland Scots ate more rabbits than the

Right *Wild boar saddle (top) with fillet (tenderloin) and chops (bottom) can be treated like a good free-range pork.*

Above *Wild rabbits proliferate in all parts of Scotland, providing excellent game meat.*

Highlanders, and a favourite way of cooking them was with onions, or else they were simply roasted. Rabbit meat was also minced (ground) and mixed with pork and onions. This mixture was shaped into a roll and also used to make soups and pies. Kingdom of Fife pie is made with rabbit and pickled pork or bacon.

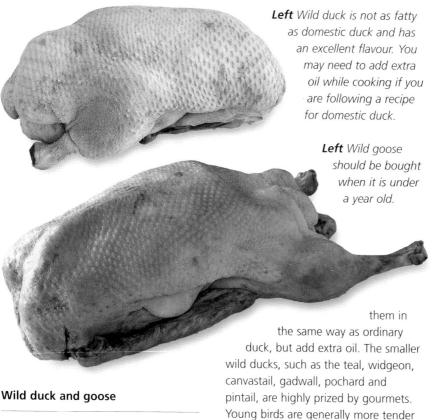

Left Wild duck is not as fatty as domestic duck and has an excellent flavour. You may need to add extra oil while cooking if you are following a recipe for domestic duck.

Left Wild goose should be bought when it is under a year old.

Wild goose makes a tasty roast. The plump Canada goose is the largest and most commonly found, although the smaller greylag, pinkfoot and whitefront are also good.

Pheasant

The diet of a pheasant does not include much heather because they do not frequent the high moorlands, so it has a mild flavour. If eaten without hanging their flavour is similar to that of chicken. After hanging, the flesh develops a mild gamey taste. The pheasant season extends from 1 October to 1 February, and they are at their best in November and December as the birds have more flavour after the first frosts. Pheasants are often bought as a brace (a cock and a hen bird). A cock usually weighs around 1.3kg/3lb and a hen about 900g/2lb. The hen is less dry than the

them in the same way as ordinary duck, but add extra oil. The smaller wild ducks, such as the teal, widgeon, canvastail, gadwall, pochard and pintail, are highly prized by gourmets. Young birds are generally more tender and older ones can be tough and need to be cooked long and slow in a stew or casserole.

Wild duck and goose

Far less fatty than the domesticated birds, wild ducks and geese can still be found in Scotland. Try to get birds that come from inland waters, rather than from saltwater coasts and marshes as the flesh can tough and salty. It is also better to eat birds before they reach a year old.
Wild ducks Mallards are the largest and the most common wild ducks. Use

Left Oven-ready cock (top) and hen pheasants can be bought from quality butchers. Although there are often small blemishes on the skin, pick a bird that looks plump and healthy.

Above Pheasants thrive in the Lowlands, and their meat is quite mildly flavoured. They are sold in pairs, a male (bottom) and a female, known as a brace. The hen is more tender and smaller than the cock and will serve three people, while the cock will serve four.

cock and tends to have more flavour. They are grilled (broiled), roasted or jugged in the same way as hare, and are also good stuffed with apples.

Grouse

The red grouse inhabits the Scottish moors where it feeds on heather, blueberries, grasses and herbs, which all impart a unique flavour to the flesh. The flavour varies according to the locality and the hanging time (usually two to seven days) and the meat is stronger than that of other grouse. They are shot from 12 August until 10 December. A native of Scotland, it is only found here and in the north of England.

Grouse flesh tends to be dry, and they were originally cooked on a spit so that they basted themselves as they turned. They can be split up the

Below Wild pheasants can be found throughout Scotland and are easy and tasty game for locals and hunters.

backbone, spatchcocked, brushed with oil and grilled for 10–15 minutes. Grouse should be roasted quickly in a hot oven. Before roasting the bird can be stuffed with cranberries to keep it moist and complement the flavour. Wrap well in streaky (fatty) bacon or brush with butter and baste during cooking. After roasting, the legs (which have a bitter flavour) are usually removed and used in stews and soups where the long cooking mellows the bitterness. The Victorians often enjoyed cold roast grouse for breakfast.

Partridge

The tasty partridge is making a comeback after many years of decline, thanks to the efforts of many estate owners and gamekeepers who have introduced both the French red-legged

Above Red-legged (left) and grey-legged partridges are two different species.

partridge and the smaller native grey partridge. The shooting season is from 1 September to 1 February. Partridge develops more flavour if it is hung well. It can be casseroled or roasted, sometimes with an onion inside, or stuffed with wild mushrooms and cooked in the same way as grouse.

Other game birds

Woodcock has a wonderfully rich flavour and is still found in many gaming reserves. It is roasted with berries and roasted root vegetables such as turnips and potatoes.
Pigeons are small and tasty, and are available all the year round, although each one provides only a small quantity of meat. Squab pigeons are the more tender young pigeons that have a good flavour and texture. They are now farmed commercially and good-quality pigeons are readily available from game butchers.

Scotland's quality meats

From the lush pastures of the Lowlands to sheep-rearing in the bleak Highlands, Scotland's meats have the reputation for excellent flavour, high quality and natural rearing conditions.

Meat is enjoyed frequently in Scotland. In the past, a soup or stew would spread a few smaller joints around a whole family, and the innards would be made into haggis, black puddings (blood sausage) and delicious pie fillings.

Above Tasty entrecôte (sirloin) steaks (top) are cut from the sirloin. The prime cut is the long, lean fillet (tenderloin) (bottom).

Beef

Scottish beef from native breeds such as the shaggy, long-haired Highland cattle or the famous Aberdeen Angus – both of which tolerate the bleak, rugged terrain and harsh weather –

Right Lamb leg and leg steaks are tender and good for roasting and barbecuing.

has achieved international renown for its superb rich full flavour and succulent texture.

Beef needs hanging to develop the flavour and tenderize the meat. Good-quality beef is dark red with a marbling of creamy coloured fat – bright red, wet-looking meat indicates that it has not been hung for long enough.

One of the oldest dishes using beef is Scotch collops, and the recipe appears in many old cookbooks. Originally the meat was thinly sliced, beaten with a rolling pin to flatten it, then seasoned with salt and pepper and fried quickly. "Scotching" meant cutting a criss-cross pattern on the meat before cooking.

Minced collops or "mince and tatties" is a much-loved dish. Minced (ground) beef is cooked very slowly with onions over a low heat until tender. Just before serving, a handful of toasted rolled oats is stirred in and the meat is served with baked or boiled potatoes. Properly made the dish is very tasty, but it is often ruined by the addition of water and cornflour (cornstarch) to thicken it.

Cold roast beef, left over from a roast joint, is often simmered with carrots in an onion gravy to make a dish known as *inky pinky*.

Cheaper, less tender cuts of beef, such as shin (shank), need long, slow cooking in liquid. Boiled beef is something of a misnomer, as the liquid should just bubble very gently for a few hours. Potted meat and meat loaves

are a speciality of Scottish cuisine and these can be bought at most butchers. Potted beef is called *potted hough*, the Scottish name for shin beef.

Forfar was an important centre of the beef trade in Angus, and a speciality of the town is Forfar Bridies, a type of pasty similar to a Cornish pasty. Filled with chopped rump (round) steak and onions, they were named after Maggie Bridie of Glamis, one of many people who sold the tasty pasties at local fairs and markets.

Mutton and lamb

Mutton has been a favourite in Scotland for hundreds of years and in 19th-century Britain, Scottish mutton and lamb were renowned for their flavour and quality. Although sheep were reared mainly for milk and wool, they were slaughtered for meat, and often salted and preserved for winter.

Traditionally, every part of the animal was used – the shoulder and *gigot* (a French term for the leg) were braised or roasted; the blood was made into black pudding (blood sausage); the kidneys were fried; the heart, head and trotters were used in broth. Other parts went to make haggis. *Powsowdie* is a very old dish of sheep's head pie or broth.

There are many breeds of sheep in Scotland. Blackface sheep, for example, are a hardy breed that can withstand

Below *Haggis is a traditional Scottish dish.*

the harshest of winters. They graze on heather-clad hills in summer and feed on hay and turnips in winter. Shetland sheep are a distinctive breed native to the Shetland Isles. The small sheep are very hardy and can weather severe conditions. Their diet of seaweed and heather, together with the salt carried on the strong winds to their pastures, gives them a unique, slightly gamey flavour, quite different from lamb derived from other breeds of sheep produced in other areas.

Salting mutton is still done in the Hebrides, Orkney, Shetland and some northern parts of the Highlands. In the Islands it is called *reested* or *reestit* mutton. The meat (sometimes cut up but always left on the bone) is cured with salt, sugar and spices (in the Highlands juniper berries are used) for up to three weeks, then hung to dry or smoked for 10 to 15 days. A small piece is sufficient to flavour a pot of soup or broth.

Traditional Scottish dishes such as Scotch broth needed long, slow cooking, as they used mutton from a mature sheep rather than young lamb as is more usual today. Mutton has a fuller, richer flavour and is gaining popularity once again, although it remains difficult to obtain.

Scotch pies, made with lamb, were originally sold in taverns and are now a national institution throughout Scotland. Mutton pies were praised by Dr Johnson on his tour of Scotland. The pies are sold by butchers and bakers and have a distinctive shape with a rim of pastry above the lid, which leaves a space that is often filled with mashed potatoes or baked beans. They are always eaten hot, never cold.

Haggis and black pudding

Both a type of sausage that would have been a major part of the staple diet in centuries past, the haggis and the black pudding (blood sausage) have become great symbols of Scottish heritage, custom and tradition. They are still enjoyed widely today, although they are more frequently bought ready-made than prepared by hand in the home.

Haggis is actually a type of sausage, of which the outer cover is discarded and only the juicy inner meat is eaten. It is composed of mutton and lamb and their offal, highly spiced and bound together with oatmeal, and packed into a sheep's stomach ready for lengthy boiling. Nowadays haggis is generally sold cooked, ready for further cooking and reheating.

Black pudding is another quintessential Scottish food. It is a blood sausage that is usually highly spiced. It is bought already poached and is then sliced and fried for breakfast or supper, or to slip into a sandwich for a tasty lunch.

Below *The nationalist poet Robert Burns immortalized the haggis in his memorable "Address to a haggis", which is recited throughout Scotland every year on Burns Night.*

Dairy and cheese

Dairy products traditionally played an important role in providing nutrients and protein in the diet. As a result, cheese, butter, milk and cream abound in the old recipes, as well as many new ones too.

Creams, milks and butter

Much of Scottish cooking is based on the flavourful addition of creams, milks or butter. Buttermilk, whey and sour milk were traditionally enjoyed as refreshing summer drinks, and buttermilk was added to mashed potatoes, porridge (oatmeal), scones and bannocks for extra flavour. In Shetland whey was fermented in oak casks for several months to produce *blaand*, a drink that has been revived and is now produced commercially.

Many traditional dishes are based on milk and cream, not only the creamy vegetables and mashed potatoes, but also the desserts and cakes. Cranachan

Below Dairy farming is strong in the Lowlands, where luscious creams and tasty local cheeses are produced.

Below The wash for Bishop Kennedy includes a generous dash of whisky, giving a lovely tasty rind.

is a delicious dessert traditionally made with fresh raspberries, oatmeal or porridge oats and fresh, thick cream. Many cakes and desserts were created with a large dollop of fresh cream in mind, such as the tarts and fruit pies and crumbles, or *frushies* as they are known. Cream and milk are also favourites in drinks, especially with whisky either as a cream liqueur or floating on top of a sumptuous Highland coffee.

Fresh flavoursome butter has been produced in Scotland for centuries. It is used in most cooked dishes, adding a rich taste. Bread, bannocks and fruit cakes are all spread liberally with soft pats of fresh butter at teatime.

A wealth of cheeses

In the past there were a great many Scottish cheeses, some of which were made in the home. They were an important source of nourishment. Dairy industrialization led to a steep decline in farmhouse cheese-making. Happily there has been a resurgence of interest in traditional and speciality cheeses made by artisan cheese-makers across the country. Superb cheeses are still made by hand, using time-honoured methods. **Crowdie** is an ancient Highland cheese made from skimmed cow's milk and is similar to cottage cheese, with a sharp, acidic flavour. Uniquely Scottish, it was once used as part-payment of rent in the Highlands. After the Clearances

Above St Andrews is a Trappist-style washed-rind cheese from Perthshire.

crowdie disappeared, but it was revived in the 1960s. It is unusual because it is half cooked. Fresh milk is left in a warm place to sour naturally, and then heated until it separates and curdles. The curds are hung up in a large square of muslin (cheesecloth) to drip. Some crowdie is mixed with double (heavy) cream before it is sold in tubs. Other types of crowdie are shaped into small logs and include *Gruth Dhu*, or Black Crowdie, which is blended with double cream then liberally coated in toasted rolled oats and black pepper. *Hramsa* is crowdie mixed with wild garlic and white and red pepper, while *Galic Hramsa* is rolled in crumbled hazelnuts and almonds.

Caboc, from the Highlands, is a soft-textured cream cheese shaped into logs and rolled in toasted pinhead oatmeal. The nubbly oatmeal contrasts well with the soft creamy cheese. The name is derived from the word *kebbock*, the old generic name for cheese.

Dunsyre Blue is an artisan-made, blue-veined, cow's-milk cheese with a creamy yet sharp flavour. It is made solely from the milk of native Ayrshire cattle, renowned for its excellence.

Lanark Blue is made from unpasteurized sheep's milk and is mottled with blue veins. Its creamy, sharp flavour is superb and the cheese has been compared favourably with the French Roquefort.

Strathdon Blue is a Highland cheese with a deliciously spicy flavour and delectable creamy smooth texture dotted with knobbly blue veins, which provide a pleasing contrast. It has won the Best Scottish Cheese at the British Cheese Awards twice in the last few years.

Cairnsmore is a prize-winning hard farmhouse cheese from Galloway. Aromatic and nutty, with the sweetness of caramel and burnt toffee, it ripens in seven to nine months.

Scottish Cheddar is mostly made from pasteurized cow's milk and is a hard cheese with a delicious nutty flavour. When young it has a mild taste, which becomes sharper and fuller flavoured as the cheese matures.

Drumloch is a full-fat hard pressed cheese similar to Cheddar, made from the milk of Guernsey cows in Scotland. It has a beautiful creamy texture, light golden colour and rich flavour.

Isle of Mull is a cream-coloured cow's-milk cheese, similar in flavour to Cheddar, but with an unmistakable tang of the sea.

Tobermory is an excellent full-flavoured, traditional unpasteurized farmhouse hard cheese, which is matured for 18 months.

Tobermory Mornish Made using sheep's milk, this is a silky smooth, semi-soft, white, mould-ripened cheese with a wonderful creamy flavour that has hints of grass and lemon.

Orkney Farmhouse Cheese, made with unpasteurized cow's milk, is renowned and has a wonderfully buttery, mellow flavour. Because of

Orkney's isolation, traditional small-scale cheese-making on farms there has continued for hundreds of years.

Inverloch, a superb hard-pressed, pasteurized goat's milk cheese coated in red wax, is made on the Isle of Gigha.

Gigha Pear and **Gigha Orange** These are innovative and attractive fruit-shaped waxed cheeses, which are a blend of Cheddar, cream cheese and flavourings such as pear liqueur and orange liqueur.

St Andrews from Perthshire is a creamy semi-soft cheese. It is one of the two Trappist-style washed-rind cheeses made in Scotland; the other is Bishop Kennedy. It has a supple, holey texture and a sweet-sour, slightly yeasty taste.

Bishop Kennedy has its origins in the medieval monasteries of France. A full-fat soft cheese, with a strong creamy taste, it is runny when ripe. The rind is washed in malt whisky to produce a distinctive orange-red crust. It has become popular in cooking.

Below Cairnsmore (top) is aromatic and nutty, while Caboc is creamy and rolled in toasted oatmeal.

From hedgerow and orchard

Flourishing for centuries in Scotland's long cool summers and fertile soil, fruits and berries play a key role in the Scottish kitchen. Wild strawberries (*Fragaria vesca*) and raspberries (*Rubus idaeus*) were once plentiful but are now scarce. The tiny berries have a magnificent flavour, different from that of today's cultivated berries.

In the past, wealthy people grew peaches in their gardens. In the 18th century, ovens built behind the garden walls supplemented the sun's heat and later in the same century, hollow walls with flues, heated by furnaces below the ground, provided a more efficient way of keeping in heat, allowing all kinds of delicate and exotic fruits to be grown. Cherries, apricots, blackcurrants, plums, gooseberries, strawberries, raspberries and blackberries were enjoyed as part of the summer diet and incorporated into recipes.

Berries

The traditional Scottish kitchen garden would have berry bushes, especially raspberries, the national favourite. In

Right Mulberries can be eaten just as they are when ripe.

Above Elderberries can be cooked in pies, tarts and fools or used to make jellies and sauces.

Tayside, which is famous for its sweet velvety raspberries and juicy strawberries, there are pick-your-own fruit farms, where people rush to pick the berries in their prime, usually in July. If you pick your own fruit, go early in the morning or choose a cool day when the fruit will be in peak condition.

All types of berry are delicate and very perishable so keep them in the refrigerator and eat them as fresh as possible. Farm shops offer very good value, as the berries are usually freshly picked. Look for firm, plump berries,

Left You will often find a bush of raspberries growing in a cottage garden or hedgerow.

but remember that very large berries often lack flavour. To enjoy them at their best, allow them to reach room temperature before eating. Don't wash them until just before eating. Rinse strawberries very gently and hull them after washing to avoid making them soggy – the hull acts as a plug.

Raspberries from Scotland have acquired an excellent reputation and have been grown commercially since the beginning of the 20th century. Over the years new varieties have been developed, such as Glen Moy and Glen Garry.

Blackberries Glossy, juicy blackberries are one of late summer's most delicious fruits, and the most common wild fruit in Britain. Blackberries are known as brambles in Scotland and in the Highlands the bush is called *an druise beannaichte* – the blessed bramble.

Tayberries are a cross between the red raspberry and a strain of blackberry. They are very juicy with a sharp taste and make particularly good jam.

Mulberries are large berries, either black or white, that grow on large dome-shaped bushes, which can be very old. They make excellent jams, jellies and sauces.

Loganberries are large juicy dark red-wine coloured berries, a cross between raspberries and dewberries (which are in the same family as blackberries). They are used to flavour stews and drinks.

Above Cranachan, a delicious blend of juicy raspberries, thick, fresh cream and rolled oats, is a firm favourite as a dessert.

Strawberries grow well in the Lowlands but have trouble ripening elsewhere. The delicious wild variety can be found in hedgerows, making wonderful treats.

Elderberries are a tasty addition to game and meat dishes. They grow on elder trees, following the blooming of the elderflower, and the berries can be used to flavour drinks and cordials.

Gooseberries are found in many kitchen gardens. The succulent bright green berries have a sharp flavour and make delicious pies and crumbles.

Below Victoria plums are large oval fruits with yellow skins flushed with scarlet and a lovely sweet juicy flesh. They are good for bottling and stewing.

Rowanberries are tiny bright orange-red berries that are added to sauces and relishes for rich game meats.
Rose hips are the seed pods for roses, and appear after the plants have finished flowering. They make excellent jellies to serve with game.

Orchard fruits

The Lowlands produce some wonderful and flavoursome orchard fruits, although the season is short. In addition to those below, peaches and cherries are also grown, if not widely.

Apples of many varieties are grown for eating and use in jams and jellies, as well as pies and crumbles.
Pears are also abundant, making fabulous preserves, jellies and pie fillings when they ripen in the autumn.
Plums grow well in the Lowlands and are a favourite in pies and crumbles, as well as with porridge (oatmeal). Victoria plums are the most commonly found.

Jams and preserves

In the 18th century, when sugar became affordable to almost everyone, it became the vogue to make jams and preserves from seasonal fruits. Costly imported fruits, particularly oranges, were also used.

Marmalades Early marmalade had a strong flavour and was so dense and sticky that a knife was needed to slice it. Early Scottish recipes called the shreds of peel "chips" and

Above Scottish marmalades are known around the world for their excellent quality and flavour.

so the product became known as chip marmalade. The Scots were the first to serve marmalade as a breakfast spread, as they believed that the peel and sugar warmed the stomach at the first meal of the day. They were also the first to produce a less thick and sticky marmalade, which became known as Scotch marmalade in England and was much in demand.

Jams and jellies have taken a prime place in the Scottish kitchen, especially those using the wealth of berries that grow wild in the countryside and are cultivated in the garden.

They were primarily made to stock the larder with fruits and berries to last the winter, by the 18th century jam-making had become more of an art-form and cooks in big estates took pride in the quality of their recipes.

Recently jam- and jelly-making has had a new lease of life. The growth in cottage industries and a growing demand for traditional, organic and non-manufactured goods have given rise to a number of small preserve-makers. They produce some excellent and delicious jams and jellies.

Wild mushrooms

Throughout Scotland's long history, wild mushrooms have been used to flavour many dishes, especially soups, stews and casseroles. They thrive in damp woods and grassy meadows, making the Scottish climate and landscape ideal for growth.

Although there are plenty of cultivated varieties available today, the flavour of wild mushrooms is far superior, with each variety having its own texture and taste.

In Scotland wild mushrooms, both fresh and dried, are becoming more easily available from specialist stores, grocers and local markets.

Button (white) mushrooms have an excellent flavour, and they sprout abundantly during the warm months, especially after rain. Commonly found, these mushrooms impart a definite, faintly sweet taste when added to soups and stews. Larger varieties are called closed-cap mushrooms.

Common field (portabello) mushrooms are pink and white when young and turn brown then almost black as they age. Small and unopened the mushrooms have a delicate flavour, while the taste of older specimens is more pronounced.

Below Field blewits add a nutty flavour to soups and stews.

Above Clockwise from top: flat or field mushrooms, chestnut mushrooms, button mushrooms, and closed-cap mushrooms.

Chanterelle mushrooms are a beautiful golden yellow with a fleshy cap, curly edge and the fragrance of apricots. They flourish in large groups in summer and autumn in woods, especially those of beech and oak. Chanterelles have a special affinity with potatoes and eggs, and are delicious in cream sauces.

Field blewits or blue leg mushrooms are found in long grass or pastureland. They have a buff-coloured cap and the flesh is quite thick and chunky, good to use in soups and stews.

Morel mushrooms rate among the finest wild mushrooms and, unlike most other edible mushrooms, appear in orchards and forests in the spring. Morels have a honeycombed

appearance and a splendid meaty, slightly nutty flavour that is enhanced by cooking in butter. Morels come in various colours – reddish, grey, black or brown – and their intense aromatic flavour is not lost when they are dried. Morels are never eaten raw, as they are likely to cause stomach upsets.

Ceps are also known as penny buns. These are highly prized with a wonderfully nutty flavour. Found in woodland, they can grow to be very big – up to 1kg (2lb 2oz). Check for maggots before eating.

St George's mushrooms are found in pastures. They have a delicious nutty flavour and meaty aroma, and can be fried, stewed or boiled.

Puffballs range in diameter from less than 2.5cm/1in to more than 30cm/12in and are among the best of the edible mushrooms. When young and firm they are delicious sliced and fried or grilled (broiled). As they mature, the interior turns yellow, which is a sign that they are no longer worth eating. The pear-shaped puffball grows on rotting logs and stumps, in late summer and early autumn. You should take great care when collecting puffball mushrooms from the wild as they can closely resemble more poisonous varieties.

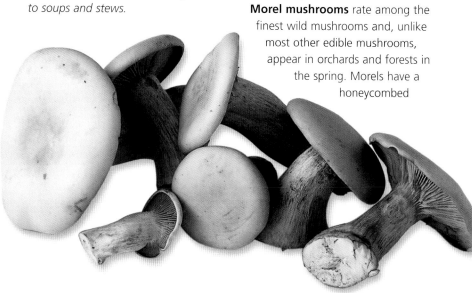

Left Tasty Chanterelles are delicious in cream sauces.

Above Ceps, also known as Penny buns, have a lovely nutty flavour.

Mushroom picking

Never be tempted to pick wild mushrooms unless you are an expert or are accompanied by a mycologist. Some deadly poisonous mushrooms look remarkably similar to edible varieties. If you add just one poisonous mushroom to a basket of edible varieties, your whole harvest will be tainted and must be disposed of.

There are many books that will help you to identify wild fungi but the best way of finding out more is by going on one of the many organized mushroom forays that are available for novice wild-mushroom enthusiasts. In Scotland there is the Scottish Wild Mushroom Code, but wherever you are picking you should act sensibly. Wildlife needs mushrooms too, so only pick what you will use. Do not pick mushrooms until the cap has opened out, and leave those that are past their best. The main part of the mushroom is below the surface; take care not to damage or trample it and not to disturb its surroundings. Sprinkle trimmings discretely in the same area as the mushroom came from.

Some mushrooms are also rare and should not be picked. Before you collect mushrooms at a nature reserve please always seek advice from the manager. Special conditions may apply to some areas where rare species are being encouraged.

Below Chanterelle mushrooms can be found in damp woodland in late summer and autumn.

Dried mushrooms

Many types of wild mushroom can be bought dried and can add excellent flavour. It takes 900g/2lb of fresh mushrooms to obtain just 90g/3½oz dried mushrooms. The flavour of dried mushrooms is concentrated and their rich, strong flavour means a little goes a long way – just 25g/1oz of dried mushrooms mixed with 450g/1lb of fresh mushrooms will flavour an entire dish. Dried wild mushrooms can be added to risottos, soups, sauces and stews, or they may be fried in butter. To reconstitute them, soak in hot water for 20–30 minutes before cooking. Use a half-water, half-milk mixture for morel mushrooms. Always add the soaking liquid to the dish, as much of the flavour remains in the liquid, but strain it first to remove any grit or dirt.

Vegetables from the kitchen garden

Medieval French monks brought many hitherto unknown varieties of fruits and vegetables, such as spinach, French (green) beans and cauliflower, to Scotland. The monks of Holyrood planted orchards and laid out gardens at the base of the Castle Rock in Edinburgh, and trained laymen in horticulture. The cultivation of vegetables and fruits spread to the gardens of the nobility and other wealthy families and by the 19th century Scottish gardeners had become internationally famous.

Green vegetables

Young summer vegetables were used to make *hairst bree*, harvest broth, which is similar to Scotch broth but without the barley. The tender sweet vegetables gave the broth a special flavour.

Kale or kail Dark green leafy kale is eaten throughout Scotland and is so central to Scottish cuisine that the word *kail* came to mean soup and even to signify the main meal of the day. Kale grows on a long stem and has curly dark green leaves but no head. It has the advantage of flourishing in Scotland's often harsh climate and is resistant to frost – in fact the flavour improves after a slight frost. Shred the leaves finely and cook for a few minutes in boiling salted water, as for cabbage. In Shetland a unique variety of kale develops a head. It is believed to have ancient Scandinavian origins.

Cabbage was a staple item of the diet in Orkney and Shetland (in common with Scandinavian countries) and was eaten as a vegetable in its own right and included in soups and stews. Cabbage was preserved for winter by being layered in barrels with fat, oats, salt and spices with a weight on top. It was then left to ferment, the result being very similar to sauerkraut.

Leeks have a delicate onion flavour. The market gardeners on the Lothian coast supplied fruit and vegetables to Edinburgh and the quality of their leeks was unsurpassed. Scottish leeks are distinct from other leeks as they have almost as much green as white, so add a good colour to broths. They are essential to the famous cock-a-leekie

Above Leeks are a crucial ingredient for traditional cock-a-leekie and potato and leek soups, as well as many stews.

soup, a broth made with chicken and leeks. Slice leeks down the middle and wash very well to remove any sand or grit. Chop and add to soups or stews.

Wild leaves

Nettles Highlanders once gathered young tender nettles in the spring to eat alone as a vegetable or in soups and broths. Young nettle leaves can be cooked in the same way as spinach. Wash them well and place in a pan with just the water clinging to the leaves. Cook over a low heat for 7–10 minutes, chopping them as they cook in the pan, then add butter, salt and pepper to taste.

Wild rocket grows prolifically in many areas, especially in the

Left From far left: white cabbage, savoy cabbage and green cabbage are usually boiled or steamed.

Above *Mashed turnips make up the traditional dish of "bashed neeps", also known as "turnip purry".*

Lowlands alongside gardens and pastures. It can be picked, washed and added to stews or made into a fresh peppery salad.

Wild garlic leaves are found in meadows and alongside pastures. They are only around for a few weeks in the year. They add a delicate, mild garlic flavour to dishes.

Root vegetables

Carrots In the days when sugar was a costly imported luxury, most people relied on honey to sweeten their food, together with the natural sweetness of root vegetables, particularly carrots. Their inherent natural sweetness and moist texture made them a successful ingredient of many delicious cakes, puddings, pies, tarts and preserves.

Turnips were introduced into Scotland in the 18th century and the Scots recognized them immediately as a tasty vegetable – unlike the English who fed them to their cattle. Several Scottish dishes use turnips and they became the traditional accompaniment to haggis.

Right *Potatoes, known in Scotland as "tatties", are commonly mashed.*

Mashed turnips were commonly known as *bashed neeps*, or *turnip purry* (from the French purée) by the gentry. Young turnips have the best flavour and texture.

Potatoes were an important crop in the west and in the Islands and by the 19th century had become a staple food. Potatoes form the basis of many old dishes and in general Scots prefer floury varieties such as Maris Piper, Golden Wonder and Kerr's Pinks. *Mealy tatties* (boiled potatoes) were cheap and filling, and were sold from carts in Scottish cites in the 19th century. *Stovies* is a very old dish consisting of sliced potatoes cooked with onions. Sometimes cheese or meat was added to make the dish more substantial. In Orkney cooked potatoes and turnips or kale were mashed together to make *clapshot*. The

Above *Parsnips are a great favourite, either mashed or roasted.*

curiously named *rumbledethumps*, from the Border region, is made with potatoes and cabbage. The name comes from "rumbled and thumped". *Colcannon* is a Highland dish of boiled cabbage, carrots, turnips and potatoes mashed with butter.

Oats and barley

Scotland's cool climate is ideal for oats and barley. Rolled oats are used in oatcakes, bread, broth and of course porridge (oatmeal). Oatcakes have a light, mealy flavour and may be thick or thin – it is a matter of personal preference. Highly nutritious, they were eaten by 14th-century soldiers to sustain them during long marches. In the past, oatcakes accompanied almost every meal and they are delicious eaten with butter, cheese or marmalade.

Oats and oatmeal

Used in a variety of foods and dishes, oats were also used to make black and white mealie puddings. Mealie pudding is a mixture of oats, onions, suet (chilled, grated shortening) and seasoning boiled in a skin or cloth; blood was added to make black pudding (blood sausage). These puddings were traditionally made in the winter when the animals were slaughtered. Skirlie was made by mixing oats, onions and suet, and frying the mixture in a pan. The noise, or skirl, as it cooked gave rise to the name. Today it is usually served with roast meat or used as a stuffing.

Above
Clockwise from top: rolled oats, oatmeal, whole oats and oat bran.

Soups and broths have an important role and a long history in Scotland's cuisine. *Brose* is an ancient dish and a distant relative of the modern Swiss muesli (granola). It was quick to

Above *Porridge (oatmeal) has now been recognized as a delicious and healthy way to start the day.*

make, nourishing and filling. A labourer or shepherd would fill a leather or wooden hoggin (wallet or pouch) with ground oats, then add water from a nearby stream or brook. The hoggin was slung on his back and the continuous warmth and movement as he worked caused the mixture to thicken and ferment. A simple meal could also be made by mixing oats with boiling water – perhaps the world's first convenience food. The term *brose* has gradually come to mean a variety of different broths thickened with rolled oats, such as *mussel brose* and *kail brose*.

Porridge came to be accepted throughout the British Empire as a breakfast dish. In the 18th century it

Right *Clockwise from left: pot barley, barley flakes and pearl barley.*

was usual to add ale or porter to the porridge, and on bitterly cold winter mornings a couple of spoonfuls of whisky were added – even for children to sustain them on their long walk to school. A bowl of milk or cream was placed next to the porridge bowl and a spoon was dipped first into the hot porridge then into the cold milk or cream. In Scotland it is still customary to add salt – never sugar – to porridge, with cold milk or thin cream as an accompaniment.

Leftover porridge was poured into the porridge drawer of the dresser and left to set, after which it was cut into slices, known as *caulders*. They were taken by farm workers to the fields and eaten in the middle of the day. Sometimes the slices were cooked alongside eggs, bacon or fish.

Quaker Oats created rolled oats in the United States in 1877. Made by steaming and rolling the oats, rolled oats have the advantage of cooking quickly, but there is some loss of flavour and nutrients due to the heat treatment. Rolled oats are particularly popular in Scotland.

Barley

Bread made with barley was widely eaten throughout Scotland until the end of the 17th century, when oats became the more popular grain, one reason being that they keep longer than barley. However, in the Highlands and Islands barley continued as a staple.

Barley is still a common thickener for broths, soups and sauces; it is a crucial ingredient of the famous Scotch broth, Scotland's favourite soup. Much of the crop today is malted and used in the making of whisky.

Bere, an ancient variety of barley, has been grown and ground for food since the Stone Age. Centuries ago this type of barley was called *bygg*, which is the name given to barley in Norway. In Orkney the crop was called corn and provided the staple food in the form of bere bannocks and home-brewed ale. Bere was used by the whisky and beer industry until the 20th century, but its higher protein and lower starch content is no longer favoured. Farmers also prefer modern types of barley, as the yield is greater than that of bere.

Bere is still cultivated in Orkney where it is kiln-dried and stone-ground to produce beremeal. Creamy coloured beremeal has a more earthy flavour than that of commercially produced barley flour. It is used to make bread and bannocks by bakers in Orkney and the Hebrides, although a small amount of wheat flour is now usually added to lighten the texture.

Buy rolled oats and barley flour in small quantities from a store with a high turnover, so you know they will be fresh. Store in an airtight container.

Below *Oatcakes are delicious spread with butter and marmalade or served with a variety of cheeses.*

Bannocks and bread

Bannocks cooked from the bakestone and the variety of savoury and sweet breads have always been a part of the Scottish diet. Recently there has been an upsurge of interest in "real" bannocks and bread, and traditional, well-flavoured bannocks and crusty breads from dedicated bakers, who are masters of their craft, are once again in demand. Their recipes go back to the first bannocks.

Bannocks

The traditional bannocks are thicker and softer than oatcakes, although similar in make-up. Their name probably comes from the Latin word for bread, *panis*. Bannocks are unique to Scotland and were originally unleavened in the days when peat was the only fuel available and every home had a

Below Bannocks are cooked on a heated bakestone in thin rounds traditionally cut into wedges.

bakestone on which the bannocks were freshly cooked or fired each day. They became less popular when domestic ovens became more widespread, but have regained a market with the recent resurgence of traditional foods and recipes.

The first breads

The advent of ovens in the 16th century led to baked loaves, and every town possessed a public bakehouse where bread dough was taken to be baked. In the more populous towns and cities those who could afford it bought their bread from the baker's store. The Baijen Hole was an ancient and famous baker's store in Edinburgh. It was renowned for its rolls, called *soutar's clods*, which had a thick crust and were made from coarse wheat flour.

In 16th-century Scotland there were four kinds of wheat bread. The best was *manche*, followed by *cheat* (trencher bread, used as a plate),

Above Rowies are buttery bread rolls traditionally eaten for breakfast with homemade jams and jellies.

ravelled and *mashlock*. Wheat was grown in the fertile Lowlands, but bread made from wheat flour was eaten only by the wealthy, right up until the early part of the 20th century, when it gradually became a staple food for everyone. Regional speciality breads developed throughout Scotland.

Rowies Aberdeen buttery rowies or butteries are very similar to French croissants, but taste saltier and are flatter in shape. They are associated with Aberdeen because the fishing fleets used to take them on their journeys into cold, rough seas. The high fat content of the rowies kept out the bitter cold and sustained the men. The rolls are quite difficult to make at home as professional bakers steam the dough before baking.

Baps (the origin of the name is unknown) are floury rolls, which today are mostly round in shape, although originally the shape and size varied from one region to another. Baps are thickly coated with flour before baking to prevent a crust forming, which allows them to rise well. Prime Minister William Gladstone's grandfather owned a small store in Edinburgh that sold baps, along with flour and oats. His

Left *Scottish morning rolls, or baps, are soft and slightly flattened.*

removed the germ and husk, meant that everyone could now afford white bread. It was sold cheaply in every corner store and a slice of bread and butter became a basic part of working-class meals.

A cutting loaf was slightly cheaper than a fresh loaf and was usually a day old when sold, as it sliced more easily than freshly baked bread.

Plain loaves were baked in batches and joined together without the use of baking tins (pans), then separated once they were cooked. A pan loaf, baked in a tin, was for the wealthier people. "Speaking pan loafy" meant speaking in an affected manner, while "a pan loaf" was a slang expression for somebody who acted posh.

In the 1950s and early 60s many of the country's small traditional bakers were ousted by the large milling companies, but there is a strong recent trend towards the tasty traditional breads of the past and many small producers are proving successful.

baps were
rumoured to be small,
and so the neighbourhood lads
nicknamed him "Sma' Baps".
Fadge is a large flat loaf or cake, sometimes with dried fruit and nuts.
Tod, or toddie, is a small round cake of bread that was given to children.
Whig (meaning wedge) is a fine wheat teabread that can be buttered.
Ankerstoek is a large loaf of rye bread.
Buttermilk bread is quick and easy to make and can be made with oats or wheat flour.

Breads for special occasions

The breads and cakes that were specially prepared for festive occasions were collectively known as *gudebread*. Selkirk bannock is a round yeasted fruit loaf, first baked in 1859 by Robbie Douglas in his bakery at Selkirk Market Place. He introduced several features that improved the local bannock. Indeed, when Queen Victoria visited Sir Walter Scott's granddaughter in 1867, she declined the splendid repast that had been prepared for her in favour of a piece of Selkirk bannock and a cup of tea.

Right *Bread made from wheat flour was only eaten by the wealthy in the Lowlands until the early 20th century.*

Milling and bread manufacture

In the mid-19th century, white flour became cheaper than brown and the introduction of roller-milling, which left only the white part of the wheat, but

A wealth of cakes

The humble bannock, cooked on a bakestone over a peat fire, had, by the 15th century, developed into a Scottish speciality, the rich fruity teabread. This was made by adding expensive dried fruits, honey, butter and spices to plain bread dough. At this time, dried fruits and sugar, which was regarded as a spice, were kept under lock and key along with other expensive spices such as ginger and pepper. These breads were served only on special occasions.

The Scottish fruitcake

In the bakehouses and kitchens of the wealthy, teabreads gave way to enormous fruitcakes baked in large ovens, which were served on important occasions. There are a great many Scottish recipes for fruitcakes.

Dundee cake No one can agree what goes to make an authentic Dundee cake and where it originated. It has been suggested that it is a descendant of Dundee gingerbread, or that the

Left The traditional round fruitcake, upon which many regional specialities were based.

recipe was devised by the marmalade makers as a means of using up the surplus orange peel. Others believe that marmalade was one of the original ingredients of the cake. Dundee cake should be lighter and more crumbly than traditional fruit

cake, not too heavily fruited, and should have the characteristic topping of whole or split almonds, without which it's not a genuine Dundee cake.

Plum cake These early cakes were shaped by hand into rounds and wrapped in pastry (known as *huff pastry*). This was then placed inside a tin hoop placed on a tin tray before baking. The pastry protected the outside of the cake from burning during the long cooking needed for such a large cake, and also, together with the tin hoop, helped to keep the cake in shape. The *huff* pastry was carefully cut off and discarded before the cake was served.

Black bun The traditional Hogmanay cake is a rich, dark fruit cake encased in pastry. Bun is the old Scots word for plum cake, as the cakes were originally made wth dried plums. The pastry protected the outside of the cake from burning during cooking and helped to keep the cake in shape. The fruit-

Left Dundee cake, with its topping of almonds, has become a favourite traditional fruit cake throughout Britain.

Above The rich, pastry-covered black bun is celebrated with a few whiskies at Hogmanay.

Above Sponge cakes came to Scotland in the 19th century, with a range of flavours and toppings.

Above Glamis cake with walnuts and dates became a popular cake to eat as part of high tea.

soaked pastry was discarded. Today the pastry is richer and is an essential part of the cake.

Sponge cakes

The early 19th century saw the introduction of coal-fired ranges with ovens and this, together with a dramatic fall in the prices of wheat and sugar, meant that Scottish women could bake at home. Plain cakes without fruit became popular and were intended to be eaten with a cup of the newly popular tea. Plain cakes were also far cheaper and less time-consuming to make than fruitcakes, and could be flavoured or decorated.

By the 19th century it was discovered that adding fat to the sponge mixture made a more substantial cake with better keeping qualities. High tea became an important meal, especially in the industrial towns. A tempting array of sponge cakes, pastries and fancies would always be on offer when visitors were expected.

Regional cakes

Every region of Scotland developed its own unique and delicious recipes for cakes and teabreads. Some of

Scotland's regional cake recipes went on to become world famous, while others virtually disappeared from baker's stores and tearooms. A large variety of regional cakes are still baked today.

Deer horns were fried cakes formed around cornet-shaped tins.

Coburg cakes were popular for their spicy taste.

Glamis cake was made with walnuts and dates, squeezed together in a loaf tin and cut into rich slices.

Montrose cakes were flavoured with rose water and nutmeg.

Below Honeys produced in the Lowlands add sweetness to many traditional cakes.

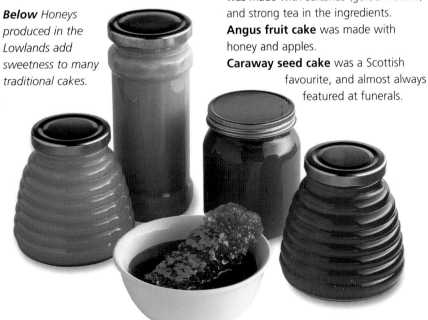

Scots snow cake used arrowroot instead of flour.

Sair heidies, from the Grampian region, were small sponge cakes wrapped in paper jackets and covered with crushed sugar crystals.

Balmoral cake was unusual because of its baked almond-paste icing.

Auld reekie plum cake was a popular cake, containing whisky and ginger as well as dried fruits.

Portree plum cake from the Isle of Skye contained stout and spices.

Kirrie loaf, a teabread from Angus, was made with sultanas (golden raisins) and strong tea in the ingredients.

Angus fruit cake was made with honey and apples.

Caraway seed cake was a Scottish favourite, and almost always featured at funerals.

Scotch whisky

Scotland's gift to the world, Scotch whisky is unique and inimitable. It requires the Scottish climate, pure water and rich peat, not to mention hundreds of years of experience in the skilful art of distilling.

The origins of whisky are lost in the mists of time. The word itself is derived from the Gaelic *uisge beatha* – the water of life. As time passed, *uisge* became *usky*, then eventually whisky. The oldest reference to whisky dates back to 1494 when "8 bolls of malt to Friar John Cor wherewith to make aquavitae" were entered in the Scottish Exchequer Rolls.

Scotland's national drink was already well established by the 15th century and by the early 1500s had also become the favoured drink of royalty. During the 17th century the popularity

of whisky grew steadily, especially in the Lowlands where many distilleries sprang up to meet the increasing demand. Highland distilleries were smaller than those of the south and supplied mainly local towns and villages.

In 1690 came the first mention of a famous whisky noted for its quality: Ferintosh, which was distilled by Forbes of Culloden. In 1784 the owner was bought out and Robert Burns immortalized the sad event:

Thee Ferintosh! O sadly lost!
Scotland laments frae coast to coast!

Cheap whisky became available in the 18th century, although it was rather nasty by all accounts, but good whisky, from Glenlivet for instance, was highly esteemed and expensive.

Whisky, especially malt whisky, is a versatile ingredient and its special taste imparts a distinctive yet subtle flavour to all kinds of dishes. Many of today's leading Scottish chefs have created marvellous recipes using whisky. Add a splash to a steaming bowl of those great stalwarts of Scottish cuisine, cock-a-leekie soup and Scotch broth. Stir a couple of spoonfuls into a marinade for meat, game or poultry. Soak dried fruits for a rich fruitcake in whisky, then feed the baked cake with whisky. Not only does whisky add a unique flavour, it also preserves and tenderizes; for instance fish and meat can be marinated in whisky before cooking. Do not be afraid to experiment by using

Left Laphroaig, made on Islay, is very peaty, and Whyte & Mackay is re-blended for a second period of maturation.

Above The barley is initially malted, which means that it is soaked in tanks of spring water, known as steeps, for two to three days.

different whiskies in a recipe; you will find that the taste of the whole dish is transformed.

Malt whisky

Aromatic, smooth and full of complex character, malt whisky is a drink of enormous variety and no two malts are the same. Single malts are the products of just one distillery and are the most highly prized. Vatted malts are a blend of malts from several distilleries within a particular region. Malt whiskies, with their complex flavours, vary in colour from palest straw to deep glowing amber and are more expensive than blended whiskies. This is partly due to their long maturation in casks that have previously contained sherry, port, rum or bourbon – which also augment their flavour and character as well as colour; for instance a fino sherry cask produces a light-coloured whisky, while an oloroso sherry cask results in a darker, strongly sherried whisky. Each region

Left The Famous Grouse and Glenmorangie are both made in the northern Highlands.

Lochnagar, produced close to Balmoral, is a typical example of a good East Highland malt.

The Lowlands produce malts which were the first whiskies to be drunk on a large scale, such as Rosebank. They have a fruity sweetness and a dry finish.

Campbeltown malts, from the Kintyre peninsula, are fully flavoured with a tang of salt, for example Springbank.

Islay produces dry, peaty and smoky malts. Some, such as Lavagulin, are powerful, while others, for example Bunnahabhain, are less so.

Above Quality Scotch whisky should be enjoyed on its own or with ice.

Blended whiskies

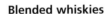

Blending malt and grain whiskies has created some excellent whiskies. Master blenders may combine more than 50 different malt and grain whiskies into a blended whisky. The normal ratio of grain to malt is 60:40. The percentage of malt used

determines the quality, flavour, smoothness and character. Each whisky used in the blending process will usually have been matured for about five years, but there are also several longer-aged blended Scotch whiskies available.

Below The casks are specially made from woods such as oak to impart a subtle flavour to the whisky.

produces its own character, often expressing age-old traditions.

Speyside is the principal whisky-producing region and makes some of the world's greatest malts – Macallan, Glenfiddich and Glenlivet to name just three. Speyside malt whiskies are sweet and can be highly perfumed, with scents of roses, apples and lemonade.

The Central Highlands produce malt whiskies that are not so sweet. They tend to have a dry finish and a fine fragrance. Edradour is one example.

West Highland malts have a mild smokiness and a dryish finish, and include such fine whiskies as Talisker from the Isle of Skye.

East Highland malts are smooth and slightly sweet, with a hint of smokiness and a dryish finish. Royal

Breakfasts

A good hearty Scottish breakfast is the ideal way
to start the morning, especially if your day involves
energetic outdoor activities. Oats take many forms,
from porridge to oatcakes, and smoked fish, such as
smoked haddock and salmon, is also popular.
The national favourite, black pudding, is a
traditional breakfast staple, often served with
eggs, bacon and rowies, a special breakfast
roll enjoyed with jam or marmalade.

Porridge

One of Scotland's oldest foods, oatmeal porridge remains a favourite way to start the day, especially during winter. Brown sugar or honey, cream and a tot of whisky are treats added for weekend breakfasts and to spoil guests in some of the best guesthouses and hotels.

Serves 4

1 litre/1¾ pints/4 cups water

115g/4oz/1 cup pinhead oatmeal

good pinch of salt

Variation Modern rolled oats can be used, in the proportion of 115g/4oz/ generous 1 cup to 750ml/1¼ pints/3 cups water, plus a sprinkling of salt. This cooks more quickly than pinhead oatmeal. Simmer, stirring to prevent sticking, for about 5 minutes. Either type of oatmeal can be left to cook overnight in the slow oven of a range.

1 Put the water, pinhead oatmeal and salt into a heavy pan and bring to the boil over a medium heat, stirring with a wooden spatula. When the porridge is smooth and beginning to thicken, reduce the heat to a simmer.

2 Cook gently for about 25 minutes, stirring occasionally, until the oatmeal is cooked and the consistency smooth. Serve hot with cold milk and extra salt, if required. It is frequently served with chopped fresh fruit.

Per portion Energy 115kcal/488kJ; Protein 3.6g; Carbohydrate 20.9g, of which sugars 0g; Fat 2.5g, of which saturates 0g; Cholesterol 0mg; Calcium 16mg; Fibre 2g; Sodium 304mg.

Potato cakes

This is the traditional method of making potato cakes on a griddle or in a heavy frying pan. Commercial versions are available throughout Scotland as thin, pre-cooked potato cakes, which are fried to eat with a full breakfast or to enjoy at high tea.

Makes about 12

675g/1½lb potatoes, peeled

25g/1oz/2 tbsp unsalted (sweet) butter

about 175g/6oz/1½ cups plain (all-purpose) flour

salt

1 Boil the potatoes in a large pan over a medium heat until tender, then drain thoroughly, replacing the pan with the drained poatoes over a low heat for a few minutes to allow any moisture to evaporate completely.

2 Mash the potatoes with plenty of salt, then mix in the butter and cool.

3 Turn out on to a floured work surface and knead in about one-third of its volume in flour, or as much as is needed to make a pliable dough.

4 Roll out to a thickness of about 1cm/½in and cut into triangles.

5 Heat a dry griddle or heavy frying pan over a low heat and cook the potato cakes on it for about 3 minutes on each side until browned. Serve hot.

Per batch Energy 1276kcal/5392kJ; Protein 30.4g; Carbohydrate 249.1g, of which sugars 6.7g; Fat 24.1g, of which saturates 13.4g; Cholesterol 53mg; Calcium 282mg; Fibre 14g; Sodium 203mg.

Rowies

These are the delicious traditional breakfast rolls served in Scottish homes, originally coming from Aberdeenshire, although they are made all over the country today and are very popular in tourist areas. They are eaten like a croissant, hot from the oven with butter or fresh cream and marmalades or jams and jellies.

Makes 16

7.5ml/1½ tsp dried yeast

15ml/1 tbsp soft light brown sugar

450ml/¾ pint/scant 2 cups warm water

450g/1lb/4 cups strong white bread flour

pinch of salt

225g/8oz/1 cup butter

115g/4oz/½ cup lard or white cooking fat

1 Mix the yeast with the sugar, dissolve in a little warm water taken from the measured amount then set aside in a warm place, lightly covered to allow some air to circulate.

2 Mix the flour in a large mixing bowl with the salt. When the yeast has bubbled up pour it into the flour with the rest of the water. Mix well to form a dough and leave in a warm place covered with a dish towel to rise until it has doubled in size, about 2 hours.

3 Cream the butter and lard or white cooking fat together in a small bowl and then divide the mixture into three portions. The mixture should be soft enough to spread easily but not warm enough to melt. If it is melting, refrigerate for 5–10 minutes.

4 When the dough has doubled in size, knock back (punch down) until its the original size. Roll it out on a floured surface to a rectangle about 1cm/½in thick. Spread a third of the butter mixture over two-thirds of the dough.

5 Fold the ungreased third of the dough over on to the greased middle third, then the other greased third into the middle, thus giving three layers. Roll this back to the original rectangle size. Leave to rest in a cool place for 40 minutes then repeat the procedure, including the resting period, twice more, to use up the butter mixture.

6 Cut the dough into 16 squares. Shape into rough circles by folding the edges in all the way around and place on a baking sheet. Leave to rise, covered with a clean dry dish towel, for 45 minutes. Meanwhile preheat the oven to 200°C/400°F/Gas 6.

7 When the rowies have risen, bake in the oven for 15 minutes until golden brown and flaky.

Per portion Energy 296kcal/1233kJ; Protein 3g; Carbohydrate 25.4g, of which sugars 1.5g; Fat 21g, of which saturates 11.4g; Cholesterol 41mg; Calcium 47mg; Fibre 1g; Sodium 96mg.

Kedgeree

Of Indian origin, kedgeree came to Scotland via England and the landed gentry. It quickly became a popular dish using smoked fish for breakfast or high tea. This is a more manageable dish than the full Scottish breakfast when feeding several people, and it is often served in guesthouses and restaurants.

Serves 4–6

450g/1lb smoked haddock

300ml/½ pint/1¼ cups milk

175g/6oz/scant 1 cup long grain rice

pinch of grated nutmeg and cayenne pepper

50g/2oz/¼ cup butter

1 onion, peeled and finely chopped

2 hard-boiled eggs

salt and ground black pepper

chopped fresh parsley, to garnish

lemon wedges and wholemeal (whole-wheat) toast, to serve

1 Poach the haddock in the milk, made up with just enough water to cover the fish, for about 8 minutes, or until just cooked. Skin the haddock, remove all the bones and flake the flesh with a fork. Set aside.

2 Bring 600ml/1 pint/2½ cups water to the boil in a large pan. Add the rice, cover closely with a lid and cook over a low heat for about 25 minutes, or until all the water has been absorbed by the rice. Season with salt and a grinding of black pepper, and the nutmeg and cayenne pepper.

3 Meanwhile, heat 15g/½oz/1 tbsp butter in a pan and fry the onion until soft and transparent. Set aside. Roughly chop one of the hard-boiled eggs, and slice the other into neat wedges.

4 Stir the remaining butter into the rice and add the flaked haddock, onion and the chopped egg. Season to taste and heat the mixture through gently (this can be done on a serving dish in a low oven if more convenient).

5 To serve, pile up the kedgeree on a warmed dish, sprinkle generously with parsley and arrange the wedges of egg on top. Put the lemon wedges around the base and serve hot with the toast.

Variation Try using leftover cooked salmon, instead of the haddock.

Per portion Energy 399kcal/1668kJ; Protein 28.9g; Carbohydrate 38g, of which sugars 2.2g; Fat 14.6g, of which saturates 7.6g; Cholesterol 181mg; Calcium 62mg; Fibre 0.5g; Sodium 974mg.

Smoked haddock with spinach and poached egg

This is a really special breakfast treat. Use young spinach leaves in season and, of course, the freshest eggs. There is something about the combination of eggs, spinach and "smoke" that really perks you up in the morning.

Serves 4

4 undyed smoked haddock fillets

milk

75ml/2½fl oz/⅓ cup double (heavy) cream

25g/1oz/2 tbsp butter

250g/9oz fresh spinach, tough stalks removed

white wine vinegar

4 eggs

salt and ground black pepper

1 Over a low heat, poach the haddock fillets in just enough milk to come halfway up the fish, shaking the pan gently to keep the fish moist, for about 5 minutes. When cooked remove the fish and keep warm.

2 Increase the heat under the milk and allow to reduce by about half, stirring occasionally. Add the cream and allow to bubble up. Season to taste with salt and pepper. The sauce should be thickened but should pour easily.

3 Heat a frying pan then add the butter. Add the spinach, stirring briskly for a few minutes. Season lightly then set aside, keeping it warm.

4 To poach the eggs, bring 4cm/1½in water to a simmer and add a few drops of vinegar. Gently crack two eggs into the water and cook for 3 minutes. Remove the first egg using a slotted spoon and rest in the spoon on some kitchen paper to remove any water. Repeat with the second egg, then cook the other two in the same way.

5 Place the spinach over the fillets and a poached egg on top. Pour over the cream sauce and serve immediately.

Per portion Energy 350kcal/1455kJ; Protein 27.5g; Carbohydrate 1.5g, of which sugars 1.4g; Fat 26.3g, of which saturates 14g; Cholesterol 277mg; Calcium 170mg; Fibre 1.3g; Sodium 969mg.

Smoked haddock and cheese omelette

This creamy, smoked haddock soufflé omelette is also known as Omelette Arnold Bennett, after the famous author who frequently dined in the Savoy Hotel in London. It is now served all over the world, using good Scottish smoked haddock and cheese.

Serves 2

175g/6oz smoked haddock fillet, poached and drained

50g/2oz/½ cup butter, diced

175ml/6fl oz/¾ cup whipping or double (heavy) cream

4 eggs, separated

40g/1½oz/⅓ cup mature (sharp) Cheddar cheese, grated

ground black pepper

watercress, to garnish

1 Remove the skin and any bones from the haddock fillet by carefully pressing down the length of each fillet with your fingertips. Discard them. Using a fork and following the grain of the flesh, flake the flesh into large chunks.

2 Melt half the butter with 60ml/4 tbsp of the cream in a fairly small non-stick pan. Wait until the mixture is hot but not boiling, and then add the chunks of flaked fish. Stir together gently, making sure that you do not break up the flakes of fish. Bring slowly to the boil, stirring continuously. Once it is boiling, cover the pan with a lid, remove from the heat and set aside to cool for at least 20 minutes.

3 Preheat the grill (broiler) to high. Mix the egg yolks with 15ml/1 tbsp of the cream. Season with ground black pepper, then stir into the fish. In a separate bowl, mix the cheese and the remaining cream. Stiffly whisk the egg whites, then fold into the fish mixture.

4 Heat the remaining butter in an omelette pan until it is slightly bubbling. Add the fish mixture and cook until it is browned underneath. Pour the cheese mixture over evenly and grill (broil) until it is bubbling.

5 Serve on a warmed plate immediately, garnished with watercress and with fresh crusty bread to accompany.

Cook's Tip

Try to buy smoked haddock that does not contain artificial colouring for this recipe. Besides being better for you, it gives the omelette a lighter, more attractive colour.

Per portion Energy 821kcal/3396kJ; Protein 36.1g; Carbohydrate 2.6g, of which sugars 2.6g; Fat 74g, of which saturates 42.6g; Cholesterol 577mg; Calcium 280mg; Fibre 0g; Sodium 1123mg.

Smoked haddock and bacon

This is a classic combination, very much associated with Scotland. The smokiness of the fish goes well with the rich flavour of the bacon – both are complemented by the creamy sauce.

Serves 4

25g/1oz/2 tbsp butter

4 undyed smoked haddock fillets

8 rashers (strips) lean back bacon

120ml/4floz/½ cup double (heavy) cream

ground black pepper

snipped fresh chives, to garnish

1 Preheat the grill (broiler) to medium. Over a gentle heat, melt the butter in a frying pan.

2 Add the haddock fillets, working in two batches if necessary, and cook gently, turning once, for about 3 minutes each side. When cooked, place in a large ovenproof dish and cover. Reserve the juices from the frying pan.

3 Grill (broil) the bacon, turning once, until just cooked through but not crispy. Leave the grill on.

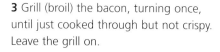

4 Return the frying pan to the heat and pour in the cream and any reserved juices from the haddock. Bring to the boil then simmer briefly, stirring occasionally. Season to taste with ground black pepper.

5 Meanwhile place two bacon rashers over each haddock fillet and place the dish under the grill (broiler) briefly. Then pour over the hot creamy sauce, garnish with snipped fresh chives and serve immediately.

Variation

Instead of topping the smoked haddock with bacon, use wilted spinach for a healthier, tasty option. Thoroughly wash a good handful of spinach for each person. Then plunge it into boiling water for 3 minutes, drain well and lay across each fillet.

Per portion Energy 391kcal/1624kJ; Protein 28.8g; Carbohydrate 0.5g, of which sugars 0.5g; Fat 30.5g, of which saturates 16.5g; Cholesterol 119mg; Calcium 40mg; Fibre 0g; Sodium 1671mg.

Creamy scrambled eggs with smoked salmon

A special treat for weekend breakfasts, eggs served this way are popular in some of
Scotland's best guesthouses and hotels and are a good alternative to the traditional fry-up.

Serves 1

3 eggs

15ml/1 tbsp single (light) cream
or milk

knob (pat) of butter

1 slice of smoked salmon,
chopped or whole, warmed

salt and ground black pepper

sprig of fresh parsley, to garnish

triangles of hot toast, to serve

1 Whisk the eggs in a bowl together
with half the cream or milk, a generous
grinding of black pepper and a little
salt to taste if you like, remembering
that the smoked salmon may be quite
naturally salty.

2 Melt the butter in a pan then add the
egg mixture and stir until nearly set.
Add the rest of the cream, which
prevents the eggs from overcooking.

3 Either stir in the chopped smoked
salmon or serve the warmed slice
alongside the egg. Serve immediately
on warmed plates.

Variation
For creamy scrambled eggs with bacon
and cheese, first cook 1 or 2 rashers
(strips) of streaky (fatty) bacon per
person in a non-stick frying pan until
crispy. Then chop the bacon, add
it to the egg mixture and scramble over
a gentle heat as above. Just before it
sets, add 25g/1oz/¼ cup grated hard
cheese, such as Cheddar, and some
freshly chopped herbs of your choice –
basil or chives work well. Mix together
quickly and serve immediately on hot
buttered toast or freshly baked bread.

Per portion Energy 447kcal/1862kJ; Protein 37.3g; Carbohydrate 0.4g, of which sugars 0.4g; Fat 33.6g, of which saturates 13.1g; Cholesterol 734mg; Calcium 128mg; Fibre 0g; Sodium 1.37g.

Black pudding with potato and apple

This traditional blood sausage has come a long way from its once humble position in Scottish cooking. Made throughout Scotland and widely available, black pudding is now extremely popular, and even features on many a contemporary restaurant menu.

Serves 4

4 large potatoes, peeled

45ml/3 tbsp olive oil

8 slices of black pudding (blood sausage), such as Clonakilty

115g/4oz cultivated mushrooms, such as oyster or shiitake

2 eating apples, peeled, cored and cut into wedges

25ml/1½ tbsp sherry vinegar or wine vinegar

15g/½oz/1 tbsp butter

salt and ground black pepper

1 Grate the potatoes, putting them into a bowl of water as you grate them. Drain and squeeze out any moisture.

2 Heat 30ml/2 tbsp of the olive oil in a large non-stick frying pan, add the grated potatoes and season. Press the potatoes into the pan with your hands.

3 Cook the potatoes until browned, then turn over and cook the other side. When cooked, slide on to a warmed plate.

4 Heat the remaining oil and sauté the black pudding and mushrooms together for a few minutes. Remove from the pan and keep warm.

5 Add the apple wedges to the frying pan and gently sauté to colour them golden brown. Add the sherry or wine vinegar to the apples, and boil up the juices. Add the butter, stir with a wooden spatula until it has melted and season to taste with salt and ground black pepper.

6 Cut the potato cake into portion-sized wedges and divide among four warmed plates. Arrange the slices of black pudding and cooked mushrooms on the bed of potato cake, pour over the apples and the warm juices and serve immediately.

Per portion Energy 247kcal/1034kJ; Protein 4.2g; Carbohydrate 28.8g, of which sugars 5.4g; Fat 13.6g, of which saturates 4g; Cholesterol 13mg; Calcium 16mg; Fibre 2.4g; Sodium 132mg.

Laver bread and bacon omelette

Laver bread is a tasty seaweed preparation perhaps more commonly associated with the Welsh, but it has been used in Scotland for centuries. Dried or canned versions are available and avoid the long preparation time, but if you prefer, use boiled spinach instead.

Makes 1 omelette

oil, to prepare the pan

3 eggs

10ml/2 tsp butter

1 rasher (strip) lean back bacon, cooked and diced

25g/1oz prepared laver bread

salt and ground black pepper

1 Heat a little oil in an omelette pan then leave for a few minutes to help season the pan. A non-stick or small curved-sided pan may also be used.

2 Break the eggs into a bowl large enough for whisking, season then whisk until the yolk and white are well combined but not frothy.

3 Pour the oil out of the pan and reheat. Add the butter, which should begin to sizzle straight away. If it does not the pan is too cool or if it burns it is too hot. Rinse out, dry and try again.

4 Pour the whisked eggs into the pan and immediately, using the back of a fork, draw the mixture towards the middle of the pan, working from the outside and using quick circular movements going around the pan.

5 As it is beginning to cook but is not quite set, put the bacon and laver bread evenly over one half of the omelette. Cook for another 30 seconds then remove from the heat.

6 Fold one side of the mixture over the side with the bacon and laver bread, leave for a minute or two, then turn out on to a warmed plate. Serve immediately while piping hot.

Per portion Energy 355kcal/1472kJ; Protein 23.6g; Carbohydrate 0.5g, of which sugars 0.4g; Fat 29.2g, of which saturates 11.4g; Cholesterol 605mg; Calcium 131mg; Fibre 0.5g; Sodium 691mg.

Lamb's kidneys with a devil sauce

This is one of those hearty dishes that the Scots are so good at, ideal as a breakfast dish, served with rice, for when you are about to go out for a day's walking or stalking game on the hills and highlands. It can also be accompanied with creamy mashed potato for a delicious yet easy-to-prepare lunch or supper.

Serves 4

12 lamb's kidneys

45ml/3 tbsp vegetable oil

15ml/1 tbsp Worcestershire sauce

15ml/1 tbsp Mushroom Sauce

pinch of cayenne pepper

175g/6oz/¾ cup butter

10ml/2 tsp English (hot) mustard

10ml/2 tsp French mustard

1 Skin the kidneys and slice them in half horizontally. Push the flesh out of the way with a finger to reveal all the white gristle. Use a sharp-pointed pair of scissors or a very sharp vegetable knife to remove the central gristly core and any fat.

Variation
These kidneys make an excellent savoury for serving at the end of a formal dinner. Spoon small portions on to rounds of fried bread. You will only need one whole kidney per person.

2 Heat the oil in a frying pan and cook the kidneys over a high heat for a few minutes on both sides, leaving them a little pink. Pour off any excess fat from the pan and set aside to allow the kidneys to cool a little.

3 Meanwhile mix together all the other ingredients in a bowl, using the back of the spoon to break up the sauces.

4 Spread the mixture over the kidneys and return to the heat. Cook gently until the butter melts, then serve.

Per portion Energy 542kcal/2246kJ; Protein 26g; Carbohydrate 1.1g, of which sugars 1g; Fat 48.3g, of which saturates 25.1g; Cholesterol 566mg; Calcium 29mg; Fibre 0g; Sodium 609mg.

Lorn sausage with red onion relish

The Firth of Lorn, the region from which this dish originated, cuts through Argyll between the island of Mull and the mainland on the west coast of Scotland. Prepared simply and traditionally in a loaf shape and chilled overnight, the sausage is then sliced before cooking. Accompanied by cranberry and red onion relish, it makes a delicious meal.

Serves 4

900g/2lb minced (ground) beef

65g/2½oz/generous 1 cup stale white breadcrumbs

150g/5oz/scant 1 cup semolina

5ml/1 tsp salt

75ml/5 tbsp water

ground black pepper

Cranberry and Red Onion Relish, to serve

1 In a large mixing bowl, combine the beef, breadcrumbs, semolina and salt together thoroughly with a fork. Pour in the water, mix again and season to taste. Pass the beef mixture through a coarse mincer (grinder) and set aside.

2 Carefully line a 1.3kg/3lb loaf tin (pan) with clear film (plastic wrap).

3 Spoon the sausage mixture into the tin, pressing it in firmly with the back of a wooden spoon. Even out the surface and fold the clear film over the top. Chill overnight.

4 When ready to cook, preheat the grill (broiler). Turn the sausage out of the tin on to a chopping board and cut into 1cm/½in slices. Grill (broil) each slice until cooked through, turning once. Alternatively, fry until cooked through, again turning once.

Cook's Tip
For the best results, use standard minced (ground) beef for these sausages rather than lean minced steak, as the higher fat content is needed to bind the ingredients together.

Per portion Energy 691kcal/2886kJ; Protein 50.1g; Carbohydrate 40.7g, of which sugars 0.4g; Fat 37.4g, of which saturates 15.6g; Cholesterol 135mg; Calcium 47mg; Fibre 1.1g; Sodium 299mg.

Soups

There has long been a tradition of soup making in Scotland. In rural areas it was usual for everyone to grow sufficient vegetables for the household in a kitchen garden, and these, plus a small amount of meat or a bone, would be added to a rich stock to make a healthy supper to feed the whole family. A huge pot would be hung over the fire, sending out the wonderful aromas of that day's soup.

Spiced creamed parsnip soup with sherry

Parsnips are a naturally sweet vegetable and the modern addition of curry powder complements this perfectly, while a dash of sherry lifts the soup into the dinner-party realm. Try swirling some natural yogurt into this deeply flavoured dish when serving.

2 Cut the parsnips into even-sized pieces, add to the pan and coat with butter. Stir in the curry powder.

3 Pour in the sherry and cover with a cartouche (see Cook's Tip) and a lid. Cook over a low heat for 10 minutes or until the parsnips are softened, making sure they do not colour.

4 Add the stock and season to taste. Bring to the boil then simmer for about 15 minutes or until the parsnips are soft. Remove from the heat. Allow to cool for a while then purée in a blender.

5 When ready to serve, reheat the soup and check the seasoning. Add a swirl of natural (plain) yogurt, if you like.

Cook's Tip
A cartouche is a circle of greaseproof (waxed) paper that helps to keep in the moisture, so the vegetables cook in their own juices along with the sherry.

Serves 4

115g/4oz/½ cup butter

2 onions, sliced

1kg /2¼lb parsnips, peeled

10ml/2 tsp curry powder

30ml/2 tbsp medium sherry

1.2 litres/2 pints/5 cups chicken or vegetable stock

salt and ground black pepper

1 Melt the butter in a pan, add the onions and sweat gently without allowing them to colour.

Per portion Energy 437kcal/1820kJ; Protein 5.9g; Carbohydrate 39.5g, of which sugars 20.2g; Fat 28.7g, of which saturates 16.8g; Cholesterol 67mg; Calcium 134mg; Fibre 12.9g; Sodium 218mg.

Leek and potato soup

This is a hearty Scottish staple, forming everything from a warming lunch to a hot drink from a flask by the loch on a cold afternoon. The chopped vegetables produce a chunky soup. If you prefer a smooth texture, press the mixture through a sieve.

Serves 4

50g/2oz/¼ cup butter

2 leeks, washed and chopped

1 small onion, peeled and finely chopped

350g/12oz potatoes, peeled and chopped

900ml/1½ pints/3¾ cups chicken or vegetable stock

salt and ground black pepper

chopped fresh parsley, to garnish

2 Add the potatoes to the pan and cook for about 2–3 minutes, then add the stock and bring to the boil. Cover and simmer for 30–35 minutes.

3 Season to taste and remove the pan from the heat. Dice and stir in the remaining butter. Garnish with the chopped parsley and serve hot.

1 Heat 25g/1oz/2 tbsp of the butter in a large pan over a medium heat. Add the leeks and onion and cook gently, stirring occasionally, for about 7 minutes, until they are softened but not browned.

Cook's Tips
• Don't use a food processor to purée this soup as it can give the potatoes a gluey consistency. The potatoes should be left to crumble and disintegrate naturally as they boil, making the consistency of the soup thicker the longer you leave them.
• If you can, make your own chicken or vegetable stock by simmering bones and vegetables in water for 2 hours and straining the liquid.

Per portion Energy 179Kcal/747kJ; Protein 3.2g; Carbohydrate 17.9g, of which sugars 4g; Fat 11g, of which saturates 6.7g; Cholesterol 27mg; Calcium 32mg; Fibre 3g; Sodium 88mg.

Cabbage and potato soup with caraway

Earthy floury potatoes are essential to the success of this soup, so choose your variety carefully. Caraway seeds come from a plant in the parsley family. They are aromatic and nutty, with a delicate anise flavour, adding a subtle accent to this satisfying dish.

Serves 4

30ml/2 tbsp olive oil

2 small onions, sliced

6 garlic cloves, halved

350g/12oz/3 cups shredded green cabbage

4 potatoes, unpeeled

5ml/1 tsp caraway seeds

5ml/1 tsp sea salt

1.2 litres/2 pints/5 cups water

1 Pour the olive oil into a large pan and soften the onion. Add the garlic and the cabbage and cook over a low heat for 10 minutes, stirring occasionally to prevent the cabbage from sticking.

2 Add the potatoes, caraway seeds, sea salt and water. Bring to the boil then simmer until all the vegetables are cooked through, about 20–30 minutes.

3 Remove from the heat and allow to cool slightly before mashing into a purée or passing through a seive.

Cook's Tip
Use floury potatoes to achieve the correct texture for this soup. King Edward or Maris Piper (US russet or Idaho) are excellent choices.

Per portion Energy 144Kcal/601kJ; Protein 3.1g; Carbohydrate 20.4g, of which sugars 8.1g; Fat 6g, of which saturates 0.9g; Cholesterol 0mg; Calcium 60mg; Fibre 3.3g; Sodium 507mg.

Avocado, spinach and sorrel soup

Sorrel, with its sharp lemony flavour, grows wild throughout the UK, Europe, North America and Asia. In some parts of Scotland it is known as "sourocks", a reference to its sharp or sour flavour. It is delicious in salads and soups.

Serves 4

30ml/2 tbsp olive oil

2 onions, chopped

1kg/2¼lb spinach

900ml/1½ pints/3¾ cups light chicken stock

4 garlic cloves, crushed with salt

1 bunch sorrel leaves

2 avocados, peeled and stoned (pitted)

1 Pour the olive oil into a large heavy pan and sweat the onions over a gentle heat until soft but not coloured. Meanwhile, wash the spinach thoroughly and remove the stalks.

2 Add the spinach to the onions and cook for about 2 minutes, stirring, to wilt the leaves. Cover and increase the heat slightly then cook for a further 3 minutes. Add the stock, cover again and simmer for about 10 minutes.

3 Add the garlic, sorrel and avocados to the soup and once heated through remove from the heat.

4 Allow the soup to cool then purée in a blender. Reheat the soup before serving with warmed crusty bread.

Cook's Tips
• Crushing garlic in salt helps to bring out the oils of the garlic and also stops any being wasted in a garlic press. Use a coarse salt and try to keep a chopping board or at least a corner of one for this sole purpose, as it is hard to get rid of the scent of garlic and it can taint other foods.
• When using avocados in soup do not let them boil as this makes them taste bitter. They are best added at the end and just heated through.
• This soup freezes for up to a month. Freeze it the day you make it.

Per portion Energy 282kcal/1161kJ; Protein 9.3g; Carbohydrate 11.4g, of which sugars 8.3g; Fat 22.1g, of which saturates 4.1g; Cholesterol 0mg; Calcium 452mg; Fibre 8.9g; Sodium 357mg.

Rocket soup with kiln-smoked salmon

Kiln-smoked salmon has actually been "cooked" during the smoking process, producing a delicious flaky texture. This is in contrast to traditional cold-smoked salmon, which is not actually cooked but does not spoil because it has been preserved first in brine.

Serves 4

15ml/1 tbsp olive oil

1 small onion, sliced

1 garlic clove, crushed

150ml/¼ pint/⅔ cup double (heavy) cream

350ml/12fl oz/1½ cups vegetable stock

350g/12oz rocket (arugula)

4 fresh basil leaves

salt and ground black pepper

flaked kiln-smoked salmon, to garnish

1 Put the olive oil in a high-sided pan over a medium heat and allow to heat up. Add the sliced onion and sweat for a few minutes, stirring continuously. Add the garlic and continue to sweat gently until soft and transparent, although you should not allow the onion to colour.

2 Add the cream and stock, stir in gently and bring slowly to the boil. Allow to simmer gently for about 5 minutes. Add the rocket, reserving a few leaves to garnish, and the basil. Return briefly to the boil and turn off the heat. Add a little cold water and allow to cool for a few minutes.

3 Purée in a blender until smooth, adding a little salt and pepper to taste. When ready to serve, reheat gently but do not allow to boil. Serve in warmed bowls with a few flakes of salmon, a leaf or two of rocket and a drizzle of virgin olive oil over the top.

Variation
Cold-smoked salmon is also very good with this soup, and can be used if you can't find the kiln-smoked variety. Simply cut a few slices into medium to thick strips and add to the hot soup. Warming the smoked salmon for a few minutes increases the flavour.

Per portion Energy 258kcal/1063kJ; Protein 6.8g; Carbohydrate 3.2g, of which sugars 2.8g; Fat 24.3g, of which saturates 13.1g; Cholesterol 56mg; Calcium 174mg; Fibre 2.1g; Sodium 395mg.

Cullen skink

The famous Cullen skink comes from the small fishing port of Cullen on the east coast of Scotland, the word "skink" meaning an essence or soup. The fishermen smoked their smaller fish and these, with locally grown potatoes, formed their staple diet.

Serves 6

1 Finnan haddock, about 350g/12oz

1 onion, chopped

bouquet garni

900ml/1½ pints/3¾ cups water

500g/1¼lb potatoes, quartered

600ml/1 pint/2½ cups milk

40g/1½oz/3 tbsp butter

salt and pepper

chopped chives, to garnish

1 Put the haddock, onion, bouquet garni and water into a large pan and bring to the boil. Skim the surface with a slotted spoon, discarding any fish skin, then cover the pan. Reduce the heat and gently poach for 10–15 minutes, until the fish flakes easily.

2 Lift the fish from the pan, using a fish slice, and remove the skin and any bones. Return the skin and bones to the pan and simmer, uncovered, for a further 30 minutes. Flake the cooked fish flesh and leave to cool.

Cook's Tip
If you can't find Finnan haddock, use a good quality smoked haddock.

3 Strain the fish stock and return to the pan, then add the potatoes and simmer for about 25 minutes, or until tender.

4 Carefully remove the poatoes from the pan using a slotted spoon. Add the milk to the pan and bring to the boil.

5 In a separate pan, mash the potatoes with the butter. A little at a time, whisk this thoroughly into the pan until the soup is thick and creamy.

6 Add the flaked fish to the pan and adjust the seasoning. Sprinkle with chives and serve immediately with fresh crusty bread.

Per portion Energy 205kcal/864kJ; Protein 16.1g; Carbohydrate 19g, of which sugars 6.4g; Fat 7.8g, of which saturates 4.7g; Cholesterol 41mg; Calcium 137mg; Fibre 1g; Sodium 132mg.

Mussel and fennel bree

Bree is the Scots word for a soup or broth, most often associated with shellfish rather like a bisque or bouillabaisse. Mussels partner particularly well with the anise flavour of Pernod or Ricard. Try to get the native Scottish mussels that are smaller with a good flavour. You will need two pans for this dish, one to cook the mussels and one for the bree.

Serves 4

1kg/2¼lb fresh mussels

1 fennel bulb

120ml/4fl oz/½ cup dry white wine

1 leek, finely sliced

olive oil

25g/1oz/2 tbsp butter

splash of Pernod or Ricard

150ml/¼ pint/⅔ cup double (heavy) cream

25g/1oz fresh parsley, chopped

1 Clean the mussels thoroughly, removing any beards and scraping off any barnacles. Discard any that are broken or open.

2 Strip off the outer leaves of the fennel and roughly chop them. Set to one side. Then take the central core of the fennel and chop it very finely. Set it aside in a separate dish or bowl.

3 Place the roughly chopped fennel leaves, the mussels and the wine in a large pan, cover and cook gently until all the mussels open, about 5 minutes. Discard any that remain closed.

4 In a second pan sweat the leek and finely chopped core of the fennel gently in the oil and butter until soft.

5 Meanwhile remove the mussels from the first pan and either leave in the shell or remove. Set aside.

6 Strain the liquor on to the leek mixture and bring to the boil. Add a little water and the pastis, and simmer for a few minutes. Add the cream and parsley and bring back to the boil.

7 Place the mussels in a serving tureen and pour over the soup. Serve with crusty bread for mopping up the juices.

Cook's Tip
Farmed or "rope-grown" mussels are easier to clean. If you use mussels with lots of barnacles you will need to remove these first.

Per portion Energy 392kcal/1624kJ; Protein 13.4g; Carbohydrate 5.7g, of which sugars 3g; Fat 33g, of which saturates 16.9g; Cholesterol 105mg; Calcium 95mg; Fibre 2.8g; Sodium 297mg.

King scallops in Jerusalem artichoke broth

In Scotland scallops are mainly found on the west coast and around the Islands. The best are hand-collected, when divers literally dive down and collect them from the seabed, which is why they can be expensive. This way, though, the divers can be selective and choose only the right size, and they do not disturb the seabed.

Serves 4

450g/1lb Jerusalem artichokes

75g/3oz/6 tbsp butter

1 large onion, chopped

5ml/1 tsp sea salt

120ml/4 fl oz/½ cup double (heavy) cream

8 fresh king scallops

chopped fresh parsley, to garnish

1 Roughly peel the artichokes, but don't be too fussy as the knobbly bits can be hard to get into and it is very time-consuming. It is most important to remove all the earth otherwise the soup can be gritty. Chop roughly.

2 Heat a pan, melt the butter and gently sweat the onions until softened but not coloured. Add the artichokes and stir to coat in the butter.

3 Cover the pan with a well-fitting lid and leave to stew gently for about 10 minutes, giving the pan a shake occasionally to prevent the artichokes from sticking to the base of the pan.

4 Pour in enough water just to cover the artichokes, and add the salt. Bring to the boil then reduce the heat and simmer gently for 30 minutes. Purée in a blender until smooth, then strain into a clean pan. Add the cream and check the seasoning.

5 Slice the scallops in two horizontally. When the soup is ready, remove from the heat and add the scallops. They will cook in the soup off the heat in a couple of minutes. Serve garnished with chopped fresh parsley, allowing four slices of scallop per person.

Per portion Energy 383kcal/1586kJ; Protein 13.5g; Carbohydrate 8.1g, of which sugars 5g; Fat 33.3g, of which saturates 20.4g; Cholesterol 106mg; Calcium 94mg; Fibre 2.1g; Sodium 280mg.

Shore crab soup

These little crabs have a velvet feel to their shell. They are mostly caught off the west coast of Scotland, although they can be quite difficult to find in fishmongers. If you have trouble finding them, you can also use common or brown crabs for this recipe.

Serves 4

1kg/2¼lbs shore or velvet crabs

50g/2oz/¼ cup butter

50g/2oz leek, washed and chopped

50g/2oz carrot, chopped

30ml/2 tbsp brandy

225g/8oz ripe tomatoes, chopped

15ml/1 tbsp tomato purée (paste)

120ml/4fl oz/½ cup dry white wine

1.5 litres/2½ pints/6¼ cups fish stock

sprig of fresh tarragon

60ml/4 tbsp double (heavy) cream

lemon juice

1 Bring a large pan of water to a rolling boil and plunge the live crabs into it. They will be killed very quickly, and the bigger the pan and the more water there is, the better. Once the crabs are dead – a couple of minutes at most – take them out of the water, place in a large bowl and smash them up. This can be done with either a wooden mallet or the end of a rolling pin.

2 Melt the butter in a heavy pan, add the leek and carrot and cook gently until soft but not coloured.

3 Add the crabs and when very hot pour in the brandy, stirring to allow the flavour to pervade the whole pan. Add the tomatoes, tomato purée, wine, stock and tarragon. Bring to the boil and simmer gently for 30 minutes.

4 Strain the soup through a metal sieve, forcing as much of the tomato mixture through as possible. (If you like you could remove the big claws and purée the remains in a blender.)

5 Return to the heat, simmer for a few minutes then season to taste. Add the cream and lemon juice, and serve.

Cook's Tip
If you don't have fish stock then water will do, or you could use some of the water used to boil the crabs initially.

Per portion Energy 419kcal/1741kJ; Protein 35.1g; Carbohydrate 3.8g, of which sugars 3.6g; Fat 25.7g, of which saturates 15.1g; Cholesterol 196mg; Calcium 252mg; Fibre 1.1g; Sodium 1122mg.

Scotch broth

Sustaining and warming, Scotch broth is custom-made for the chilly Scottish weather, and makes a delicious winter soup anywhere. Traditionally, a large pot of it is made and this is dipped into throughout the next few days, the flavour improving all the time.

Serves 6–8

1kg/2¼lb lean neck (US shoulder or breast) of lamb, cut into large, even-sized chunks

1.75 litres/3 pints/7½ cups cold water

1 large onion, chopped

50g/2oz/¼ cup pearl barley

bouquet garni

1 large carrot, chopped

1 turnip, chopped

3 leeks, chopped

1 small white cabbage, finely shredded

salt and ground black pepper

chopped fresh parsley, to garnish

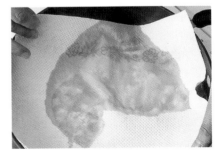

1 Put the lamb and water in a large pan over a medium heat and gently bring to the boil. Skim off the scum with a spoon. Add the onion, pearl barley and bouquet garni, and stir in thoroughly.

2 Bring the soup back to the boil, then reduce the heat, partly cover the pan and simmer gently for a further 1 hour. Make sure that it does not boil too furiously or go dry.

3 Add the remaining vegetables to the pan and season with salt and ground black pepper. Bring to the boil, partly cover again and simmer for about 35 minutes, until the vegetables are tender.

4 Remove the surplus fat from the top of the soup with a sheet of kitchen paper. Serve the soup hot, garnished with chopped parsley, with chunks of fresh bread.

Per portion Energy 387kcal/1619kJ; Protein 36.2g; Carbohydrate 17.7g, of which sugars 9.1g; Fat 19.5g, of which saturates 8.8g; Cholesterol 127mg; Calcium 86mg; Fibre 4.3g; Sodium 157mg.

First courses

With Scotland's extensive coastline, lochs and rivers, its first courses are often based on smoked and fresh fish and shellfish, from the simple raw oyster to king scallops and langoustines in delicate sauces. The sensational smoked salmons that are now being produced provide a sumptuous start to any meal, simply sprinkled with ground black pepper and a squeeze of fresh lemon. Smoked products, game and wonderful cheeses also make delicious first courses.

Asparagus with lime butter dip

In Scotland asparagus has the shortest of seasons, just six weeks, but it is worth the wait and while it is at its freshest you should find as many ways as possible to enjoy it. This recipe is based on the traditional butter sauce but it has lime added to lift the flavour. The dip can be used for most kinds of shellfish too.

Serves 4

40 medium asparagus spears

1 litre/1¾ pints/4 cups water

15g/½oz coarse salt

For the lime butter dip

90ml/6 tbsp dry white wine

90ml/6 tbsp white wine vinegar

3 shallots or 1 onion, finely chopped

225g/8oz/1 cup very cold unsalted (sweet) butter, cut into chunks

juice of 1 lime

salt and ground black pepper

lime wedges, to serve

1 Wash the asparagus spears and trim the bases off evenly to give about 10cm/4in lengths. Bring a pan of water to the boil, add the salt then plunge in the asparagus. Cook for about 7 minutes or until you can just spear a stem with a knife and the blade slips out easily. Drain immediately and set aside, keeping the asparagus warm.

2 A stainless steel pan with a handle is essential for the lime butter dip. If you are using a gas ring make sure the flame does not come round the side of the pan, as the sauce can burn easily. Combine the wine and vinegar in the pan with the shallots or onion, and simmer until the liquid has reduced to about 15ml/1 tbsp.

3 Off the heat, vigorously whisk in the butter until the sauce thickens. Whisk in the lime juice until thoroughly combined. Taste the sauce and adjust the seasoning if necessary.

4 Arrange ten asparagus spears per serving on warmed individual plates. Coarsely grind some black pepper over the top. Serve the warm lime butter dip in a bowl for handing round or in four small bowls.

Cook's Tips
• There are two important points to remember when you add the butter to the sauce. Firstly, don't allow the sauce to boil. If the butter is taking a long time to melt, put the pan back over a gentle heat to speed it up. Secondly, you must not stop whisking until the butter is completely incorporated.
• You can use the asparagus trimmings to make soup or a lovely rich stock for stews or casseroles.

Variations
This butter dip is a simple but effective sauce for shellfish. Variations include using cider instead of vinegar and orange or lemon juice instead of lime juice. Adding fish stock when reducing gives a strong fish flavour.

Per portion Energy 527kcal/2166kJ; Protein 7.8g; Carbohydrate 6.7g, of which sugars 6.1g; Fat 50.9g, of which saturates 31.5g; Cholesterol 128mg; Calcium 84mg; Fibre 4.5g; Sodium 1841mg.

Lanark Blue and walnut salad

Lanark Blue is a blue cheese made from ewe's milk by Humphrey Errington on his farm near Biggar, south of Edinburgh. It is based on the French Roquefort but has a creamy texture and tangy flavour all its own. This is a delicious fresh-tasting first course but can be served without the figs as a cheese course.

Serves 4

mixed salad leaves

4 fresh figs

115g/4oz Lanark Blue, cut into small chunks

75g/3oz/¾ cup walnut halves

For the dressing

45ml/3 tbsp walnut oil

juice of 1 lemon

salt and ground black pepper

1 Mix all the dressing ingredients together in a bowl. Whisk briskly until thick and emulsified.

Cook's Tip
Look for dark green salad leaves, such as lamb's lettuce and rocket (arugula), and reds, such as lollo rosso, as well as some crunchy leaves, such as Little Gem (Bibb), to add interest.

Variation
The figs may be replaced with ripe nectarines or peaches if you prefer. Wash and cut in half, discard the stone, then cut each half into three or four slices. If the skin is tough, you may need to remove it.

2 Wash and dry the salad leaves then tear them gently into bitesize pieces. Place in a mixing bowl and toss with the dressing. Transfer to a large serving dish or divide among four individual plates, ensuring a good balance of colour and texture on each plate.

3 Cut the figs into quarters and add to the salad leaves.

4 Sprinkle the cheese over, crumbling it slightly. Then sprinkle over the walnuts, breaking them up roughly in your fingers as you go.

Per portion Energy 415kcal/1726kJ; Protein 10.6g; Carbohydrate 26.6g, of which sugars 26.4g; Fat 30.3g, of which saturates 7.3g; Cholesterol 22mg; Calcium 286mg; Fibre 4.5g; Sodium 383mg.

Langoustines with saffron and tomato

The best langoustines come from the west coast of Scotland, where everything from a tiny shrimp to just smaller than a lobster is called a prawn. Langoustines, also known as Dublin Bay prawns or Norway lobsters, look like miniature lobsters, although they taste more like jumbo prawns or shrimp, and these can be substituted if you prefer.

Serves 4

5ml/1 tsp sea salt

20 live langoustines or Dublin Bay prawns (jumbo shrimp)

1 onion

15ml/1 tbsp olive oil

pinch of saffron threads

120ml/4fl oz/½ cup dry white wine

450g/1lb ripe fresh or canned tomatoes, roughly chopped

chopped fresh flat leaf parsley, to garnish

salt and ground black pepper

1 Bring a large pan of water to the boil, add the salt and plunge the shellfish into the pan. Let the water return to the boil then transfer the shellfish to a colander to cool.

Variation
You can also use other kinds of shellfish for this dish, such as mussels or clams. You will need to adjust the cooking times. Lobster also goes well in this recipe if you are serving a large number of people for a special occasion.

2 When cooled, shell the langoustines or prawns and reserve four heads with two claws each. Keep the rest of the shells, heads and claws to make a flavourful stock for the sauce.

3 Chop the onions. Heat a large heavy pan and add 15ml/1 tbsp olive oil. Gently fry the chopped onion to soften.

4 Stir in the saffron threads. Then add the shellfish debris, including the heads and the pincers. Stir to mix thoroughly and then reduce the heat.

5 Add the wine and then the tomatoes. Simmer to soften the tomatoes – this will take about 5 minutes. Do not allow the mixture to become too dry; add water if necessary.

6 Strain through a sieve, pushing the debris to get as much moisture out as possible. The resulting sauce should be light in texture; if it's too thick add some water. Check the seasoning.

7 Add the langoustines or prawns and warm over a gentle heat for a few minutes. Serve in warmed soup plates garnished with the reserved langoustine or prawn heads and scattered with chopped fresh flat leaf parsley.

Cook's Tip
Crushing the langoustine or prawn shell debris with a rolling pin before adding it to the pan helps to extract more flavour into the juices.

Per portion Energy 107kcal/449kJ; Protein 9.8g; Carbohydrate 4.9g, of which sugars 4.5g; Fat 3.4g, of which saturates 0.6g; Cholesterol 98mg; Calcium 54mg; Fibre 1.3g; Sodium 598mg.

Langoustines with garlic butter

There is nothing quite like the smell of garlic butter melting over shellfish. Freshly caught langoustines or jumbo shrimp are ideal for this simple yet extremely tasty first-course dish. Serve with plenty of fresh crusty white bread to soak up the delicious garlicky juices.

Serves 4

2 garlic cloves

5ml/1 tsp coarse salt

10ml/2 tsp chopped fresh flat leaf parsley, plus extra to garnish (optional)

250g/9oz/generous 1 cup butter, softened

juice of 2 lemons

pinch of cayenne pepper

20 freshly caught langoustines or Dublin Bay prawns (jumbo shrimp), cooked and peeled

ground black pepper

1 Preheat the grill (broiler) to medium. Using a blender or food processor, blend the garlic cloves, salt and chopped parsley until quite well mixed. Then add the butter, lemon juice and cayenne pepper and blend again until all the ingredients are thoroughly combined.

2 Scrape the butter mixture out of the food processor and into a bowl.

3 Place the langoustines or prawns on a metal baking tray and put a blob of garlic butter on each one. Place under the preheated grill for about 5 minutes, or until the shellfish are cooked and the butter is bubbling.

4 Lift five shellfish on to each plate and spoon over the collected pan juices. Serve immediately with a grind or two of black pepper and garnished with chopped fresh flat leaf parsley if you like. Accompany with fresh bread for mopping up the juices.

Cook's Tip

To cook the langoustines or prawns, plunge them into boiling water until the water returns to the boil and then drain and cool. Shell them by pulling off the head, legs and outer shell. Reserve a few heads to garnish, if you like.

Per portion Energy 616kcal/2552kJ; Protein 29.7g; Carbohydrate 4.9g, of which sugars 0.6g; Fat 53.3g, of which saturates 33.1g; Cholesterol 192mg; Calcium 68mg; Fibre 0.5g; Sodium 1098mg.

Grilled oysters with highland heather honey

Heather honey is very fragrant, the pollen gathered by bees late in the season when the heather on the moors is in full flower. Beekeepers in Scotland will take their hives up to the hills once the spring and early summer blossoms are over, so the flavour is more intense.

Serves 4

1 bunch spring onions (scallions), washed

20ml/4 tsp heather honey

10ml/2 tsp soy sauce

16 fresh oysters

1 Preheat the grill (broiler) to medium. Chop the spring onions finely, removing any coarser outer leaves.

2 Place the heather honey and soy sauce in a bowl and mix. Then add the finely chopped spring onions and mix them in thoroughly.

3 Open the oysters with an oyster knife or a small, sharp knife, taking care to catch the liquid in a small bowl. Leave the oysters attached to one side of the shell. Strain the liquid to remove any pieces of broken shell, and set aside.

4 Place a large teaspoon of the honey and spring onion mixture on top of each oyster.

5 Place under the preheated grill until the mixture bubbles, which will take about 5 minutes. Take care when removing the oysters from the grill as the shells retain the heat. Make sure that you don't lose any of the sauce from inside the oyster shells.

6 Allow the oysters to cool slightly before serving with slices of bread to soak up the juices. Either tip them straight into your mouth or lift them out with a spoon or fork.

Per portion Energy 81kcal/343kJ; Protein 9.2g; Carbohydrate 9.1g, of which sugars 6.9g; Fat 1.2g, of which saturates 0.2g; Cholesterol 46mg; Calcium 121mg; Fibre 0.3g; Sodium 588mg.

Dressed crab with asparagus

Crab is the juiciest and most flavoursome seafood, possibly better even than lobster and considerably cheaper. This dish is a combination of two paragons: crab as the king of seafood and asparagus as a prince among vegetables.

Serves 4

24 asparagus spears

4 dressed crabs

30ml/2 tbsp mayonnaise

15ml/1 tbsp chopped fresh parsley

1 Cook the asparagus as for Asparagus with Lime Butter Dip), but when cooked plunge the stems into iced water to stop them from cooking further. Drain them when cold and pat dry with kitchen paper.

2 Scoop out the white crab meat from the shells and claws and place it in a bowl. If you can't find fresh crabs, you can use the same amount of canned or frozen white crab meat.

3 Add the mayonnaise and chopped fresh parsley and combine with a fork. Place the mixture into the crab shells and add six asparagus spears per serving. Serve with crusty bread.

Per portion Energy 207kcal/859kJ; Protein 19.5g; Carbohydrate 3g, of which sugars 2.8g; Fat 13g, of which saturates 1.9g; Cholesterol 72mg; Calcium 157mg; Fibre 2.6g; Sodium 540mg.

Hot crab soufflés

These delicious little soufflés must be served as soon as they are ready, so seat your guests at the table before taking the soufflés out of the oven. Use local freshly caught crabs if possible, although canned or frozen will do if necessary.

Serves 6

50g/2oz/¼ cup butter

45ml/3 tbsp fine wholemeal (whole-wheat) breadcrumbs

4 spring onions (scallions), finely chopped

15ml/1 tbsp Malaysian or mild Madras curry powder

25g/1oz/¼ cup plain (all-purpose) flour

105ml/7 tbsp coconut milk or milk

150ml/¼ pint/⅔ cup whipping cream

4 eggs, separated, plus 2 extra egg whites

225g/8oz white crab meat

mild green Tabasco sauce, to taste

salt and ground black pepper

1 Use a little of the butter to grease six ramekins or a 1.75 litre/3 pint/7½ cup soufflé dish. Sprinkle in the fine wholemeal breadcrumbs, roll the dish(es) around to coat the base and sides completely, then tip out the excess breadcrumbs. Preheat the oven to 200°C/400°F/Gas 6.

2 Melt the remaining butter in a pan, add the spring onions and Malaysian or mild Madras curry powder and cook over a low heat for about 1 minute, until softened. Stir in the flour and cook for 1 minute more.

3 Gradually add the coconut milk or milk and cream, stirring continuously until each batch is thoroughly absorbed. Cook over a low heat until the mixture is smooth and thick.

4 Off the heat, stir in the egg yolks, then the crab meat. Season with salt, black pepper and Tabasco sauce.

5 In a grease-free bowl, beat the egg whites stiffly with a pinch of salt. Using a metal spoon, stir one-third into the crab mixture to lighten it; fold in the rest. Spoon into the dish(es).

6 Bake in the preheated oven until well risen and golden brown, and firm to the touch. Individual soufflés will be ready in 8 minutes; a large soufflé will take 15–20 minutes. Serve immediately.

Variation
Lobster or salmon can be used instead of crab in these soufflés. Cook the fish before adding it to the mixture.

Per portion Energy 234kcal/972kJ; Protein 11.8g; Carbohydrate 8.7g, of which sugars 1.8g; Fat 17.1g, of which saturates 9.3g; Cholesterol 97mg; Calcium 37mg; Fibre 0.3g; Sodium 322mg.

Mussels with Musselburgh leeks

Musselburgh is a former fishing port near Edinburgh, famous for its oyster beds and its leeks – a short, stumpy variety with huge green tops and an excellent flavour.

Serves 4

1.3kg/3lb mussels

1 leek, cut into 5cm/2in lengths

50g/2oz/¼ cup butter

1 onion, finely chopped

pinch of saffron threads

150ml/¼ pint/⅔ cup dry white wine

1 bay leaf

sprig of fresh thyme

6 black peppercorns

100ml/3½fl oz/scant ½ cup double (heavy) cream

ground black pepper

chopped fresh parsley, to garnish

1 Scrub the mussels in plenty of cold water and discard any that are broken or remain open when tapped lightly. Remove the beard by pulling hard towards the pointed tip of the mussel. Use as small, sharp knife to scrape off any barnacles.

2 Thoroughly wash the leek, discard any tough outer leaves and cut into fine strips or batons.

3 Melt the butter in a heavy pan then sweat the onion gently until soft. Add the saffron threads and stir for a few minutes, then add the leek batons and allow to wilt slightly. Add the mussels with the wine, herbs and peppercorns. Cover and steam over a medium heat until the mussel shells open, about 5 minutes. Discard any that remain closed.

4 Remove the lid from the pan and add the cream. Simmer rapidly to allow the sauce to thicken slightly. Remove the bay leaf and thyme, and stir well to mix the leek around.

5 Serve immediately in warmed bowls, with a grind or two of black pepper and garnished with lots of chopped fresh parsley. Provide hot, crusty bread for mopping up the sauce.

Per portion Energy 332kcal/1379kJ; Protein 17.6g; Carbohydrate 1.9g, of which sugars 1.6g; Fat 25.7g, of which saturates 15.2g; Cholesterol 100mg; Calcium 214mg; Fibre 0.2g; Sodium 288mg.

Sea trout mousse

This deliciously creamy mousse makes a little sea trout go a long way. It is equally good
made with salmon if sea trout is not available.

Serves 6

250g/9oz sea trout fillet

120ml/4fl oz/½ cup fish stock

2 gelatine leaves or 15ml/1 tbsp
powdered gelatine

juice of ½ lemon

30ml/2 tbsp dry sherry or dry
vermouth

30ml/2 tbsp freshly grated Parmesan

300ml/½ pint/1¼ cups
whipping cream

2 egg whites

15ml/1 tbsp sunflower oil

salt and ground white pepper

For the garnish

5cm/2in piece cucumber, with peel,
thinly sliced

6 small sprigs fresh dill or chervil,
plus extra, chopped

1 Place the sea trout fillet in a shallow
pan. Pour in the fish stock and heat
to simmering point. Poach the fish for
about 3–4 minutes, until lightly cooked.
Lift the trout out and set it aside to cool
slightly. Strain the stock into a jug
(pitcher), then add the gelatine to the
hot stock and stir until dissolved
completely. Set aside to cool.

2 When the trout is cool enough to
handle, remove the skin and flake the
flesh. Pour the stock into a food
processor. Process briefly, then gradually
add the flaked trout, lemon juice, sherry
or vermouth and Parmesan through the
feeder tube, continuing to process the
mixture until smooth. Scrape into a
large bowl and leave to cool completely.

3 Lightly whip the cream then fold it
into the cold trout mixture. Season to
taste, then cover with clear film (plastic
wrap) and chill until the mousse is
beginning to set.

4 Beat the egg whites with a pinch of
salt until softly peaking. Stir one-third
into the trout mixture to lighten it, then
fold in the rest.

5 Lightly grease six ramekin dishes with
the sunflower oil. Divide the mousse
among the ramekins and level the
surface. Place in the refrigerator for 2–
3 hours, until set. Just before serving,
arrange a few slices of cucumber and a
small herb sprig on each mousse and
add a little chopped dill or chervil.

Per portion Energy 286kcal/1181kJ; Protein 12g; Carbohydrate 1.5g, of which sugars 1.5g; Fat 25.2g, of which saturates 13.9g; Cholesterol 58mg; Calcium 94mg; Fibre 0g; Sodium 111mg.

Marinated smoked haddock fillets

This simple dish is also excellent made with kipper fillets. Rum has always been popular on the west coast where it arrived from the Caribbean into the Glasgow ports.

2 Whisk together the mustard, lemon juice and some ground black pepper. Add the oil gradually, whisking continuously. Pour two-thirds of the dressing over the fish. Cover the dish with clear film (plastic wrap) and leave the fish to marinate for 2 hours in a cool place. Sprinkle with the rum and leave for 1 hour more.

3 Cook the potatoes in boiling salted water until tender. Drain, cut in half and place in a bowl. Cool a little, then toss in the remaining dressing. Stir in the chopped fresh dill, cover and set aside.

4 Slice the haddock thinly, as for smoked salmon, or leave whole if you like. Arrange on small plates and spoon over some marinade and onion rings. Pile the potato halves on one side of each plate and garnish each portion with a sprig of dill. Serve chilled or at room temperature.

Cook's Tip
Try to get a large, thick haddock fillet. If all you can find are small pieces, you can still make the dish, but serve the pieces whole instead of slicing them.

Variation
In some parts of the Highlands and Islands, whisky is used instead of rum. A good whisky with a subtle flavour would be best for this delicate dish.

Serves 6

450g/1lb undyed smoked haddock fillet, skinned

1 onion, very thinly sliced into rings

5–10ml/1–2 tsp Dijon mustard

30ml/2 tbsp lemon juice

90ml/6 tbsp olive oil

45ml/3 tbsp dark rum

12 small new potatoes, scrubbed

30ml/2 tbsp chopped fresh dill, plus 6 sprigs to garnish

ground black pepper

1 Cut the fish fillet in half lengthways. Check for and remove any bones by pressing gently with your fingertips and thumb all the way down. Arrange the pieces in a single layer in a shallow non-metallic dish. Sprinkle the onion rings evenly over the top.

Per portion Energy 212kcal/884kJ; Protein 15.3g; Carbohydrate 7.7g, of which sugars 1.3g; Fat 11.7g, of which saturates 1.7g; Cholesterol 27mg; Calcium 37mg; Fibre 0.9g; Sodium 577mg.

Smoked haddock pâté

Arbroath smokies are small haddock that are beheaded and gutted but not split before being salted and hot-smoked. You can also use kippers or any smoked fish for this recipe.

Serves 6

3 large Arbroath smokies, approximately 225g/8oz each

275g/10oz/1¼ cups soft cheese

3 eggs, beaten

30–45ml/2–3 tbsp lemon juice

ground black pepper

sprigs of chervil, to garnish

lettuce and lemon wedges, to serve

1 Preheat the oven to 160°C/325°F/ Gas 3. Butter six ramekin dishes. Lay the smokies in a baking dish and heat through in the oven for 10 minutes.

2 Remove the fish from the oven, carefully remove the skin and bones then flake the flesh into a bowl.

3 Mash the fish with a fork then work in the cheese, then the eggs. Add lemon juice and pepper to taste.

4 Divide the fish mixture among the ramekin dishes and place them in a large roasting pan. Pour hot water into the roasting pan to come halfway up the dishes. Bake in the oven for 30 minutes, until just set.

5 Leave to cool for 2–3 minutes, then run a sharp knife around the edge of each dish and carefully invert the pâté on to warmed plates. Garnish with chervil sprigs and serve with the lettuce leaves and lemon wedges.

Per portion Energy 206kcal/859kJ; Protein 25.3g; Carbohydrate 1.7g, of which sugars 0.1g; Fat 11g, of which saturates 5.8g; Cholesterol 153mg; Calcium 82mg; Fibre 0g; Sodium 940mg.

Haddock and smoked salmon terrine

This substantial terrine makes a superb dish for a summer buffet, accompanied by dill mayonnaise or a fresh mango salsa. Serve with a light, crisp salad.

**Serves 10–12 as a first course,
6–8 as a main course**

15ml/1 tbsp sunflower oil,
for greasing

350g/12oz oak-smoked salmon

900g/2lb haddock fillets, skinned

2 eggs, lightly beaten

105ml/7 tbsp crème fraîche

30ml/2 tbsp drained capers

30ml/2 tbsp drained soft green or
pink peppercorns

salt and ground white pepper

crème fraîche, peppercorns, fresh
dill and rocket (arugula), to garnish

1 Preheat the oven to 200°C/400°F/
Gas 6. Grease a 1 litre/1¾ pint/4 cup
loaf tin (pan) or terrine with the oil. Use
half of the salmon to line the tin or
terrine, letting some of the ends
overhang the mould. Reserve the
remaining smoked salmon.

Variation
Use any thick white fish fillets for this
terrine – try halibut or Arctic bass. Cod
is also good, although it is better to
use a firm, chunky piece that will not
crumble easily after being cooked. You
could also use fresh salmon for a truly
salmony flavour.

2 Cut two long slices of haddock the
length of the tin or terrine and set
aside. Cut the rest of the haddock into
small pieces. Season all the haddock.

3 Combine the eggs, crème fraîche,
capers and peppercorns in a bowl.
Season, then stir in the small pieces of
haddock. Spoon the mixture into the tin
or terrine until one-third full. Smooth
the surface with a spatula.

4 Wrap the reserved long haddock
fillets in the reserved smoked salmon.
Lay them on top of the fish mixture in
the tin or terrine.

5 Fill the tin or terrine with the rest of
the fish mixture, smooth the surface
and fold the overhanging pieces of
smoked salmon over the top. Cover
tightly with a double thickness of foil.
Tap the terrine to settle the contents.

6 Stand the terrine in a roasting pan
and pour in boiling water to come
halfway up the sides. Place in the
preheated oven and cook for 45
minutes–1 hour.

7 Take the terrine out of the roasting
pan, but do not remove the foil cover.
Place two or three large heavy tins on
the foil to weight it and leave until cold.
Chill in the refrigerator for 24 hours.

8 About 1 hour before serving, lift off
the weights and remove the foil.
Carefully invert the terrine on to a
serving plate and lift off the terrine.
Serve the terrine in thick slices with
crème fraîche, peppercorns, fronds of
dill and rocket leaves.

Per portion Energy 187kcal/785kJ; Protein 27.5g; Carbohydrate 0.3g, of which sugars 0.2g; Fat 8.5g, of which saturates 3.7g; Cholesterol 95mg; Calcium 31mg; Fibre 0g; Sodium 735mg.

Mallard pâté

Mallard ducks are shot during the game season, which in Scotland is during the winter months. This recipe needs two days to prepare, as the birds need to be briefly cooked and allowed to rest overnight before making the rest of the pâté.

Serves 4

2 young mallards

a little groundnut (peanut) oil

185g/6½oz streaky (fatty) bacon

300g/11oz wild duck livers

10ml/2 tsp salt

ground black pepper

pinch each of grated nutmeg, ground ginger and ground cloves

275ml/9fl oz/generous 1 cup double (heavy) cream

4 egg yolks

37.5ml/2½ tbsp brandy

50g/2oz/scant ⅓ cup sultanas (golden raisins)

1 Preheat the oven to 240°C/475°F/Gas 9. Remove the legs from the ducks. Season the birds and sprinkle with oil. Roast in the preheated oven for 15 minutes then remove from the oven and leave to rest, overnight if possible.

2 The next day, preheat the oven to 190°C/375°F/Gas 5. Put the bacon, livers, salt, pepper and spices into a blender and purée to a smooth cream.

3 Add the cream, egg yolks and brandy, and purée for a further 30 seconds. Push the mixture through a sieve into a mixing bowl and add the sultanas.

4 Remove the breasts from the ducks and skin them. Dice the meat finely then mix into the liver mixture.

5 Put the mixture in a terrine, cover with foil and cook in the oven in a roasting pan of hot water for 40–50 minutes. The centre should be slightly wobbly. Cool then chill for at least 4 hours. Serve with toast.

Per portion Energy 771kcal/3203kJ; Protein 48.5g; Carbohydrate 9.8g, of which sugars 9.8g; Fat 59.3g, of which saturates 28.4g; Cholesterol 636mg; Calcium 81mg; Fibre 0.3g; Sodium 1782mg.

Strawberry and smoked venison salad

The combination of strawberries, balsamic vinegar and smoked venison creates a perfect ménage à trois. The tang of the vinegar sets off the sweetness of the strawberries, which must be ripe, and adds a fruity contrast to the rich, dry, smoky venison.

Serves 4

12 ripe Scottish strawberries

2.5ml/½ tsp caster (superfine) sugar

5ml/1 tsp balsamic vinegar

8 thin slices of smoked venison

mixed salad leaves

For the dressing

10ml/2 tsp olive oil

5ml/1 tsp balsamic vinegar

splash of strawberry wine (optional)

salt and ground black pepper

1 Slice the strawberries vertically into three or four pieces then place in a bowl with the sugar and balsamic vinegar. Leave for 30 minutes.

Cook's Tips
• Suitable salad leaves include lollo rosso for colour, rocket (arugula) and lamb's lettuce (corn salad) for a peppery flavour and colour, and Little Gem (Bibb) for crunch.
• The sugar brings out the moisture in the strawberries, which combines with the balsamic vinegar to creates a lovely shiny coat. Do not leave them to stand for too long as they can become tired looking, 30 minutes is about right.

2 Meanwhile, make the dressing by placing the olive oil and balsamic vinegar in a small bowl and whisking them together with the wine, if you are using it. Add salt and ground black pepper to taste.

3 Cut the smoked venison into little strips. Mix the salad leaves together then toss with the dressing. Distribute the salad leaves among four plates, sprinkle with the strawberries and venison and serve immediately.

Per portion Energy 116kcal/486kJ; Protein 11.6g; Carbohydrate 3.1g, of which sugars 3.1g; Fat 6.8g, of which saturates 1.2g; Cholesterol 25mg; Calcium 16mg; Fibre 0.6g; Sodium 31mg.

Fish and shellfish

The sea, the loch and the river have always provided the mainstay of the diet in the Highlands and Islands of Scotland, where the rugged mountains provide little in the way of food and nourishment. Salmon is perhaps the king of Scottish fish, and the rivers are renowned fishing centres for the best in leaping fresh wild salmon. Some fishing villages up and down the coasts and on the Islands still bring in a daily catch, with haddock, sea trout, lobsters, crabs and prawns, although there has been a decline in the fishing industry due to overfishing.

Clam stovies

Clams are now harvested in the lochs, especially in Loch Fyne where some of the best Scottish clams are grown on ropes. Limpets or cockles can also be used if you can buy them fresh or collect them yourself along the seashore.

Serves 4

2.5 litres/4 pints/10 cups clams

potatoes (see step 3)

oil, for greasing

chopped fresh flat leaf parsley, to garnish

50g/2oz/¼ cup butter

salt and ground black pepper

1 Wash the clams and soak them overnight in fresh cold water. This will clean them out and get rid of any sand and other detritus.

2 Preheat the oven to 190°C/375°F/ Gas 5. Put the clams into a large pan, cover with water and bring to the boil. Add a little salt then simmer until the shells open. Reserve the cooking liquor. Shell the clams, reserving a few whole.

3 Weigh the shelled clams. You will need three times their weight in unpeeled potatoes.

4 Peel and slice the potatoes thinly. Lightly oil the base and sides of a flameproof, ovenproof dish. Arrange a layer of potatoes in the base of the dish, add a layer of the clams and season with a little salt and ground black pepper. Repeat until the ingredients are all used, finishing with a layer of potatoes on top. Finally, season lightly.

5 Pour in some of the reserved cooking liquor to come about halfway up the dish. Dot the top with the butter then cover with foil. Bring to the boil on the stove over a medium-high heat, then bake in the preheated oven for 2 hours until the top is golden brown.

6 Serve hot, garnished with chopped fresh flat leaf parsley.

Per portion Energy 320kcal/1348kJ; Protein 17.3g; Carbohydrate 36.7g, of which sugars 3.3g; Fat 12.6g, of which saturates 7g; Cholesterol 57mg; Calcium 188mg; Fibre 2.9g; Sodium 262mg.

Steamed mussels with spinach salsa

Mussels are an under used shellfish, and have the advantages of combining well with lots of different flavours and being quite inexpensive compared to other kinds of seafood. The colours of this dish work well if you leave the mussels in the half-shell.

Serves 4

64 mussels

4 bunches fresh spinach

8 ripe tomatoes, blanched and peeled

2 spring onions (scallions), finely chopped

dash of white wine

For the salsa

120ml/4fl oz/½ cup olive oil

2 garlic cloves, crushed

30ml/2 tbsp chopped fresh coriander (cilantro)

115g/4oz/½ cup butter

salt and ground black pepper

1 Clean the mussels using a hard brush or a small, sharp knife. Remove any beards from the outside and discard any mussels with broken shells or that are open. Leave them to soak in a bowl of fresh slightly salted cold water for at least 30 minutes before cooking.

2 Wash the spinach thoroughly and remove the stalks. Cut the tomatoes into quarters, remove the seeds and dice finely.

3 Put the mussels and spring onion into a pan, add the wine and cover. Steam for a few minutes until the shells open then remove from the pan and leave to cool. Discard any that remain closed.

4 Meanwhile, make the salsa. Place the juices that were used to steam the mussels in a bowl and whisk them together with the oil to create an emulsion, then add the tomatoes, garlic and coriander.

5 To assemble, break off one shell and loosen the mussel in the other. Cook the spinach in a frying pan with the butter until just wilting (then season with salt and ground black pepper. Distribute among four warmed plates, arrange the shelled mussels on top and spoon over the salsa.

Per portion Energy 258kcal/1070kJ; Protein 9g; Carbohydrate 4.6g, of which sugars 4.5g; Fat 22.8g, of which saturates 8.4g; Cholesterol 42mg; Calcium 181mg; Fibre 2.4g; Sodium 244mg.

King scallops with bacon

This is the simplest of dishes, combining bacon and scallops with brown butter which has just begun to burn but not quite. It gives a tasty dish a lovely nutty smell, which is why the French call this dish "noisette" – nutty.

Serves 4

12 rashers (strips) streaky (fatty) bacon

12 scallops

225g/8oz/1 cup unsalted (sweet) butter

juice of 1 lemon

30ml/2 tbsp chopped fresh flat leaf parsley

ground black pepper

1 Preheat the grill (broiler) to high. Wrap a rasher of bacon around each scallop so it goes over the top and not round the side.

2 Cut the butter into chunks and put it in a small pan over a low heat.

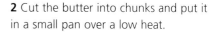

3 Meanwhile grill (broil) the scallops with the bacon facing up so it protects the meat. The bacon fat will help to cook the scallops. This will take only a few minutes; once they are cooked set aside and keep warm.

4 Allow the butter to turn a nutty brown colour, gently swirling it from time to time. Just as it is foaming and darkening, take off the heat and add the lemon juice. Be warned, it will bubble up quite dramatically.

5 Place the scallops on warmed plates, dress with plenty of chopped fresh parsley and pour the butter over.

Cook's Tip
Get the scallops on to warmed plates just as the butter is coming to the right colour, then add the lemon juice.

Per portion Energy 665kcal/2749kJ; Protein 24.4g; Carbohydrate 2.7g, of which sugars 0.6g; Fat 62g, of which saturates 34.7g; Cholesterol 189mg; Calcium 51mg; Fibre 0.5g; Sodium 1240mg.

Queenies with smoked Ayrshire bacon

This recipe uses the classic combination of scallops with bacon, but this time using princess scallops – known locally as "Queenies" – which are cooked with a flavoursome cured bacon known as smoked Ayrshire bacon.

Serves 4

6 rashers (strips) smoked Ayrshire bacon, cut into thin strips

5ml/1 tsp ground turmeric

28 princess scallops

1 sprig each of parsley and thyme

1 bay leaf

6 black peppercorns

150ml/¼ pint/⅔ cup dry white wine

75ml/2½fl oz/⅓ cup double (heavy) cream

30ml/2 tbsp chopped fresh chives, to garnish

1 Using a pan with a close-fitting lid, fry the bacon in its own fat until well cooked and crisp. Remove the bacon.

2 Reduce the heat, stir the turmeric into the juices and cook for 1–2 minutes.

3 Add the scallops to the pan with the herbs and peppercorns. Carefully pour in the wine (it will steam) and then cover with the lid. The scallops will only take a few minutes to cook. Test them by removing a thick one and piercing with a sharp knife to see if they are soft. Once they are cooked, remove from the pan and keep warm.

4 Stir in the cream and increase the heat to allow the sauce to simmer. This should be a light sauce; if it becomes too thick then add a little water.

5 Serve the scallops in warmed bowls or on plates with the sauce ladled over. Sprinkle with the crisp bacon and garnish with chopped fresh chives.

Per portion Energy 353kcal/1476kJ; Protein 36.5g; Carbohydrate 4.8g, of which sugars 0.5g; Fat 18.4g, of which saturates 9.1g; Cholesterol 106mg; Calcium 51mg; Fibre 0g; Sodium 904mg.

East Neuk lobster with wholegrain mustard and cream

The East Neuk of Fife is the "corner" of Fife on the east coast of Scotland, an area bounded by the sea almost all around. From Elie to St Andrews, there is a proliferation of fishing villages, which in their time provided the vast majority of jobs in the area. Today Pittenweem is the only real fishing port with its own fish and shellfish market.

Serves 2

1 lobster, approximately 500g/1¼lb

10ml/2 tsp butter

splash of whisky (grain not malt)

1 shallot or ½ onion, finely chopped

50g/2oz button (white) mushrooms

splash of white wine

175ml/6fl oz/¾ cup double (heavy) cream

5ml/1 tsp wholegrain mustard

10ml/2 tsp chopped fresh chervil and a little tarragon

60ml/4 tbsp breadcrumbs

50g/2oz/¼ cup butter, melted

salt and ground black pepper

1 Cook the lobster in boiling salted water for about 7 minutes then set aside to cool.

Cook's Tip
You can use a precooked lobster or prepared lobster meat for this recipe if you prefer.

2 Once cool, cut the lobster down the middle, top to bottom, and remove the intestines down the back.

3 Remove the meat from the tail, taking care not to let it break into pieces.

4 Cut the tail meat into slanted slices. Remove the meat from the claws, keeping it as whole as possible. Wash the two half-shells out and set aside.

5 Heat a frying pan over a low heat, add the butter and wait for it to bubble. Gently add the lobster meat and colour lightly (don't overcook or it will dry out). Pour in the whisky. If you have a gas hob, allow the flames to get inside the pan to briefly flame the pieces and burn off the alcohol; if the hob is electric, don't worry as it isn't vital. Remove the lobster meat.

6 Add the chopped shallot or onion and the mushrooms, and cook gently over a medium-low heat for a few minutes until soft and the onion or shallot is transparent. Add a little white wine, then the cream, and allow to simmer to reduce to a light coating texture. Then add the mustard and the chopped herbs and mix well. Season to taste with a little salt and freshly ground black pepper. Meanwhile preheat the grill (broiler) to high.

7 Place the two lobster half-shells on the grill pan. Distribute the lobster meat evenly throughout the two half-shells and spoon the sauce over. Sprinkle with breadcrumbs, drizzle with melted butter and brown under the preheated grill. Serve immediately.

Per portion Energy 812kcal/3357kJ; Protein 23.6g; Carbohydrate 12g, of which sugars 3.7g; Fat 74.9g, of which saturates 46g; Cholesterol 287mg; Calcium 127mg; Fibre 0.9g; Sodium 580mg.

Grilled lobster with tarragon cream

Lobsters are readily available in Scotland; look out for them in the fishmongers in fishing villages, as you can choose your own live lobster, freshly caught that day. Lobsters are at their best prepared simply to make the most of their firm sweet meat. Fresh herbs, cream and melted butter are among the most suitable accompaniments.

Serves 4

2 live lobsters, approximately 675–800g/1½–1¾lb

grated rind of 1 orange

75g/3oz/6 tbsp unsalted (sweet) butter

pinch of cayenne pepper

50ml/2fl oz/¼ cup whipping cream

2 sprigs of fresh tarragon

salt and ground black pepper

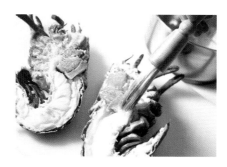

3 Melt the butter and brush it liberally over the four half lobsters, covering all the exposed flesh. Season lightly with salt and a little cayenne pepper.

5 Put the lobsters under the preheated grill for about 7 minutes and then pour off the juices into the cream and tarragon. Stir them in gently.

1 Dispatch or freeze the lobsters before cooking, if you like (see Cook's Tip), then bring a large pan of water to the boil over a high heat. Add the grated orange rind and plunge the whole lobsters into the pan. Bring the water back to a rolling boil then boil for about 5 minutes.

2 Drain the lobsters and leave to cool. Once cooled, split the lobsters in two down the middle with a sharp knife. Remove the stomach sac from the head and the intestine tract, which runs down the tail. Remove the claws and crack them open. Remove the meat and place it in the head.

4 Preheat the grill (broiler) to high. Pour the cream into a pan over a low heat and add the sprigs of tarragon, stirring it in gently. Bring the cream to just below boiling point, turn the heat right down and then leave the cream to infuse the flavours and aromas of the tarragon for 10 minutes.

Cook's Tip

If you are worried about dispatching a live lobster then either plunge a small sharp knife through the back of its head prior to boiling or place it in the deep freeze for 20 minutes before boiling; the cold makes them sleepy and they don't feel the heat as they are plunged into the pan of water.

6 Add the buttery lobster juices from the grill pan and turn the heat up a fraction. Bring the cream mixture to the boil, whisking to combine the buttery lobster juices with the tarragon cream. Strain the sauce.

7 Place half a lobster on each warmed serving plate, and gently spoon over the cream sauce, letting it spill over on to the plate. Serve immediately.

Variation

Lobster also goes well with other fresh herbs. Wild garlic works well for this dish; use a few sprigs in the same way as the tarragon. Fresh dill also gives a lovely flavour. Chop it finely before adding it to the cream.

Per portion Energy 284kcal/1180kJ; Protein 20.8g; Carbohydrate 0.8g, of which sugars 0.8g; Fat 22.1g, of which saturates 13.2g; Cholesterol 153mg; Calcium 91mg; Fibre 0.6g; Sodium 421mg.

Flaky smoked salmon with warm new potatoes

A type of smoked salmon that has remained true to itself down the ages while retaining its distinctive flavour is Salar, made on the island of South Uist in the Outer Hebrides. It is a flaky smoked salmon and this is achieved by smoking the fish closer to the heat source. The result is a delicious, moist, full-flavoured smoked fish, perfect in this dish.

Serves 4

12 small new potatoes

4 x Salar flaky salmon steaks, about 75g/3oz each

mixed salad leaves

a little olive oil

a few fresh basil leaves, torn, to garnish

For the dressing

10ml/2 tsp balsamic vinegar

20ml/4 tsp virgin olive oil

1 Cook the potatoes until just done, then drain and leave to cool until you can handle them.

2 Meanwhile, for the dressing, mix the balsamic vinegar and olive oil together. Toss the mixed salad leaves in the dressing then divide between four individual serving plates.

Cook's Tip
Choose small, tasty new potatoes, such as baby Maris Piper or King Edwards. Make sure that they are not overcooked as they need to retain some crispness.

3 Cut the potatoes in two and mix with a little olive oil. The warmth of the potatoes will create a great smell and bring out the flavour.

4 Arrange the potatoes over the salad leaves and place the smoked salmon on top. Garnish with a few torn fresh basil leaves and serve with crusty bread.

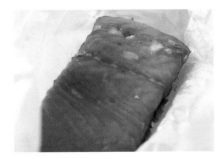

Per portion Energy 322kcal/1342kJ; Protein 17.3g; Carbohydrate 20.1g, of which sugars 1.6g; Fat 19.6g, of which saturates 3.1g; Cholesterol 38mg; Calcium 23mg; Fibre 1.3g; Sodium 48mg.

Baked salmon with watercress sauce

The quintessential Scottish centrepiece, the whole baked salmon makes a stunning focal point for a buffet. Baking it in foil is easier than poaching and retains the melting quality. Decorating the fish with thin slices of cucumber adds to this Highland delight.

Serves 6–8

2–3kg/4½–6½lb salmon, cleaned, with head and tail left on

3–5 spring onions (scallions), thinly sliced

1 lemon, thinly sliced

1 cucumber, thinly sliced

salt and ground black pepper

sprigs of fresh dill, to garnish

lemon wedges, to serve

For the sauce

3 garlic cloves, chopped

200g/7oz watercress leaves, finely chopped

40g/1½oz/¾ cup finely chopped fresh tarragon

300g/11oz/1¼ cups mayonnaise

15–30ml/1–2 tbsp lemon juice

200g/7oz/scant 1 cup unsalted (sweet) butter

1 Preheat the oven to 180°C/350°F/ Gas 4. Rinse the salmon and lay it on a large piece of foil. Stuff the fish with the sliced spring onions and lemon. Season with salt and black pepper.

2 Loosely fold the foil around the fish and fold the edges over to seal. Bake in the preheated oven for about 1 hour.

3 Remove the fish from the oven and leave it to stand, still wrapped in the foil, for about 15 minutes. Then gently unwrap the foil parcel and set the salmon aside to cool.

4 When the fish has cooled, carefully lift it on to a large plate, still covered with lemon slices. Cover the fish tightly with clear film (plastic wrap) and chill for several hours in the refrigerator.

5 Remove the lemon slices from the top of the fish. Use a blunt knife to lift up the edge of the skin and carefully peel the skin away from the flesh, avoiding tearing the flesh. Pull out any fins at the same time. Carefully turn the salmon over and repeat on the other side. Leave the head on for serving, if you wish. Discard the skin.

Variation
If you prefer to poach the fish rather than baking it, you will need to use a fish kettle. Place the salmon on the rack in the kettle. Cover the salmon completely with cold water, place the lid over to cover, and slowly bring to a simmer. Cook for 5–10 minutes per 450g/1lb until tender.

6 To make the sauce, put the garlic, watercress, tarragon, mayonnaise and lemon juice in a food processor or bowl, and process or mix to combine.

7 Melt the butter then add to the watercress mixture a little at a time, processing or stirring until the butter has been incorporated and the sauce is thick and smooth. Cover and chill.

8 Arrange the cucumber slices in overlapping rows along the length of the fish, so that they look like large fish scales. You can also slice the cucumber diagonally to produce longer slices for decoration. Trim the edges with scissors. Serve the fish, garnished with dill and lemon wedges, with the watercress sauce alongside.

Cook's Tip
Do not prepare the sauce more than a few hours ahead of serving as the watercress will discolour.

Per portion Energy 1044kcal/4323kJ; Protein 51.6g; Carbohydrate 1.4g, of which sugars 1.2g; Fat 92.4g, of which saturates 28.5g; Cholesterol 231mg; Calcium 135mg; Fibre 0.7g; Sodium 558mg.

Salmon with herb butter

A delicious fish with a delicate flavour, salmon needs to be served simply. Here, fresh dill and lemon are combined to make a slightly piquant butter.

2 Spoon the butter on to a piece of baking parchment and roll up, smoothing with your hands into a sausage shape. Twist the ends tightly, wrap in clear film (plastic wrap) and put in the freezer for 20 minutes, until firm.

3 Meanwhile, preheat the oven to 190°C/375°F/Gas 5. Cut out four squares of foil to encase the salmon steaks and grease with butter. Place a salmon steaks into the centre of each.

Serves 4

50g/2oz/¼ cup butter, softened, plus extra for greasing

finely grated rind of 1 lemon

15ml/1 tbsp lemon juice

15ml/1 tbsp chopped fresh dill

4 salmon steaks

2 lemon slices, halved

4 sprigs of fresh dill

salt and ground black pepper

1 Place the butter, lemon rind, lemon juice and chopped fresh dill in a small bowl and mix together with a fork until blended. Season to taste with salt and ground black pepper.

4 Remove the herb butter from the freezer and slice into eight rounds. Place two rounds on top of each salmon steak with a halved lemon slice in the centre and a sprig of dill on top. Lift up the edges of the foil and crinkle them together until well sealed. Place on a baking tray.

5 Bake for 20 minutes. Place the unopened parcels on warmed plates. Open the parcels and slide the contents on to the plates with the juices.

Per portion Energy 409kcal/1700kJ; Protein 35.6g; Carbohydrate 0.2g, of which sugars 0.2g; Fat 29.6g, of which saturates 9.8g; Cholesterol 114mg; Calcium 47mg; Fibre 0.2g; Sodium 156mg.

Salmon fishcakes

The secret of a good fishcake is to make it with freshly prepared fish and potatoes, homemade breadcrumbs and plenty of interesting seasoning.

Serves 4

450g/1lb cooked salmon fillet

450g/1lb freshly cooked potatoes, mashed

25g/1oz/2 tbsp butter, melted

10ml/2 tsp wholegrain mustard

15ml/1 tbsp each chopped fresh dill and chopped fresh flat leaf parsley

grated rind and juice of ½ lemon

15g/½oz/1 tbsp plain (all-purpose) flour

1 egg, lightly beaten

150g/5oz/generous 1 cup dried breadcrumbs

60ml/4 tbsp sunflower oil

salt and ground white pepper

rocket (arugula) leaves and fresh chives, to garnish

lemon wedges, to serve

1 Flake the cooked salmon, watching carefully for and discarding any skin and bones. Place the flaked salmon in a bowl with the mashed potato, melted butter and wholegrain mustard. Mix well then stir in the chopped fresh dill and parsley, lemon rind and juice. Season to taste.

2 Divide the mixture into eight portions and shape each into a ball, then flatten into a thick disc. Dip the fish cakes first in flour, then in egg and finally in breadcrumbs, making sure they are evenly coated.

3 Heat the oil in a frying pan until very hot. Fry the fishcakes in batches until golden brown and crisp all over. As each batch is ready, drain on kitchen paper and keep hot.

4 Warm some plates and then place two fishcakes on to each warmed plate, one slightly on top of the other. Garnish with rocket leaves and chives, and serve with lemon wedges.

Cook's Tip
Almost any fresh white or hot-smoked fish is suitable; smoked cod and haddock are particularly good. A mixture of smoked and unsmoked fish also works well.

Per portion Energy 586kcal/2453kJ; Protein 29.8g; Carbohydrate 49.9g, of which sugars 3.2g; Fat 31g, of which saturates 7.2g; Cholesterol 117mg; Calcium 79mg; Fibre 1.3g; Sodium 266mg.

Coulibiac

Wild salmon was very plentiful in Scotland in the 19th century, although the rise in gaming and fishing led to an Act of Parliament being passed banning the gentry from feeding their staff on salmon more than three times a week. This wonderful pie was probably one of the ways in which the staff would enjoy it.

Serves 4

50g/2oz/¼ cup butter

1 small onion, finely chopped

175g/6oz/scant 1 cup long grain rice

350ml/12fl oz/1½ cups chicken stock

1 bay leaf

olive oil

175g/6oz button (white) mushrooms

450g/1lb ready-made puff pastry

2.25kg/5lb salmon, skinned and filleted

dash of dry white wine

chopped fresh fennel

3 eggs, boiled until firm and sliced

egg wash, made by whisking 1 egg with a little milk

salt and ground black pepper

For the hollandaise sauce

3 egg yolks

30ml/2 tbsp white wine vinegar

115g/4oz/½ cup butter, diced

1.5ml/¼ tsp salt

pinch of ground black pepper

1 Preheat the oven to 180°C/350°F/Gas 4. In a small ovenproof pan, melt half the butter then cook the onion until translucent. Add the rice and stir. Add the stock and a pinch of salt. Bring to the boil and add the bay leaf. Cover and cook in the preheated oven for 20 minutes. When cooked gently fluff up the rice with a fork and leave to cool.

2 Slice the mushrooms finely. Heat the remaining butter with a little olive oil in a second pan and quickly fry the mushrooms. Set aside to cool.

3 Roll out the puff pastry into a square, long enough for a fillet and leaving 2.5cm/1in at each end. Sprinkle half the rice in a strip across the centre of the pastry. Cover with one salmon fillet, moisten with a little wine then season with salt and ground black pepper, and sprinkle over the chopped fresh fennel.

4 Cover the salmon with half the sliced egg and half the cooked mushrooms and a few spoonfuls of the rice. Then lay the second salmon fillet on top, adding another splash of wine and seasoning again with salt and ground black pepper. Place another layer of sliced egg over the top, sprinkle the rest of the mushrooms over, and finish by adding the remaining rice.

5 Brush the edges of the pastry with the egg wash, fold the pastry over and seal. Decorate with any pastry trimmings, if you like, and brush egg wash all over.

6 Allow to rest in a cool place for an hour. Meanwhile preheat the oven to 220°C/425°F/Gas 7. Bake the coulibiac in the preheated oven for about 40 minutes. If the pastry browns too quickly, turn down the heat. Allow to rest for 10 minutes before serving.

7 Make the hollandaise sauce. Put the egg yolks and vinegar in the top of a double boiler. Stir until thoroughly combined. Place the pan on the base pan filled with hot, but not boiling, water and heat gently, stirring, until the yolks begins to thicken. Add a piece of butter and whisk over a gentle heat until the butter has melted. Gradually add the remaining butter, whisking until the sauce thickens. Remove from the heat and stir in the salt and ground black pepper.

8 Use a serrated bread knife to cut the coulibiac and slice across its width. Hot and moist, it is delicious served with salad or a green vegetable with the hollandaise sauce. It is also excellent cold with a fresh salad.

Per portion Energy 1005kcal/4190kJ; Protein 50.7g; Carbohydrate 77.9g, of which sugars 2.4g; Fat 56.6g, of which saturates 7.8g; Cholesterol 244mg; Calcium 139mg; Fibre 0.7g; Sodium 521mg.

Herrings in oatmeal

Herrings have a wonderfully strong flavour and are ideal for simple recipes. Traditional to the Northern Isles and the east coast, these herrings coated in oats make for hearty meals, and are also easy to prepare and cook.

Serves 4

175ml/6fl oz/¾ cup thick mayonnaise

15ml/1 tbsp Dijon mustard

7.5ml/1½ tsp tarragon vinegar

4 herrings, approximately 225g/8oz each

juice of 1 lemon

115g/4oz/generous 1 cup medium rolled oats

salt and ground black pepper

1 Place the mayonnaise in a small mixing bowl and add the mustard and vinegar. Mix thoroughly and then chill for a few minutes.

2 Place one fish at a time on a chopping board, cut side down, and open out. Press gently along the backbone with your thumbs. Turn the fish over and carefully lift away the backbone.

3 Squeeze lemon juice over both sides of the fish, then season with salt and ground black pepper. Fold the fish in half, skin side outwards.

4 Preheat the grill (broiler) to medium hot. Place the rolled oats on a plate then coat each herring evenly in the oats, pressing it in gently.

5 Place the herrings on a grill rack and grill (broil) the fish for 3–4 minutes on each side, until the skin is golden brown and crisp and the flesh flakes easily when the fish is cut into. Serve immediately on warmed plates with the mustard sauce handed round in a separate dish or bowl.

Per portion Energy 755kcal/3143kJ; Protein 36.7g; Carbohydrate 32.6g, of which sugars 0.6g; Fat 54g, of which saturates 9.3g; Cholesterol 98mg; Calcium 149mg; Fibre 3g; Sodium 459mg.

Mackerel with gooseberry relish

Off Scotland's west coast it is still possible to fish for mackerel yourself and quite often at the weekends part-time fishermen can be found selling fresh mackerel at the harbours. Mackerel is very good for you, and the tart gooseberries give you a serving of fruit too.

Serves 4

4 whole mackerel

60ml/4 tbsp olive oil

For the sauce

250g/9oz gooseberries

25g/1oz/2 tbsp soft light brown sugar

5ml/1 tsp wholegrain mustard

salt and ground black pepper

1 For the sauce, wash and trim the gooseberries and then roughly chop them, so there are some pieces larger than others.

2 Cook the gooseberries in a little water with the sugar in a small pan. A thick and chunky purée will form. Add the mustard and season to taste with salt and ground black pepper.

Cook's Tips
• Turn the grill (broiler) on well in advance as the fish need a fierce heat to cook quickly. If you like the fish but hate the smell, try barbecuing outside.
• The foil lining in the grill pan is to catch the smelly drips. Simply roll it up and throw it away afterwards, leaving a nice clean grill pan.

3 Preheat the grill (broiler) to high and line the grill pan with foil. Using a sharp knife, slash the fish two or three times down each side then season and brush with the olive oil.

4 Place the fish in the grill pan and grill (broil) for about 4 minutes on each side until cooked. You may need to cook them for a few minutes longer if they are particularly large. The slashes will open up to speed cooking and the skin should be lightly browned. To check that they are cooked properly, use a small sharp knife to pierce the skin and check for uncooked flesh.

5 Place the mackerel on warmed plates and spread generous dollops of the gooseberry relish over them. Pass the remaining sauce around at the table.

Per portion Energy 576kcal/2390kJ; Protein 38.1g; Carbohydrate 8.4g, of which sugars 8.4g; Fat 43.5g, of which saturates 8.2g; Cholesterol 108mg; Calcium 43mg; Fibre 1.5g; Sodium 128mg.

Plaice fillets with sorrel and lemon butter

Sorrel is a wild herb that is now grown commercially. It is very good in salads and, roughly chopped, partners this slightly sweet-fleshed fish very well. Plaice – such a pretty fish with its orange spots and fern-like frills – is a delicate fish that works well with this sauce. Cook it simply like this to get the full natural flavours of the ingredients.

Serves 4

200g/7oz/scant 1 cup butter

500g/1¼lb plaice fillets, skinned and patted dry

30ml/2 tbsp chopped fresh sorrel

90ml/6 tbsp dry white wine

a little lemon juice

1 Heat half the butter in a large frying pan and, just as it is melted, place the fillets skin side down. Cook briefly, just to firm up, reduce the heat and turn the fish over. The fish will be cooked in less than 5 minutes. Try not to let the butter brown or allow the fish to colour.

2 Remove the fish fillets from the pan and keep warm between two plates. Cut the remaining butter into chunks. Add the chopped sorrel to the pan and stir. Add the wine then, as it bubbles, add the butter, swirling it in piece by piece and not allowing the sauce to boil. Stir in a little lemon juice.

3 Serve the fish with the sorrel and lemon butter spooned over, with some crunchy green beans and perhaps some new potatoes, if you like.

Variation
Instead of using sorrel, you could try this recipe with tarragon or thyme.

Per portion Energy 494kcal/2047kJ; Protein 25.7g; Carbohydrate 0.5g, of which sugars 0.5g; Fat 43.3g, of which saturates 26.4g; Cholesterol 170mg; Calcium 98mg; Fibre 0.3g; Sodium 501mg.

Quenelles of sole

Traditionally, these light fish "dumplings" are made with pike, but they are even better made with sole or other white fish. If you are feeling extravagant, serve them with a creamy shellfish sauce studded with crayfish tails or prawns. They make a great lunchtime meal or late-night supper, with bread and a crisp salad.

Serves 6

450g/1lb sole fillets, skinned and cut into large pieces

4 egg whites

600ml/1 pint/2½ cups double (heavy) cream

freshly grated nutmeg

salt and ground black pepper

chopped fresh parsley, to garnish

For the sauce

1 small shallot, finely chopped

60ml/4 tbsp dry vermouth

120ml/4fl oz/½ cup fish stock

150ml/¼ pint/⅔ cup double (heavy) cream

50g/2oz/¼ cup butter, diced

1 Check the sole for stray bones, then put the pieces in a food processor. Season. Switch the machine on and, with the motor running, add the egg whites one at a time through the feeder tube to make a smooth purée. Press the purée through a metal sieve placed over a bowl. Stand the bowl of purée in a larger bowl and surround it with plenty of crushed ice or ice cubes.

2 Whip the cream until very thick, but not stiff. Gradually fold it into the fish mixture. Season, then stir in nutmeg to taste. Cover the bowl and refrigerate for several hours.

3 To make the sauce, combine the shallot, vermouth and fish stock in a small pan. Bring to the boil and cook until reduced by half. Add the cream and boil until it has a thick consistency.

4 Strain and return to the pan. Whisk in the butter, one piece at a time, until the sauce is creamy. Season and keep hot, but do not allow to boil.

5 Bring a wide shallow pan of lightly salted water to the boil, then reduce the heat so that the water surface barely trembles. Using two tablespoons dipped in hot water, shape the fish mousse into ovals. As each quenelle is shaped, slip it into the simmering water.

6 Poach the quenelles in batches for 8–10 minutes, until just firm to the touch but still slightly creamy inside. Lift out using a slotted spoon, drain on kitchen paper and keep hot. When all the quenelles are cooked, arrange them on warmed plates. Pour the sauce around, garnish with parsley and serve.

Per portion Energy 771kcal/3180kJ; Protein 17.7g; Carbohydrate 3.3g, of which sugars 3g; Fat 75.4g, of which saturates 46.1g; Cholesterol 227mg; Calcium 89mg; Fibre 0.1g; Sodium 195mg.

Halibut with leek and ginger

Generally fish needs to be absolutely fresh, but halibut needs to mature for a day or two to bring out the flavour. Halibut is normally taken from the Atlantic, but some of the boats on the east coast of Scotland will catch smaller ones, bringing in a catch so fresh you need to refrigerate the fish for a day or so before cooking.

3 Dry the halibut steaks on kitchen paper. Heat a large pan with the olive oil and add 50g/2oz/¼ cup of the butter. As it begins to bubble place the fish steaks carefully in the pan, skin side down. Allow the halibut to colour – this will take 3–4 minutes. Then turn the steaks over, reduce the heat and cook for about a further 10 minutes.

4 Remove the fish from the pan, set aside and keep warm. Add the leek and ginger to the pan, stir to mix then allow the leek to soften (they may colour slightly but this is fine). Once softened, season with a little salt and ground black pepper. Cut the remaining butter into small pieces then, off the heat, gradually stir into the pan.

5 To serve, place the halibut steaks on individual warmed plates and strew the leek and ginger mixture over the fish. Accompany with mashed potato.

Serves 4

2 leeks

50g/2oz piece fresh root ginger

4 halibut steaks, approximately 175g/6oz each (see Cook's Tip)

15ml/1 tbsp olive oil

75g/3oz/6 tbsp butter

Cook's Tips

• Ask your fishmonger for flattish halibut steaks and not too thick as you want to cook them in a pan on the stove and not in the oven. Also ask him or her to skin them for you.
• It doesn't matter if you leave a bit of skin on the ginger if it is very knobbly.

1 Trim the leeks, discarding the coarse outer leaves, the very dark green tops and the root end. Cut them into 5cm/2in lengths then slice into thin matchsticks. Wash thoroughly.

2 Peel the fresh ginger as best you can then slice it very thinly and cut the slices into thin sticks.

Per portion Energy 364kcal/1520kJ; Protein 39.1g; Carbohydrate 2.7g, of which sugars 2.1g; Fat 21.9g, of which saturates 10.8g; Cholesterol 101mg; Calcium 75mg; Fibre 1.9g; Sodium 221mg.

Crusted garlic and wild thyme monkfish

Monkfish is a lovely juicy fish; it is hard to believe that until recently it was thrown back into the sea or sold breaded as "scampi" because its firm texture was not fashionable. Now it is considered a prime fish that needs simple cooking. Garlic is excellent with it as are aromatic herbs such as wild thyme and fennel.

Serves 4

4 monkfish tails (see Cook's Tip)

garlic and herb butter (see Langoustines with Garlic Butter, but use wild thyme or bog myrtle in place of parsley)

115g/4oz/generous 1 cup dried breadcrumbs (see Cook's Tip)

salt and ground black pepper

2 Season the fish with salt and freshly ground black pepper. Using your fingertips, rub the garlic butter liberally all over, ensuring that you have pushed a good quantity into each of the diagonal slashes.

3 Sprinkle on the breadcrumbs, place on a baking tray and bake for 10–15 minutes. The cooked tails should be golden brown, with white slashes where the cuts have opened up to reveal the succulent flesh inside.

1 Preheat the oven to 220°C/425°F/Gas 7. Make two or three diagonal slashes down each side of the fish, working from the bone to the edge.

Cook's Tips
• Buy monkfish tails weighing about 250g/9oz each. Ask your fishmonger to trim off all the skin and purple membrane surrounding the fillets but to leave the fish on the bone.
• The best breadcrumbs are made with day-old bread. Break the bread up with your fingers and then roughly in a food processor to make coarse breadcrumbs. Leave to dry out further overnight. The next day process the dried bread again to obtain fine dry crumbs. If you are really fussy you can then pass them through a coarse sieve to produce a very fine crumb.

Per portion Energy 272kcal/1130kJ; Protein 11.4g; Carbohydrate 9.9g, of which sugars 0.5g; Fat 21.1g, of which saturates 13.1g; Cholesterol 62mg; Calcium 26mg; Fibre 0.3g; Sodium 258mg.

Gratin of cod with wholegrain mustard

Whilst the cod crisis continues in Scottish waters, those in north-west Europe are advised not to eat Atlantic cod. However, you can now buy good-quality farmed cod and elsewhere in the world cod or its local equivalents are still available. If you need an alternative then a thick, flaky-textured, moist white-fleshed fish is what is required.

Serves 4

4 cod steaks, approximately
175g/6oz each

200g/7oz/1¾ cups grated Cheddar
cheese, such as Isle of Mull

15ml/1 tbsp wholegrain mustard

75ml/5 tbsp double (heavy) cream

salt and ground black pepper

1 Preheat the oven to 200°C/400°F/
Gas 6. Check the fish for bones. Butter
the base and sides of an ovenproof dish
then place the fish fillets skin side down
in the dish and season.

2 In a small bowl, mix the grated
cheese and mustard together with
enough cream to form a spreadable but
thick paste. Make sure that the cheese
and mustard are thoroughly blended to
ensure an even taste. Season lightly
with salt and ground black pepper.

3 Spread the cheese mixture thickly and
evenly over each fish fillet, using it all
up. Bake in the preheated oven for
20 minutes. The top will be browned
and bubbling and the fish underneath
flaky and tender. Serve immediately
on warmed plates.

Per portion Energy 445kcal/1852kJ; Protein 46g; Carbohydrate 0.4g, of which sugars 0.4g; Fat 27.7g, of which saturates 17.3g; Cholesterol 157mg; Calcium 395mg; Fibre 0g; Sodium 474mg.

West coast fisherman's stew

Many of the little ports on the west coast of Scotland still land a small catch and often there will be a box of bits and pieces, perhaps a monkfish or some small haddock, a few prawns and small crabs. Therein lies a feast waiting to be made.

Serves 4

30ml/2 tbsp olive oil

1 large onion, roughly chopped

1 leek, roughly chopped

2 garlic cloves, crushed

450g/1lb ripe tomatoes, roughly chopped

5ml/1 tsp tomato purée (paste)

1.3kg/3lb fish bones

a piece of pared orange peel

a few parsley stalks and fennel fronds

1 bay leaf

250ml/8fl oz/1 cup dry white wine

whisky or pastis, such as Pernod (optional)

1kg/2¼lb mixed fish fillets, such as salmon, sole and haddock, cut into chunks, and prepared shellfish

salt and ground black pepper

chopped fresh parsley, to garnish

2 Put in the fish bones, orange peel, herbs and wine, and add a little salt and ground black pepper. Then add enough water just to cover. Bring to a gentle boil then reduce the heat and simmer for 30 minutes.

3 Strain the soup into a clean pan, pressing the juices out of the solid ingredients with the back of a spoon.

4 Bring the liquid back to the boil and check for seasoning and texture. If you like, add a splash of whisky or Pernod. The fish takes just minutes to cook so add the firmer, larger pieces first, such as monkfish or salmon and mussels in the shell, and end with delicate scallops or prawn (shrimp) tails. Do not allow the stew to boil once you add the fish.

5 Serve in warmed soup plates, garnished with chopped fresh parsley.

1 Heat the olive oil in a large pan then sweat the onion and leek until soft. Add the garlic, tomatoes and tomato purée, and cook for 5 minutes.

Per portion Energy 341kcal/1432kJ; Protein 47.5g; Carbohydrate 6.5g, of which sugars 5.8g; Fat 7.8g, of which saturates 1.2g; Cholesterol 115mg; Calcium 53mg; Fibre 2.3g; Sodium 165mg.

Pale smoked haddock flan

The classic combination of potatoes and smoked fish is reworked in pastry. Always ask your fishmonger for "pale" smoked rather than "yellow" haddock as the latter tends to have been dyed to look bright and often has not been smoked properly at all.

Serves 4

For the pastry

225g/8oz/2 cups plain (all-purpose) flour

pinch of salt

115g/4oz/1½ cup cold butter, cut into chunks

cold water, to mix

For the filling

2 pale smoked haddock fillets (approximately 200g/7oz)

600ml/1 pint/2½ cups full-fat (whole) milk

3–4 black peppercorns

sprig of fresh thyme

150ml/¼ pint/⅔ cup double (heavy) cream

2 eggs

200g/7oz potatoes, peeled and diced

ground black pepper

1 Preheat the oven to 200°C/400°F/ Gas 6. Use a food processor to make the pastry. Put the flour, salt and butter into the food processor bowl and process until the mixture resembles fine breadcrumbs. Pour in a little cold water (you will need about 40ml/8 tsp but see Cook's Tip) and continue to process until the mixture forms a ball. If this takes longer than 30 seconds add a dash or two more water. Take the pastry ball out of the food processor, wrap in clear film (plastic wrap) and leave to rest in a cool place for about 30 minutes.

2 Roll out the dough and use to line a 20cm/8in flan tin (quiche pan). Prick the base of the pastry all over with a fork then bake blind in the preheated oven for 20 minutes.

3 Put the haddock in a pan with the milk, peppercorns and thyme. Poach for 10 minutes. Remove the fish from the pan and flake into small chunks. Allow the poaching liquor to cool.

4 Whisk the cream and eggs together thoroughly, then whisk in the cooled poaching liquid.

5 Layer the flan case with the flaked fish and diced potato, seasoning with black pepper.

6 Pour the cream mixture over the top. Put the flan in the oven and bake for 40 minutes, until lightly browned on top and set.

Cook's Tip
Different flours absorb water at different rates. A traditional rule of thumb is to use the same number of teaspoons of water as the number of ounces of flour, but some flours will require less water and others more, so add the water gradually. If you add too much water, the pastry will become unworkable and you will need to add more flour.

Variation
This recipe is also delicious if you add hard boiled eggs, chopped into quarters or eighths before adding the potatoes.

Per portion Energy 734kcal/3064kJ; Protein 23.8g; Carbohydrate 58.4g, of which sugars 8.2g; Fat 46.8g, of which saturates 27.9g; Cholesterol 225mg; Calcium 280mg; Fibre 2.3g; Sodium 636mg.

Meat and venison

Scottish beef is renowned throughout the world for its natural rearing environment, producing excellent quality meats with succulent flavours. Excellent steaks and prime cuts of beef constitute a large part of the gourmet cuisine, either in traditional pies and stews or with sumptuous sauces using local ingredients. Lamb and pork dishes are also enjoyed, especially in the Lowlands. Traditionally vension was game, forming the trophy dinner of a successful hunt. These days vension is farmed, producing succulent meat that is widely available for making some wonderful traditional fare.

Haggis with clapshot cake

Haggis is probably the best known of all Scottish traditional dishes, not least because of the famous Burns poem which is recited the world over in front of a haggis at suppers celebrating the poet. This is the traditional haggis recipe served with turnip and potato clapshot – a variation on the "haggis with neeps and tatties" theme.

Serves 4

1 large haggis, approximately 800g/1¾lb

450g/1lb peeled turnip or swede (rutabaga)

225g/8oz peeled potatoes

120ml/4fl oz/½ cup milk

1 garlic clove, crushed with 5ml/1 tsp salt

175ml/6fl oz/¾ cup double (heavy) cream

freshly grated nutmeg

ground black pepper

butter, for greasing

1 Preheat the oven to 180°C/350°F/ Gas 4. Wrap the haggis in foil, covering it completely and folding over the edges of the foil.

Cook's Tip

If you are serving haggis on Burns Night (January 25th), you need to bring the haggis whole to the table on a platter and cut it open reciting the famous Burns poem (see page 28). This is done in honour of Robert Burns, the celebrated Scottish poet.

2 Place the haggis in a roasting pan with about 2.5cm/1in water. Heat through in the preheated oven for 30–40 minutes.

3 Slice the turnip or swede and potatoes quite finely. A mandolin or food processor is quite handy for the turnip or swede as both vegetables tend to be hard and difficult to cut finely with a knife.

4 Put the sliced vegetables in a large pan and add the milk and garlic. Stir gently and continuously over a low heat until the potatoes begin to break down and exude their starch and the liquid thickens slightly.

5 Add the cream and nutmeg and grind some black pepper into the mixture. Stir gently but thoroughly. Slowly bring to the boil, reduce the heat and simmer gently for a few minutes.

6 Butter a deep round 18cm/7in dish or a small roasting pan. Transfer the vegetable mixture to the dish or pan. It shouldn't come up too high as it will rise slightly and bubble.

7 Bake in the oven for about 1 hour, or until you can push a knife easily through the cake. The top should be nicely browned by this time. If it is becoming too brown on top, cover it with foil and continue baking. If it is not browned enough after 1 hour of cooking, place it under a hot grill (broiler) for a few minutes.

8 Remove the foil from the haggis, place on a warmed serving dish and bring out to the table for your guests to witness the cutting. Use a sharp knife to cut through the skin then spoon out the haggis on to warmed plates. Serve the clapshot cake in slices with the haggis, spooning any juices over.

Per portion Energy 918kcal/3819kJ; Protein 24.9g; Carbohydrate 55.3g, of which sugars 8.5g; Fat 67.9g, of which saturates 30.2g; Cholesterol 244mg; Calcium 180mg; Fibre 3.1g; Sodium 1586mg.

Haggis, potato and apple tart

Here is another way to serve your haggis, with just a little refinement and the extra sumptuousness of puff pastry. Apple combines very well with haggis as its tart and sweet taste cuts through the richness of the meat.

3 Place the smaller pastry disc on a baking tray and spread half the potatoes over it, leaving a rim of about 2cm/¾in all the way round.

4 Cut the haggis open and crumble the meat on top. Slice the apple into circles and spread all over the haggis. Then top with the rest of the potatoes.

Serves 4

450g/1lb peeled potatoes, sliced

1 garlic clove, crushed with 1 tsp salt

freshly grated nutmeg

400g/14oz ready-made puff pastry

300g/11oz haggis

2 cooking apples, cored

1 egg, beaten

salt and ground black pepper

1 Preheat the oven to 220°C/425°F/ Gas 7. Slice the potatoes and mix with the crushed garlic. Season with a little freshly grated nutmeg and salt and ground black pepper.

2 Roll out the puff pastry into two discs, one about 25cm/10in in diameter and the other a little larger.

Cook's Tip
Use a fairly sharp-tasting variety of apple, such as Cox's Orange Pippin or cooking apples.

5 Brush the egg all around the exposed pastry rim then place the other pastry circle on top, pushing down on the rim to seal. Use a fork to tidy up the edges and then press down around the edge again to create a firm seal. Leave to rest for 10 minutes.

6 Brush over with more egg and bake the tart in the preheated oven for 10 minutes to set the pastry. Then reduce the oven temperature to 200°C/400°F/Gas 6 and bake for a further 40 minutes until evenly browned and cooked. Serve in slices.

Per portion Energy 698kcal/2919kJ; Protein 15.8g; Carbohydrate 72.9g, of which sugars 6.1g; Fat 41.2g, of which saturates 5.8g; Cholesterol 68mg; Calcium 88mg; Fibre 1.9g; Sodium 901mg.

Angus pasties

Aberdeen Angus beef is the traditional filling for pasties, as it is such a well-known breed, but any really good-quality beef may be used. These pasties are perfect served either cold or warmed for lunch or as a snack, and make great picnic food.

Makes 10

For the pastry

900g/2lb/8 cups plain (all-purpose) flour

225g/8oz/1 cup butter

225g/8oz/1cup lard or white cooking fat

pinch of salt

For the filling

1.2kg/2½lb rump (round) steak

225g/8oz/1¾ cups beef suet (US chilled, grated shortening)

5 onions, finely chopped

salt and ground black pepper

1 Preheat the oven to 200°C/400°F/Gas 6. Using a mixer, place the flour in the mixing bowl and blend in the butter and lard or white cooking fat using the dough hook. Add salt and mix to a stiff dough, adding water gradually as needed. Leave the pastry ball to rest in clear film (plastic wrap) for 30 minutes.

2 Meanwhile, trim the meat of any excess fat and cut into 1cm/½in squares. Chop the suet finely then mix with the meat and onions. Season.

3 Divide the pastry into ten equal sized pieces. Roll out each piece into an oval, not too thinly, and divide the meat mixture among them at one end, leaving an edge for sealing. Dampen the edges of each oval with cold water and fold the pastry over the filling.

4 Seal carefully – use a fork to make sure the edges are stuck together securely. Make a hole in the top of each pasty. Place on a greased baking sheet and bake in the preheated oven for 45 minutes. Serve hot, or allow to cool and refrigerate.

Per portion Energy 1131kcal/4714kJ; Protein 37.7g; Carbohydrate 84.8g, of which sugars 4.5g; Fat 74.5g, of which saturates 37.9g; Cholesterol 171mg; Calcium 162mg; Fibre 3.9g; Sodium 232mg.

Fillet steak with pickled walnut sauce

This is a traditional way of cooking beef, which makes it go a little further with the use of the onions. Fillet mignons are the small pieces from the end of the fillet, known as "collops" in Scotland. If you prefer, you can use Mushroom Sauce instead of pickled walnuts.

Serves 4

15ml/1 tbsp vegetable oil

75g/3oz/6 tbsp butter

8 slices of beef fillet (fillet mignon)

4 onions, sliced

15ml/1 tbsp pickled walnut juice

salt and ground black pepper

1 Heat the oil and half the butter in a frying pan and cook the steaks until almost done. Keep them warm.

2 Once you have taken your steaks out of the pan, melt the remaining butter then add the sliced onions. Increase the heat and stir to brown and soften the onions, scraping the base of the pan.

3 Add the pickled walnut juice and cook for a few minutes. Season to taste with salt and ground black pepper. Serve the beef on warmed plates and spoon the onions and juices over.

Per portion Energy 490kcal/2036kJ; Protein 43.4g; Carbohydrate 6.1g, of which sugars 4.3g; Fat 32.6g, of which saturates 17g; Cholesterol 167mg; Calcium 31mg; Fibre 1.1g; Sodium 219mg.

Collops of beef with shallots

Once again, the beef is paired with the sweetness of onions – a combination you will find time and again in traditional Scottish cooking. In this dish shallots are being used, left whole to impart a wonderful texture and flavour to the meal.

Serves 4

4 fillet steaks (beef tenderloin)

15ml/1 tbsp olive oil

50g/2oz/¼ cup butter

20 shallots, peeled

5ml/1 tsp caster (superfine) sugar

150ml/¼ pint/⅔ cup beef stock

salt and ground black pepper

1 Take the steaks out of the refrigerator well before you need them and dry with kitchen paper. Heat the oil and butter in a large frying pan then cook the steaks as you like them.

2 Once cooked remove the steaks from the pan and keep warm. Put the shallots in the pan and brown lightly in the meat juices. Add the sugar and then the stock. Reduce the heat to low and allow the liquid to evaporate, shaking the pan from time to time to stop the shallots from sticking.

3 The shallots will end up slightly soft, browned and caramelized with a shiny glaze. Season to taste with salt and ground black pepper.

4 Serve the steaks on warmed plates and spoon over the caramelized shallots and juices from the pan.

Per portion Energy 424kcal/1767kJ; Protein 43.2g; Carbohydrate 6.1g, of which sugars 4.6g; Fat 25.4g, of which saturates 12.5g; Cholesterol 149mg; Calcium 27mg; Fibre 0.9g; Sodium 166mg.

Roast fillet of beef with wild garlic hollandaise

Perhaps the most magnificent of Scottish dishes is the fillet steak, cooked to perfection and served with a luxurious sauce. Wild garlic, also known as ramsons, grows all over Britain, Europe and Scandinavia, though unfortunately not in the United States (see Variation for alternatives). The aroma is unmistakable and can be smelt from a distance – very garlicky.

Serves 4

4 fillet steaks (beef tenderloin)

15ml/1 tbsp olive oil

5ml/1 tsp butter

15ml/1 tbsp dry white wine

2 egg yolks

250g/9oz/generous 1 cup butter, melted

20 wild garlic leaves

squeeze of lemon juice (optional)

salt and ground black pepper

1 Dry the steaks using kitchen paper and set aside.

2 Heat a heavy pan with a good handle then add the oil and butter. Just as the butter is bubbling up, place the steaks in the pan. Keep the pan hot and brown the meat all over to seal in the juices, then reduce the heat to cook the meat to whatever stage of pinkness you want; 6 minutes will make them medium rare.

3 Remove the steaks from the pan and keep warm between two plates.

4 Allow the pan to cool for a few minutes then pour in the wine. If it bubbles up as you pour it in, wait for the pan to cool a little more before pouring in the rest.

5 Whisk the egg yolks until smooth and blended, then whisk them into the wine over a low heat, taking care that they don't scramble. They should foam and thicken slightly. Remove them from the heat if they begin to firm up.

Variation
If you are finding it hard to get fresh wild garlic, or it is out of season, you can use a garlic clove instead, chopped finely and added at the end in the same way as the leaves. For a richer flavour, roast a bulb of garlic in its skin and scoop out the flesh to flavour the sauce. Add a finely sliced wild leek or onion to the sauce to provide a lovely texture and to enhance the flavour.

6 Then, off the heat, slowly pour in the melted butter, a little bit to start with, whisking all the time. (You may not wish to add all the whey from the butter as it tends to make the sauce less thick.) This is where the handle comes in, and putting the pan on a damp cloth will help to stop it from moving about.

7 Rinse the wild garlic leaves thoroughly and drain on kitchen paper. Shred them finely and stir gently into the hollandaise. Season to taste with salt and ground black pepper. If you want a sharper taste, add a squeeze or two of fresh lemon juice.

8 Using prewarmed plates, place one steak on each, in the centre. Then spoon the wild garlic hollandaise over the top, letting it spill over on to the side of the plate. Serve with roast potatoes and steamed vegetables.

Per portion Energy 744kcal/3076kJ; Protein 33.8g; Carbohydrate 0.6g, of which sugars 0.6g; Fat 67.1g, of which saturates 38.6g; Cholesterol 328mg; Calcium 42mg; Fibre 0.3g; Sodium 459mg.

Beef with chanterelle mushrooms

The trick here is to use really good beef with no fat and to rapidly fry the dried pieces quickly so the outside is well browned and the inside very rare. Chanterelle mushrooms are the most delicious wild mushrooms, yellowy orange and resembling inverted umbrellas. They are often found wild in pine woods in Scotland, Northern Europe and North America.

Serves 4

115g/4oz chanterelle mushrooms

2 rump (round) steaks, 175g/6oz each, cut into strips

45ml/3 tbsp olive oil

1 garlic clove, crushed

1 shallot, finely chopped

60ml/4 tbsp dry white wine

60ml/4 tbsp double (heavy) cream

25g/1oz/2 tbsp butter

salt and ground black pepper

chopped fresh parsley, to garnish

Cook's Tips

• Mushrooms should ideally never be washed in water as they will absorb too much moisture.

• When browning meat in a hot pan don't put too much in at once as this lowers the temperature too quickly and the meat will poach instead of fry. Put in a few pieces at first, then wait 10–15 seconds before adding more.

1 Clean the mushrooms. If you have collected them from the wild cut off the ends where they have come from the ground and, using kitchen paper, wipe off any leaf matter or moss that may be adhering to them. Cut the mushrooms in half through the stalk and cap.

2 Dry the beef thoroughly on kitchen paper. Heat a large frying pan over a high heat then add 30ml/2 tbsp olive oil. Working in batches (see Cook's Tips) put the meat in the pan and quickly brown on all sides.

3 Remove the meat, which should still be very rare, from the pan, set aside and keep warm. Add the remaining olive oil to the pan and reduce the heat. Stir in the garlic and shallots and cook, stirring, for about 1 minute. Then increase the heat and add the mushrooms. Season and cook until the mushrooms just start to soften. Add the wine, bring to the boil and add the cream. As the liquid thickens, return the beef to the pan and heat through.

4 Remove the pan from the heat and swirl in the butter without mixing fully. Serve on warmed plates, garnished with chopped fresh parsley.

Per portion Energy 415kcal/1725kJ; Protein 29.9g; Carbohydrate 0.7g, of which sugars 0.6g; Fat 31g, of which saturates 14.2g; Cholesterol 122mg; Calcium 21mg; Fibre 0.4g; Sodium 124mg.

Dundee beef stew

Dundee is famously known as the home of marmalade, and this stew is flavoured with it. The red wine quite possibly also came into Dundee's busy port even though the majority must have come into Leith, the larger port for Edinburgh further south. This stew is excellent served with warming creamy mashed potatoes.

Serves 4

900g/2lb stewing beef

50g/2oz/½ cup plain (all-purpose) flour

2.5ml/½ tsp paprika

30ml/2 tbsp vegetable oil

225g/8oz onions, peeled and chopped

50g/2oz/½ stick butter

100g/4oz button (white) mushrooms, quartered

2 garlic cloves, crushed with a little salt

15ml/1 tbsp bitter marmalade

300ml/½ pint/1¼ cups red wine

150ml/¼ pint/⅔ cup beef stock

salt and ground black pepper

1 Preheat the oven to 180°C/350°F/ Gas 4. Cut the meat into 2.5cm/1in cubes. Season the flour with salt, black pepper and the paprika, spread it on a tray and coat the meat in it.

3 Transfer the meat to a casserole. Brown the onions in the original pan, adding a little butter if they seem too dry. Add to the casserole.

2 Heat a large pan, add the vegetable oil and brown the meat. Do this in batches if your pan is small.

4 Keeping the pan hot, add the rest of the butter and brown the mushrooms then transfer to the casserole.

5 Add the rest of the ingredients to the casserole and bring to the boil, stirring to combine the marmalade and evenly distribute the meat and mushrooms. Cover the casserole and place in the preheated oven for about 3 hours, until the meat is tender. Serve with creamy mashed potatoes.

Per portion Energy 544kcal/2276kJ; Protein 53.3g; Carbohydrate 17.1g, of which sugars 6.2g; Fat 24.1g, of which saturates 10.4g; Cholesterol 177mg; Calcium 53mg; Fibre 1.5g; Sodium 242mg.

Beef stew with oysters and Belhaven beer

Oysters have been collected from the waters south of Edinburgh since Roman times. They were very cheap and readily available in the 18th and 19th centuries, with "oyster lassies" wandering through the streets of Edinburgh selling them, calling their familiar cry, "Wha'll o' caller ou?" – "Who will have fresh oysters?"

Serves 4

1kg/2¼lb rump (round) steak

6 thin rashers (strips) streaky (fatty) bacon

12 oysters

50g/2oz/½ cup plain (all-purpose) flour

generous pinch of cayenne pepper

butter or olive oil, for greasing

3 shallots, finely chopped

300ml/½ pint/1¼ cups Belhaven Best beer

salt and ground black pepper

1 Preheat the oven to 180°C/350°F/ Gas 4. You need thin strips of beef for this recipe, so place the steaks one at a time between sheets of clear film (plastic wrap) and beat it with a rolling pin until it is flattened and thin. Slice the meat into 24 thin strips, wide enough to roll around an oyster.

2 Stretch the bacon rashers lengthways by placing them on a chopping board and, holding one end down with your thumb, pulling them out using the thick side of a sharp knife. Cut each rasher into four pieces.

3 Remove the oysters from their shells, retaining the liquid from inside their shells in a separate container. Set aside.

4 Cut each oyster in half lengthways and roll each piece in a strip of bacon, ensuring that the bacon goes around at least once and preferably covers the oyster at each end. Then roll in a strip of beef so no oyster is visible.

5 Season the flour with the cayenne pepper and salt and black pepper, then roll the meat in it.

6 Lightly grease a large flameproof casserole with butter or olive oil. Sprinkle the shallots evenly over the base. Place the floured meat rolls on top, evenly spaced.

7 Slowly pour over the beer, bring to the boil then cover and cook in the oven for 1½–2 hours.

8 The flour from around the meat will have thickened the stew sauce and produced a lovely rich gravy. Serve with creamy mashed potatoes and fresh steamed vegetables.

Cook's Tip
To open the oysters use an oyster knife, grasping the oyster in your other hand with a dish towel. If you don't have an oyster knife, use a small knife or a pen knife, although you should be careful of cutting yourself as the blade can easily slip.

Variation
Belhaven Best, beautifully honey coloured, is a draught (draft) ale. You could substitute your favourite ale or even Guinness if you prefer. If you want to create the dish without beer, use a good beef stock. Half a glass of red wine would also make a good addition if you are using stock.

Per portion Energy 528kcal/2208kJ; Protein 61.4g; Carbohydrate 12.7g, of which sugars 2.5g; Fat 24.4g, of which saturates 10.1g; Cholesterol 182mg; Calcium 52mg; Fibre 0.6g; Sodium 634mg.

All-in-the-pot beef stew

This recipe harks back to the idea of cooking everything in one pot over a fire in the hearth, the traditional way of preparing food in the small Scottish farm or cottage. It makes a superb alternative to a Sunday roast and is more forgiving as the beef, being boiled, can sit and wait while you have that extra glass of wine before lunch.

Serves 8

25g/1oz/2 tbsp butter, softened

25g/1oz/¼ cup plain (all-purpose) flour

1.6kg/3½lb silverside (pot roast), boned and rolled

450g/1lb small whole onions, peeled

450g/1lb small carrots, peeled and cut in two

8 celery sticks, peeled and cut in four

12 small potatoes

30ml/2 tbsp chopped fresh parsley

1 Make a beurre manié by combining the butter and flour thoroughly. This will be used to thicken the sauce.

2 Put the beef in a large pan, pour in cold water to cover and put on the lid. Bring to the boil and simmer for 2 hours, topping up with boiling water.

3 After 2 hours add the prepared vegetables to the pan and simmer for a further 30 minutes, until the vegetables are just cooked.

4 Remove the beef and vegetables from the pan, arrange on a serving dish and keep warm. Ladle about 350ml/12fl oz/ 1½ cups of the cooking liquor into a clean pan and bring to the boil. Whisk in the beurre manié to thicken it and add the chopped fresh parsley.

5 When ready to eat, pour the sauce over the beef and vegetables, retaining some to pass round the table. Serve the meat in thick slices, accompanied by a healthy serving of the vegetables.

Per portion Energy 875kcal/3656kJ; Protein 89.8g; Carbohydrate 38.5g, of which sugars 16.7g; Fat 41.1g, of which saturates 17.7g; Cholesterol 231mg; Calcium 121mg; Fibre 6.3g; Sodium 358mg.

Mutton hotpot

Another traditional cottage favourite, this mutton hotpot would have been a Sunday treat
in the remote Highlands. Mutton is hard to come by today but it really is worth looking out
for. Try your local farmers' market or ask your butcher if he could get it for you. It often has
a superior flavour to lamb, although it does require longer, slower cooking.

Serves 6

6 mutton chops

6 lamb's kidneys

1 large onion, sliced

450g/1lb potatoes, sliced

600ml/1 pint/2½ cups dark stock

salt and ground black pepper

1 Preheat the oven to 180°C/350°F/
Gas 4. Trim the mutton chops, leaving a
little fat but no bone. Slice the kidneys
in two horizontally and remove the fat
and core with sharp scissors.

2 Place three of the chops in a deep
casserole and season well with salt and
ground black pepper.

3 Add a layer of half the kidneys, then
half the onion and finally half the
potatoes. Season lightly.

4 Repeat the process, seasoning as you
go and making sure that you finish with
an even layer of potatoes.

5 Heat the stock and pour it into
the casserole, just about covering
everything but leaving the potatoes
just showing at the top. Cover and
cook in the preheated oven for 2 hours,
removing the lid for the last 30 minutes
to allow the potatoes to brown.

Variation
If you prefer, you can use lamb chops
instead. Use 2 chops per person and
reduce the cooking time by 30 minutes
as lamb does not need 2 hours.

Per portion Energy 626kcal/2629kJ; Protein 76.9g; Carbohydrate 23.1g, of which sugars 5g; Fat 25.8g, of which saturates 11.6g; Cholesterol 374mg; Calcium 76mg; Fibre 2g; Sodium 269mg.

Griddled loin of lamb with barley risotto

A loin of lamb is taken from the back or the saddle, and it should be completely clear of fat or gristle so you are getting pure meat. Good lamb needs little cooking – remember to take it out of the refrigerator well before you cook it to raise it to room temperature as it will then cook more quickly. Always pat the meat dry before putting it on a griddle pan.

Serves 4

a little olive oil

750ml/1¼ pints/3 cups chicken stock

75g/3oz/6 tbsp butter

1 onion, finely chopped

225g/8oz/1 cup barley

50g/2oz Bonnet cheese

3 loins of lamb

salt and ground black pepper

virgin olive oil, to serve

1 Prepare a cast-iron ridged griddle or heavy pan by brushing it with olive oil. Bring the stock to the boil. Melt the butter in a pan, and sweat the onion.

2 Add the barley to the pan and stir to coat well with the olive oil.

3 Add about one-third of the stock. Bring to the boil then reduce the heat, stirring all the time until the liquid is absorbed by the barley. Add half of the remaining stock and continue to stir and absorb. Finally add the rest of the stock, stirring all the time. You will create a thick, creamy mixture, with the barley still having a little "bite" to it. You may need more or less liquid depending on the barley; if you need more just add boiling water.

4 Grate the cheese and add to the barley when it has absorbed all the stock. Stir in well, season with salt and ground black pepper, and keep warm.

5 Heat the griddle or heavy pan until very hot. Brush the lamb with olive oil and season with salt and pepper. Sear the lamb quickly all over to brown it, then reduce the heat and cook for a further 8 minutes, turning occasionally. Leave it in a warm place to rest for 5 minutes.

6 Serve by carving thickish slices from each loin at an angle. You should get four slices from each loin, giving three per person. Add a splash of virgin olive oil to the risotto, place a mound of risotto on each warmed plate and prop the slices of lamb on it.

Per portion Energy 827kcal/3460kJ; Protein 49.8g; Carbohydrate 53.2g, of which sugars 2.2g; Fat 47.7g, of which saturates 25.2g; Cholesterol 223mg; Calcium 55mg; Fibre 0.5g; Sodium 348mg.

Braised shoulder of lamb with dulse

Dulse is a sea vegetable or seaweed and is used traditionally for flavouring dishes, especially lamb and mutton. On the Outer Hebrides the sheep will graze near the seashore and will actually eat the seaweed as well. Soay sheep, a hardy breed, feed almost exclusively on it and the flavour of their meat is improved by it too.

Serves 4

1.8kg/4lb shoulder of lamb, bone in and well trimmed of fat

30ml/2 tbsp vegetable oil

250g/9oz onions

25g/1oz/2 tbsp butter

pinch of caster (superfine) sugar

500ml/scant pint water

50g/2oz dried dulse

1 bay leaf

salt and ground black pepper

1 Preheat the oven to 180°C/350°F/ Gas 4, if necessary (see Step 5). Season the lamb all over.

2 Place a pan, big enough to hold the lamb and with a lid, on the stove. When hot, add the oil and brown the lamb all over. This can be a little difficult, as there are bits you really can't reach with the bone in, but brown as much as you can.

Cook's Tip
Press the onion hard through the sieve when straining the sauce, and if it is a bit thin boil it for a short while to reduce slightly.

3 Remove the lamb from the pan and drain off the excess fat, reserving it in case you need extra for the sauce. Peel the onions, cut in half and slice – not too finely – into half rounds.

4 Return the pan to a medium heat and add the butter. When it has melted completely, add the sliced onions with the sugar and a little salt and ground black pepper. Stir to coat with the butter then colour, without burning, for about 9 minutes.

5 Place the lamb on top of the onions, add the water, dulse and bay leaf, and season again. Cover and bring to the boil. Cook for 2 hours either over a very low heat or in the oven if the pan will fit and has ovenproof handles.

6 Remove the lamb from the pan, set aside and keep warm. Check the sauce for consistency, adding some of the reserved fat if necessary. Strain and adjust the seasoning. Slice the lamb and serve with the sauce.

Per portion Energy 677kcal/2808kJ; Protein 43.5g; Carbohydrate 5.2g, of which sugars 3.7g; Fat 53.7g, of which saturates 23.7g; Cholesterol 194mg; Calcium 48mg; Fibre 1.3g; Sodium 188mg.

Collops of venison with rowan sauce

A slice of meat is called a collop in Scotland, where it makes a popular, easy-to-prepare and nutritious meal. Rowan berries come from the mountain ash, which grows all over Britain, parts of Europe and as a shade tree in the USA. The berries make a light red jelly with a sharp flavour that partners venison perfectly.

Serves 4

4 venison haunch steaks, about 200g/7oz each

15ml/1 tbsp vegetable oil

50g/2oz/¼ cup butter

15ml/1 tbsp rowan jelly

120ml/4fl oz/½ cup red wine

salt and ground black pepper

1 Bring the steaks out of the refrigerator a few hours prior to cooking, so that they will cook more quickly. Before cooking, dry the steaks on kitchen paper and season with salt and ground black pepper.

2 Heat a heavy pan and add the oil and half the butter. Cook the haunch steaks as you would a sirloin or fillet, browning both sides and then reducing the heat to complete the cooking.

3 When cooked to your liking, remove the steaks from the pan, set them aside and keep warm.

4 Mix together the rowan jelly and wine and then add to the pan, stirring to bring up the meat juices and dissolve the jelly. Once the jelly has melted, season the sauce with salt and ground black pepper then, off the heat, swirl in the remaining butter. Serve the steaks on warmed plates with the sauce poured over.

Per portion Energy 355kcal/1488kJ; Protein 44.5g; Carbohydrate 2.7g, of which sugars 2.7g; Fat 17.4g, of which saturates 8.4g; Cholesterol 127mg; Calcium 15mg; Fibre 0g; Sodium 189mg.

Roast venison

Venison has been eaten in Scotland for generations, by kings, lairds and ordinary people, hunted and poached in equal measure. Today the wild deer are culled regularly to keep the stocks healthy and excellent wild meat is available through game dealers. There are also a number of deer farms, which produce meat of a very high quality.

Serves 4

1 venison haunch, approximately 2.75kg/6lb

30ml/2 tbsp olive oil

25g/1oz/2 tbsp butter

225g/8oz bacon, diced

salt and ground black pepper

For the marinade

1 onion, sliced

2 carrots, peeled and sliced

60ml/4 tbsp olive oil

1 bottle red wine

2 garlic cloves, crushed

1 bay leaf

5 black peppercorns

sprig of rosemary

6 juniper berries

For the sauce

15ml/1 tbsp plain (all-purpose) flour

15ml/1 tbsp butter, softened

150ml/¼ pint/⅔ cup port

15ml/1 tbsp rowan jelly

1 Marinade the meat two days before cooking. Cook the onion and carrots in the olive oil, without allowing them to colour. Then put the mixture into a non-metallic container that is large enough to hold the venison. Add the other ingredients. Put the haunch in and leave for two days, turning regularly to coat all sides.

2 When ready to cook, preheat the oven to 160°C/325°F/Gas 3. Remove the haunch from the marinade and dry with kitchen paper.

3 Put a large casserole, into which the haunch will fit with the lid on, over a high heat and add the oil and butter. Brown the bacon and then the haunch, browning it all over.

4 In another pan, reduce the marinade by half by boiling it rapidly and then strain over the haunch. Cover and cook for 30 minutes per 450g/1lb. When cooked, remove and keep warm, covered in foil so it does not dry out.

5 Strain the juices into a pan and boil rapidly. Make a beurre manié by mixing the flour and butter together and whisk it into the boiling liquor. Simmer until reduced by half. Add the port and the rowan jelly, adjust the seasoning, if necessary, and serve.

Per portion Energy 978kcal/4132kJ; Protein 167.1g; Carbohydrate 11.1g, of which sugars 7.3g; Fat 25.2g, of which saturates 8.8g; Cholesterol 383mg; Calcium 52mg; Fibre 0.2g; Sodium 442mg.

Venison pie

This is a variation on cottage or shepherd's pie and the result, using rich venison, is particularly tasty – a hearty treat after an energetic day hiking through the Highlands. Serve with lightly steamed green vegetables such as kale or cabbage.

Serves 6

30ml/2 tbsp olive oil

2 leeks, washed, trimmed and chopped

1kg/2¼lb minced (ground) venison

30ml/2 tbsp chopped fresh parsley

300ml/½ pint/1¼ cups game consommé

salt and ground black pepper

For the topping

1.4kg/3¼lb mixed root vegetables, such as sweet potatoes, parsnips and swede (rutabaga), coarsely chopped

15ml/1 tbsp horseradish sauce

25g/1oz/2 tbsp butter

1 Heat the oil in a pan over a medium heat. Add the leeks and cook for about 8 minutes, or until they are softened and beginning to brown.

2 Add the minced venison to the pan and cook over a medium heat, stirring frequently, for about 10 minutes or until the venison is thoroughly browned all over.

3 Add the chopped fresh parsley and stir it in thoroughly, then add the consommé and salt and ground black pepper. Stir well. Bring the mixture to the boil over a medium heat, then reduce the heat to low, cover and simmer gently for about 20 minutes, stirring occasionally.

4 Meanwhile, preheat the oven to 200°C/400°F/Gas 6 and prepare the pie topping. Cook the chopped root vegetables in boiling salted water to cover for 15–20 minutes.

Variation
This pie can be made with other minced (ground) meats, such as beef, lamb or pork. You may need to adapt the cooking times for these, depending on the type and quantity that you use, although the basic recipe remains the same. You can also use other types of game meats for this pie, such as finely chopped or minced rabbit or hare.

5 Drain the vegetables and put them in a bowl. Mash them together with the horseradish sauce, butter and plenty of ground black pepper.

6 Spoon the venison mixture into a large ovenproof dish and cover the top evenly with the mashed vegetables. It is often easier to spoon it over in small quantities rather than pouring it on and then smoothing it out.

7 Bake in the preheated oven for 20 minutes, or until piping hot and beginning to brown. Serve immediately, with steamed green vegetables.

Cook's Tip
• Use wild venison if possible as it has the best flavour and the lowest fat. If you can't get it, then use farmed venison, which will work well in this dish. Look for organic farmed vension.
• If leeks aren't available, then use a large onion and chop it coarsely.

Per portion Energy 307kcal/1291kJ; Protein 39.8g; Carbohydrate 13.2g, of which sugars 12.5g; Fat 12g, of which saturates 4.1g; Cholesterol 93mg; Calcium 154mg; Fibre 5.8g; Sodium 176mg.

Smoked venison with garlic mashed potatoes

Smoked venison is one of Scotland's lesser known treasures, and it can be used in many different ways. The best smoked venison is, of course, from wild animals taken from the moors and hills. The only smoker in Scotland to smoke wild venison is Rannoch Smokery in Perthshire. This warming dish makes an ideal supper or lunch.

Serves 4

675g/1½lb peeled potatoes

175ml/6fl oz/¾ cup milk

1 garlic clove

10ml/2 tsp sea salt

olive oil, for greasing and to serve

75ml/2½fl oz/⅓ cup double (heavy) cream

115g/4oz sliced smoked venison

salad leaves, to garnish

1 Preheat the oven to 180°C/350°F/ Gas 4. Slice the potatoes thinly using a sharp knife or mandolin. Place in a pan and pour in the milk.

2 Crush the garlic with the sea salt using the side of a knife. Stir the mixture into the potatoes. Bring to the boil over a gentle heat, stirring occasionally, until the starch comes out of the potatoes and the milk begins to thicken.

3 Grease the inside of a large gratin dish with a little olive oil.

4 Add the cream to the potatoes and, stirring gently so the potatoes don't break up, combine well. Allow to just come to the boil again then pour the mixture carefully into the ovenproof gratin dish.

5 Place the dish in the preheated oven for about 1 hour until lightly browned and tender.

6 To serve, scoop the potato on to warmed plates and put a pile of smoked venison on top, adding a splash of olive oil over each serving. Garnish with salad leaves.

Cook's Tips
• Use good tasty potatoes, such as King Edward or Maris Piper, for this dish (US russet or Idaho).
• If you are feeling generous, you could use more smoked venison.

Per portion Energy 281kcal/1180kJ; Protein 15.6g; Carbohydrate 29.5g, of which sugars 4.5g; Fat 12g, of which saturates 6.1g; Cholesterol 25mg; Calcium 80mg; Fibre 1.7g; Sodium 1050mg.

Venison stew

This simple yet deeply flavoured stew makes a wonderful supper dish, incorporating rich red wine and sweet redcurrant jelly with the depth of the bacon. Venison is popular in Scotland but you could substitute good-quality beef, if you prefer. Venison is a very lean meat, so bacon is included in this dish to provide some fat for the sauce.

Serves 4

1.3kg/3lb stewing venison (shoulder or topside), trimmed and diced

50g/2oz/¼ cup butter

225g/8oz piece of streaky (fatty) bacon, cut into 2cm/¾in lardons

2 large onions, chopped

1 large carrot, peeled and diced

1 large garlic clove, crushed

30ml/2 tbsp plain (all-purpose) flour

½ bottle red wine

dark stock (see Step 4)

1 bay leaf

sprig of fresh thyme

200g/7oz button (white) mushrooms, sliced

30ml/2 tbsp redcurrant jelly

salt and ground black pepper

1 Dry the venison thoroughly using kitchen paper. Set to one side.

2 Melt the butter in a large, heavy pan then brown the bacon lardons over a medium-high heat, stirring occasionally. Reduce the heat slightly to medium and add the onions and carrot, stir in and brown lightly.

3 Add the venison to the pan along with the garlic and stir into the mixture. Sprinkle on the flour and mix well.

4 Pour in the wine and dark stock to cover, along with the herbs, mushrooms and redcurrant jelly.

5 Cover the pan and simmer over a low heat until the meat is cooked, approximately 1½–2 hours. Serve immediately with creamy mashed potato and green vegetables of your choice.

Cook's Tip
This dish can be cooked and then left until required – a couple of days if need be. The flavours will be enhanced if it has been left for a while. Simply reheat and serve when needed.

Per portion Energy 727kcal/3045kJ; Protein 83.8g; Carbohydrate 17.5g, of which sugars 14.4g; Fat 31.3g, of which saturates 13.8g; Cholesterol 226mg; Calcium 70mg; Fibre 2.9g; Sodium 985mg.

Poultry and game

Central to the traditional Scottish way of life, poultry
and game have always played a key role, from the
hunt dining halls to the remote cottages of the
Highlands and Islands. Poultry was reared in the
back yard of every home and croft, from chickens
and hens to ducks and geese, all providing eggs
every day and a roast for special occasions. Game –
from pheasant to rabbit – was available to rich and
poor alike. The Highlands and glens teemed with
wild birds ready to be taken home, plucked or
skinned and made into a glorious banquet.

Stoved chicken

The word "stoved" is derived from the French *étuver* – to cook in a covered pot – and originates from the time of the Franco/Scottish Alliance in the 17th century. Instead of buying chicken joints, you can also choose either chicken thighs or chicken drumsticks.

Serves 4

900g/2lb potatoes, cut into 5mm/¼in slices

2 large onions, thinly sliced

15ml/1 tbsp chopped fresh thyme

25g/1oz/¼ stick butter

15ml/1 tbsp oil

2 large bacon rashers (strips), chopped

4 large chicken joints, halved

1 bay leaf

600ml/1 pint/2½ cups chicken stock

salt and ground black pepper

1 Preheat the oven to 150°C/300°F/ Gas 2. Make a thick layer of half the potato slices in the base of a large, heavy casserole, then cover with half the onion. Sprinkle with half the thyme and salt and ground black pepper.

2 Heat the butter and oil in a large frying pan then brown the bacon and chicken. Using a slotted spoon, transfer the chicken and bacon to the casserole. Reserve the fat in the pan.

3 Tuck the bay leaf in between the chicken. Sprinkle the remaining thyme over, then cover with the remaining onion, followed by a neat layer of overlapping potato slices. Season.

4 Pour the stock into the casserole. Brush the top layer of the sliced potatoes with the reserved fat from the frying pan, then cover tightly and cook in the preheated oven for about 2 hours, until the chicken is thoroughly cooked and tender.

5 Preheat the grill (broiler) to high. Uncover the casserole and place under the grill and cook until the slices of potato are beginning to brown and crisp. Serve hot.

Variation
You can use tarragon instead of the thyme: French tarragon has a superior flavour to the Russian variety.

Per portion Energy 630kcal/2653kJ; Protein 69.2g; Carbohydrate 48.2g, of which sugars 8.9g; Fat 19.2g, of which saturates 7.2g; Cholesterol 195mg; Calcium 57mg; Fibre 3.9g; Sodium 574mg.

Hunter's chicken

This tasty dish sometimes has strips of green pepper in the sauce instead of the mushrooms. It is excellent served with creamy mashed potatoes, and can be great for a lunch or late supper with a good chunk of fresh crusty bread.

Serves 4

30ml/2 tbsp olive oil

15g/½oz/1 tbsp butter

4 chicken portions, on the bone

1 large onion, thinly sliced

400g/14oz can chopped tomatoes

150ml/¼ pint/⅔ cup red wine

1 garlic clove, crushed

1 rosemary sprig, finely chopped, plus extra whole sprigs to garnish

115g/4oz fresh field (Portobello) mushrooms, thinly sliced

salt and ground black pepper

1 Heat the oil and butter in a large, flameproof casserole until foaming. Add the chicken portions and fry for 5 minutes. Remove the chicken pieces and drain on kitchen paper.

2 Add the sliced onion and cook gently, stirring frequently, for about 3 minutes then stir in the tomatoes and red wine.

3 Add the crushed garlic and chopped rosemary and season. Bring to the boil, stirring continuously.

4 Return the chicken to the casserole and turn to coat with the sauce. Cover with a tightly fitting lid and simmer gently for 30 minutes.

5 Add the fresh mushrooms to the casserole and stir well to mix into the sauce. Continue simmering gently for 10 minutes, or until the chicken is tender. Taste and add more salt and ground black pepper if necessary. Garnish with the fresh rosemary sprigs. Serve hot, with creamy mashed potatoes or crusty white bread and butter, if you like.

Per portion Energy 386kcal/1622kJ; Protein 53.6g; Carbohydrate 4.5g, of which sugars 4.1g; Fat 14.5g, of which saturates 4.5g; Cholesterol 155mg; Calcium 28mg; Fibre 1.5g; Sodium 141mg.

Chicken and mushroom pie

Chicken pie is a favourite throughout Scotland, especially in the Lowlands where farmyard chickens provide a plentiful supply of fresh, free-range birds. If you can find them, use wild mushrooms, such as cep mushrooms or field blewits, to intensify the flavours.

Serves 6

50g/2oz/¼ cup butter

30ml/2 tbsp plain (all-purpose) flour

250ml/8fl oz/1 cup hot chicken stock

60ml/4 tbsp single (light) cream

1 onion, coarsely chopped

2 carrots, sliced

2 celery sticks, coarsely chopped

50g/2oz fresh (preferably wild) mushrooms, quartered

450g/1lb cooked chicken meat, cubed

50g/2oz/½ cup fresh or frozen peas

salt and ground black pepper

beaten egg, to glaze

For the pastry

225g/8oz/2 cups plain (all-purpose) flour

1.5ml/¼ tsp salt

115g/4oz/½ cup cold butter, diced

65g/2½oz/⅓ cup white vegetable fat (shortening), diced

90–120ml/6–8 tbsp chilled water

1 To make the pastry, sift the flour and salt into a bowl. Rub in the butter and white vegetable fat until the mixture resembles breadcrumbs. Sprinkle with 90ml/6 tbsp chilled water and mix until the dough holds together. If the dough is too crumbly, add a little more water, 15ml/1 tbsp at a time.

2 Gather the dough into a ball and flatten it into a round. Wrap in clear film (plastic wrap) so that it is airtight and chill in the refrigerator for at least 30 minutes.

3 Preheat the oven to 190°C/375°F/ Gas 5. To make the filling, melt half the butter in a heavy pan over a low heat. Whisk in the flour and cook until bubbling, whisking constantly. Add the hot stock and whisk over a medium heat until the mixture boils. Cook for 2–3 minutes, then whisk in the cream. Season to taste with salt and ground black pepper, and set aside.

4 Heat the remaining butter in a large non-stick frying pan and cook the onion and carrots over a low heat for about 5 minutes. Add the celery and mushrooms and cook for a further 5 minutes, until they have softened. Add the cooked chicken and peas and stir in thoroughly.

5 Add the chicken mixture to the hot cream sauce and stir to mix. Adjust the seasoning if necessary. Spoon the mixture into a 2.5 litre/4 pint/2½ quart oval baking dish.

6 Roll out the pastry on a floured surface to a thickness of about 3mm/⅛in. Cut out an oval 2.5cm/1in larger all around than the dish. Lay the pastry over the filling. Gently press around the edge of the dish to seal, then trim off the excess pastry. Crimp the edge of the pastry by pushing the forefinger of one hand into the edge and, using the thumb and forefinger of the other hand, pinch the pastry. Continue all round the pastry edge.

7 Press together the pastry trimmings and roll out again. Cut out mushroom shapes with a sharp knife and stick them on to the pastry lid with a little of the beaten egg. Glaze the lid with beaten egg and cut several slits in the pastry to allow the steam to escape.

8 Bake the pie in the preheated oven for about 30 minutes, until the pastry has browned. Serve hot.

Cook's Tip
Using a combination of butter and white vegetable fat gives shortcrust pastry a lovely crumbly texture.

Per portion Energy 600kcal/2501kJ; Protein 23.7g; Carbohydrate 38.8g, of which sugars 3.7g; Fat 40g, of which saturates 21.8g; Cholesterol 132mg; Calcium 92mg; Fibre 2.7g; Sodium 226mg.

Chicken with summer vegetables and tarragon

This is an all-in-the-pot dish, with the chicken cooking liquor providing the stock for the rest of the cooking and the sauce. Summer vegetables are wonderfully packed with flavour, and it is up to you to pick the selection you prefer.

Serves 4

1.8kg/4lb boiling fowl (stewing chicken)

1 onion, peeled, studded with 6 cloves

1 bay leaf

a sprig each of thyme and parsley

10 black peppercorns

12 small potatoes, washed

8 small shallots, peeled

vegetables of your choice, such as carrots, courgettes (zucchini), broad (fava) beans and peas

25g/1oz/2 tbsp butter

30ml/2 tbsp plain (all-purpose) flour

60ml/4 tbsp chopped fresh tarragon

1 Wash the chicken and dry with kitchen paper. Place in a large pan with the onion, bay leaf, thyme, parsley and peppercorns, with water to cover. Stir to mix in all the ingredients and bring to the boil over a high heat. Reduce the heat and simmer gently for 1½ hours. Skim off the froth occasionally as the bird is boiling and make sure the chicken is covered, topping up with water if necessary.

2 Meanwhile prepare all the vegetables and place them in rows on a tray in order of cooking time, from the longest to the shortest.

3 Once cooked remove the chicken from the pan and keep warm. Remove all the seasonings, either with a slotted spoon or by straining the mixture, then bring the cooking liquor back to the boil, skimming off any fat that may have appeared on the top.

4 Start to cook the vegetables in the liqour, putting the potatoes in first for a few minutes, then adding the shallots and carrots, if using, and finally the green vegetables that take no time at all – mangetouts, for example, should go in when the potatoes are cooked. When the vegetables are cooked, place the chicken on a serving dish and surround with all the vegetables.

5 In a small pan melt the butter, add the flour and stir to create a roux. Slowly add some liquor from the large pan until a sauce is created – about 600ml/1 pint/2½ cups – and allow to simmer for a few minutes to reduce down and strengthen the flavour. At the last moment stir in the chopped fresh tarragon then ladle the sauce over the chicken and vegetables. Bring to the table and serve immediately.

Per portion Energy 713kcal/2973kJ; Protein 51.2g; Carbohydrate 39.3g, of which sugars 13g; Fat 40g, of which saturates 12.9g; Cholesterol 261mg; Calcium 103mg; Fibre 5.4g; Sodium 251mg.

Roast young grouse

As with venison, rowan jelly goes well with this meat. Young grouse can be identified by their pliable breastbone, legs and feet, and their claws will be sharp. They have very little fat so bacon is used here to protect the breasts during the initial roasting.

Serves 2

2 young grouse

6 rashers (strips) bacon

2 sprigs of rowanberries or
1 lemon, quartered, plus
30ml/2 tbsp extra rowanberries
(optional)

50g/2oz/¼ cup butter

150ml/¼ pint/⅔ cup red wine

150ml/¼ pint/⅔ cup water

5ml/1 tsp rowan jelly

salt and ground black pepper

1 Preheat the oven to 200°C/400°F/ Gas 6. Wipe the grouse with kitchen paper and place in a roasting pan. Lay the bacon over the breasts.

2 If you have rowanberries, place one sprig in the cavity of each grouse as well as a little butter. Otherwise put a lemon quarter in each cavity.

3 Roast the grouse in the preheated oven for 10 minutes, then remove the bacon and pour in the wine. Return to the oven for 10 minutes.

4 Baste the birds with the juices and cook for a further 5 minutes. Remove the birds from the pan and keep warm. Add the water and rowan jelly to the pan and simmer gently until the jelly melts. Strain into another pan, add the rowanberries, if using, and simmer until the sauce just begins to thicken. Season with salt and ground black pepper.

Cook's Tip
Grouse is traditionally served with bread sauce and game chips but Skirlie is excellent too.

Per portion Energy 423kcal/1763kJ; Protein 43.8g; Carbohydrate 1.5g, of which sugars 1.5g; Fat 24g, of which saturates 10.8g; Cholesterol 51mg; Calcium 43mg; Fibre 0g; Sodium 902mg.

Braised farm pigeon with elderberry wine

Elderberry wine is made commercially by several companies in Scotland and is just one of many things that can be made from the tree. The berries are bitter on their own but make a deep, rich, almost port-like wine. Pigeons are best in the autumn.

Serves 4

4 pigeons

15ml/1 tbsp plain (all-purpose) flour

30ml/2 tbsp olive oil, plus extra if needed

1 onion, chopped

225g/8oz button (white) mushrooms, sliced

250ml/8fl oz/1 cup dark stock

100ml/3½fl oz/scant ½ cup elderberry wine

salt and ground black pepper

kale, to serve (optional)

1 Preheat the oven to 170°C/325°F/ Gas 3. Season the pigeons inside and out with salt and black pepper and roll liberally in the flour. Heat a heavy pan over a medium heat, add the olive oil and wait for it to bubble slightly. Brown the pigeons lightly all over, then transfer them to a casserole dish.

2 Brown the onion and then the mushrooms in the same pan, still over a medium heat, adding more oil if necessary. Add the vegetables to the casserole with the pigeon and mix around well.

3 Pour in the stock, elderberry wine and just enough water to cover. Bring to the boil, cover tightly with a lid and cook in the preheated oven for 2 hours, until the pigeons are tender.

4 Remove the birds from the casserole and keep warm. Boil the cooking liquor rapidly to thicken slightly. Return the pigeons to the pan and heat through. Serve with kale, if you like.

Variation
This recipe suits most game birds, so if you can't find pigeon, or it is the wrong season, you can use partridge, woodcock, pheasant or even wild duck or goose.

Per portion Energy 296kcal/1237kJ; Protein 31g; Carbohydrate 6.8g, of which sugars 2.5g; Fat 14.3g, of which saturates 0.1g; Cholesterol 0mg; Calcium 35mg; Fibre 1g; Sodium 117mg.

Grey partridge with lentils and sausage

Grey partridge is indigenous to Scotland, although it is often called the English partridge, and is slightly smaller than the European red-legged variety. The wonderful rich flavour is complemented by the lovely earthy flavour of the Puy lentils.

Serves 4

450g/1lb/2 cups Puy lentils

75g/3oz/6 tbsp butter

15ml/1 tbsp vegetable oil

4 grey partridges

2 venison sausages

1 garlic clove, peeled but left whole

250ml/8fl oz/1 cup stock

salt and ground black pepper

1 Preheat the oven to 180°C/350°F/ Gas 4. Wash the lentils then simmer them in water for about 10 minutes to soften slightly. Drain then set aside.

2 Melt one-third of the butter with the oil in a large ovenproof frying pan and place the partridges, breast side down, in the pan. Brown both breasts lightly.

3 Set the partidges on their backs, season lightly with salt and ground black pepper and cook in the preheated oven for 15 minutes.

4 When cooked, remove the partridges from the oven, allow to cool for a few minutes then remove the legs. Keep the rest warm.

5 Put the large frying pan back on the hob and brown the two sausages. Add the Puy lentils and garlic and stir to coat in the juices from the partridges and the sausages. Then add the stock and simmer for a few minutes. Place the partridge legs on top of the lentil mixture and return to the oven for a further 15 minutes.

6 Remove the pan from the oven and set aside the partridge legs and sausages. Discard the garlic. Season the lentils with salt and ground black pepper, and if there is still a lot of liquid remaining, boil over a low heat to evaporate a little of the excess moisture. Then, off the heat, gradually swirl in the remaining butter.

7 Remove the breasts from the carcasses and set aside. Cut the sausages into pieces and stir into the lentil mixture.

8 To serve, place a leg on individual warmed plates, put the lentils on top and then the breast, sliced lengthways, on top of the lentils.

Per portion Energy 1309kcal/5495kJ; Protein 152.1g; Carbohydrate 59.4g, of which sugars 2.2g; Fat 53g, of which saturates 20.1g; Cholesterol 55mg; Calcium 255mg; Fibre 10.2g; Sodium 761mg.

Pan-fried pheasant with oatmeal and cream sauce

Rolled oats are often used for coating fish before pan-frying, but this treatment is equally good with tender poultry, game and other meats. Sweet, slightly tangy redcurrant jelly is used to bind the oatmeal to the tender pheasant breast fillets.

Serves 4

115g/4oz/generous 1 cup medium rolled oats

4 skinless, boneless pheasant breasts

45ml/3 tbsp redcurrant jelly, melted

50g/2oz/¼ cup butter

15ml/1 tbsp olive oil

45ml/3 tbsp wholegrain mustard

300ml/½ pint/1¼ cups double (heavy) cream

salt and ground black pepper

1 Place the rolled oats on a plate and season with salt and ground black pepper. Brush the skinned pheasant breasts with the melted redcurrant jelly, then turn them in the oats to coat evenly. Shake off any excess oats and set aside.

2 Heat the butter and oil in a frying pan until foaming. Add the pheasant breasts and cook over a high heat, turning frequently, until they are golden brown on all sides. Reduce the heat to medium and cook for a further 8–10 minutes, turning once or twice, until the meat is thoroughly cooked.

3 Add the mustard and cream, stirring to combine with the cooking juices. Bring slowly to the boil then simmer for 10 minutes over a low heat, or until the sauce has thickened to a good consistency. Serve immediately.

Per portion Energy 847kcal/3520kJ; Protein 37.1g; Carbohydrate 30.1g, of which sugars 9.1g; Fat 59g, of which saturates 35.1g; Cholesterol 129mg; Calcium 105mg; Fibre 2g; Sodium 205mg.

Pheasant and wild mushroom ragoût

Although not indigenous to Scotland, pheasant has become so much a part of the autumnal landscape that it is hard to imagine them not there. With their proud strutting and red eye mascara they are stunning to look at, as well as making very good eating.

Serves 4

4 pheasant breasts, skinned

12 shallots, halved

2 garlic cloves, crushed

75g/3oz wild mushrooms, sliced

75ml/2½fl oz/⅓ cup port

150ml/¼ pint/⅔ cup chicken stock

sprigs of fresh parsley and thyme

1 bay leaf

grated rind of 1 lemon

200ml/7fl oz/scant 1 cup double (heavy) cream

salt and ground black pepper

1 Dice and season the pheasant breasts. Heat a little oil in a heavy pan and colour the pheasant meat quickly. Remove from the pan and set aside.

2 Add the shallots to the pan, fry quickly to colour a little then add the garlic and sliced mushrooms. Reduce the heat and cook gently for 5 minutes.

3 Pour the port and stock into the pan and add the herbs and lemon rind. Reduce a little. When the shallots are nearly cooked add the cream, reduce to thicken then return the meat. Allow to cook for a few minutes before serving.

Cook's Tip

Serve with pilaff rice: fry a chopped onion, stir in 2.5cm/1in cinnamon stick, 2.5ml/½ tsp crushed cumin seeds, 2 crushed cardamom pods, a bay leaf and 5ml/1 tsp turmeric. Add 225g/8oz/ generous 1 cup long grain rice. Stir until well coated. Pour in 600ml/1 pint/2½ cups boiling water, cover then simmer gently for 15 minutes. Transfer to a serving dish, cover with a dish towel and leave for 5 minutes.

Per portion Energy 530kcal/2200kJ; Protein 34.1g; Carbohydrate 7.4g, of which sugars 5.9g; Fat 33g, of which saturates 20.2g; Cholesterol 69mg; Calcium 91mg; Fibre 1.1g; Sodium 114mg.

Rabbit salad with ruby chard

Chard is a delicious vegetable and can be used in place of spinach in so many recipes. The stalks are longer and thicker than spinach and the leaf has a great colour, especially the ruby varieties, which is a deep red. Prepare it as you would spinach. Rabbits are plentiful in Scotland and are a traditional favourite. This quick method is only good for the saddle.

4 Remove the rabbit from the pan and return the pan to the hob, add the butter and, as soon as it is melted, throw the chard in all at once. (It may be heaped up but will soon wilt down.) Season with salt and ground black pepper and toss to coat well with the butter. Once it has wilted – about 3 minutes – it is ready.

Serves 4

15ml/1 tbsp groundnut (peanut) oil

2 saddles of rabbit, each weighing approximately 250g/9oz

mixed salad leaves

salad dressing

50g/2oz/¼ cup butter

225g/8oz ruby chard leaves (stalks removed)

salt and ground black pepper

1 Heat a frying pan and pour in the oil, allowing it to get quite hot. Dry and season the saddles of rabbit and place them skin side down. Reduce the heat and brown lightly in the pan.

2 Turn the saddles over on to the rib side, cover and cook over a very low heat for about 7 minutes. Turn off the heat, and leave to rest.

3 Make a salad using colourful leaves. Toss with your dressing and place in the centre of four individual plates.

5 Slice the rabbit fillets from the back of the saddle and take the small fillets from underneath as well. Cut thinly and strew evenly over the salad. Place the warm chard on top and serve.

Cook's Tip
In Scotland the thick stalks of chard are often cut off and stirred into a white sauce as a separate side dish. Cut them off raw and steam them for 5–6 minutes then arrange on a serving dish and cover with a white sauce as you would do with asparagus.

Per portion Energy 287kcal/1192kJ; Protein 29g; Carbohydrate 1g, of which sugars 0.9g; Fat 18.5g, of which saturates 9.1g; Cholesterol 115mg; Calcium 126mg; Fibre 1.2g; Sodium 238mg.

Saddle of rabbit with asparagus

Some of the best asparagus comes from near Glamis in Angus in the east of the country where a little extra sunlight produces stems with juicy, succulent flavours. This is not like the white asparagus of Europe, which is grown underground, but a better-flavoured, more satisfying green variety, which grows above the soil.

Serves 4

2 saddles of rabbit

75g/3oz/6 tbsp butter

sprig of fresh rosemary

45ml/3 tbsp olive oil

10 asparagus spears

200ml/7fl oz/scant 1 cup chicken stock, plus extra for cooking the asparagus (see Step 5)

salt and ground black pepper

1 Preheat the oven to 200°C/400°F/ Gas 6. Trim the rabbit saddles, removing the membrane and the belly flaps.

2 Heat an ovenproof pan then add 50g/2oz/4 tbsp of the butter. Season the saddles and brown them lightly all over, by frying them gently in the butter for a few minutes on each side.

3 Tuck the rosemary underneath the saddles, with the fillets facing up, and put in the oven for 10 minutes.

4 Meanwhile, in a second pan, heat the olive oil then add the asparagus spears. Make sure they are coated in the oil and leave them to sweat gently for a few minutes.

5 Add enough stock to just cover the asparagus and bring to a gentle boil. Allow the liquid to evaporate to a light glaze and the asparagus will be cooked.

6 Remove the rabbit from the oven and leave to rest for 5 minutes. Remove any fat from the pan then add the measured stock. Bring to the boil, scraping up any bits from the base of the pan. Reduce the liquid by about a half, then remove from the heat and whisk in the remaining butter. Strain through a sieve and set aside.

7 Take the meat off the saddles in slices lengthways and place on a warmed serving dish. Serve with the asparagus on top and the sauce spooned over.

Per portion Energy 406kcal/1684kJ; Protein 33.7g; Carbohydrate 0.6g, of which sugars 0.6g; Fat 29.8g, of which saturates 13.4g; Cholesterol 146mg; Calcium 43mg; Fibre 0.4g; Sodium 215mg.

Rabbit with apricots

Rabbit is a delicious meat, richer and more tasty than chicken, but with a similar colouring and texture. The gamey flavours go very well in many dishes, especially those with fruits and berries. Once a staple of the countryside, enjoyed by farmers and hunting parties alike, it is now available from good butchers and some fishmongers too.

Serves 4

2 rabbits

30ml/2 tbsp plain (all-purpose) flour

15ml/1 tbsp vegetable oil

90g/3½oz streaky (fatty) bacon, cut into thin pieces

10 baby (pearl) onions, peeled but kept whole

200ml/7fl oz/scant 1 cup dry white wine

1 bay leaf

12 dried apricots

salt and ground black pepper

1 Ask your butcher to joint the rabbits, providing two legs and the saddle cut in two. Sprinkle the flour over a dish, season with salt and ground black pepper and mix well into the flour. Roll the rabbit pieces in it one by one to coat lightly all over, shaking off any excess flour. Set aside.

2 Heat a heavy pan and add the oil. Brown the rabbit pieces all over then remove from the pan. Brown the bacon followed by the onions.

3 Place the browned rabbit pieces, bacon and onions in a casserole. Pour the wine into the heavy pan and, over a low heat, scrape up all the bits from the base of the pan. Add a little water, bring to the boil and pour over the rabbit in the casserole, adding more water if needed to just cover.

4 Add the bay leaf and bring to the boil. Allow to simmer gently for 40 minutes until the rabbit is tender.

5 Remove the rabbit and onions from the pan and set aside, keeping them warm. Put the apricots into the pan and boil rapidly until the cooking liquor thickens slightly. Remove the bay leaf and check the seasoning. You can now either return the rabbit and onions to the pan as it is and heat before serving, or you can purée the apricots in the cooking liquor and pour the resulting rich sauce over the rabbit.

Cook's Tip
This dish is best reheated and served the next day so that the flavours can develop overnight.

Per portion Energy 481kcal/2022kJ; Protein 60.2g; Carbohydrate 22.5g, of which sugars 21.4g; Fat 13.8g, of which saturates 6.1g; Cholesterol 223mg; Calcium 153mg; Fibre 3.9g; Sodium 417mg.

Roast hare with beetroot and crowdie

Hares are not the easiest of things to get hold of but in some parts of Scotland they are often available. This sauce goes well with venison too. Crowdie is a cream cheese made on every homestead up to the middle of the last century. For a less rich dish you could use plain yogurt in place of the crowdie at the end.

Serves 4

2 saddles of hare

10ml/2 tsp olive oil

350g/12oz cooked beetroot (beets)

30ml/2 tbsp chopped shallot

30ml/2 tbsp white wine vinegar

50g/2oz/¼ cup crowdie

5ml/1 tsp English mustard

salt and ground black pepper

For the marinade

600ml/1 pint/2½ cups red wine

1 carrot, finely diced

1 onion, finely diced

generous pinch of mixed herbs

pinch of salt

8 peppercorns

8 juniper berries

2 cloves

1 Using a flexible knife, remove the membrane covering the saddles. Mix all the ingredients for the marinade together and coat the saddles then leave for one day, turning occasionally.

2 Preheat the oven to 240°C/475°F/ Gas 9. Take out and dry the saddles with kitchen paper. Strain the marinade through a sieve and set aside.

3 Heat the olive oil in a large ovenproof pan. Brown the saddles all over then cook in the preheated oven for 10–15 minutes. They should still be pink. Leave in a warm place to rest.

4 Remove most of the fat from the pan then add the beetroot. Cook for 1–2 minutes then add the shallot and cook for about 2 minutes to soften.

5 Add the vinegar and 30ml/2 tbsp of the marinade and stir in thoroughly. Reduce the liquid until a coating texture is nearly achieved. Reduce the heat to low and add the crowdie. Whisk it in until completely melted, then add the mustard and season to taste. Set aside and keep warm.

6 To serve, remove the fillets from the top and bottom of the saddles and slice lengthways. Place on four warmed plates and arrange the beetroot mixture on top. Reheat the sauce, without boiling, and hand round separately.

Per portion Energy 352kcal/1471kJ; Protein 41g; Carbohydrate 9.6g, of which sugars 8.7g; Fat 13.1g, of which saturates 6.5g; Cholesterol 136mg; Calcium 84mg; Fibre 1.9g; Sodium 255mg.

Loin of wild boar with bog myrtle

Wild boar used to roam the hills of Scotland centuries ago and when the kings of Scotland came for their summer holidays to Falkland Palace, Fife, they would go out hunting for them. Today they no longer exist in the wild but are farmed as a rare breed of pig. Their meat is similar to pork in that it has a sweetness to it, and the crackling is fantastic.

Serves 4

1 loin of wild boar, approximately 2.75kg/6lb

10ml/2 tsp salt

1 onion, roughly chopped

1 carrot, peeled and roughly chopped

150ml/¼ pint/⅔ cup dry vermouth

10ml/2 tsp English mustard

handful of bog myrtle, or a few sprigs of fresh rosemary, if you prefer

salt and ground black pepper

1 Ask your butcher to take the loin off the bone and then to tie it back on and to make 2cm/¾in cuts through the skin from top to bottom at 5cm/2in intervals. This will make the crackling easier to slice when you come to carve. Allow the loin to sit at room temperature for at least an hour prior to cooking. Preheat the oven to 220°C/425°F/Gas 7.

2 Rub the salt all over the skin of the boar, easing it slightly into the cuts made by the butcher.

3 Place the chopped vegetables and herbs in a lightly oiled roasting pan.

4 Put the loin on top of the vegetables and herbs, with the skin facing up, and roast in the oven for 40 minutes.

5 Reduce the oven temperature to 180°C/350°F/Gas 4 and cook for another 40 minutes. Remove from the oven and cut the meat from the bones – this should just be a matter of cutting the string. Set the meat aside to rest for at least 20 minutes.

6 Meanwhile make the gravy. Pour or spoon off the excess fat from the roasting pan but try to retain the juices, which will be under the fat.

7 Put the roasting pan on the stove over a low heat and add the vermouth and mustard. Stir well to mix thoroughly, scraping the base of the pan to incorporate the cooked flavours.

8 Just as it comes to the boil, pour the gravy into a clean pan, along with the bones, herbs and vegetables. Swill out the roasting pan with a little water and add this to the new pan, making sure that you have all the juices. Simmer the gravy in the new pan for about 5 minutes.

9 Remove the bones and strain the juices into the gravy pan. Test the seasoning, adding salt and ground black pepper if necessary.

10 Serve the loin in slices, each slice with a strip of the crackling, and pass around the gravy in a separate dish.

Cook's Tip
The crackling is particularly good and can be broken off in chunks because of the cuts made prior to cooking. The meat can be carved separately.

Per portion Energy 530kcal/2221kJ; Protein 81.9g; Carbohydrate 6.7g, of which sugars 5.7g; Fat 15.5g, of which saturates 5.3g; Cholesterol 236mg; Calcium 109mg; Fibre 1.9g; Sodium 1309mg.

Side dishes

Almost as tasty as the main course itself, the vegetables and salads in Scottish cuisine provide an often healthy or hearty accompaniment to every meal. The richly flavoured green vegetables, including kale, chard, spinach and cabbage, are excellent served on their own or with a sauce. No meal is complete, however, without those robust root vegetables: turnip, swede, parsnip, carrot and the versatile favourite, the potato.

Clapshot

This root vegetable dish is excellent with haggis or on top of shepherd's pie in place of just potato. Turnips give an earthy flavour, and swede introduces a sweet accent. It is also slightly less heavy than mashed potato, which is good for a lighter meal or supper.

Serves 4

450g/1lb potatoes

450g/1lb turnips or swede (rutabaga)

50g/2oz/¼ cup butter

50ml/2fl oz/¼ cup milk

5ml/1 tsp freshly grated nutmeg

30ml/2 tbsp chopped fresh parsley

salt and ground black pepper

1 Peel the potatoes and turnips or swede, then cut them into evenly sized small chunks. You will need a large sharp knife for the turnips.

2 Place the chopped vegetables in a pan and cover with cold water. Bring to the boil over a medium heat, then reduce the heat and simmer until both vegetables are cooked, which will take about 15–20 minutes. Test the vegetables by pushing the point of a sharp knife into one of the cubes; if it goes in easily and the cube begins to break apart, then it is cooked.

3 Drain the vegetables through a colander. Return to the pan and allow them to dry out for a few minutes over a low heat, stirring occasionally to prevent any from sticking to the base of the pan.

4 Melt the butter with the milk in a small pan over a low heat. Mash the dry potato and turnip or swede mixture, then add the milk mixture. Grate in the nutmeg, add the parsley, mix thoroughly and season to taste. Serve immediately with roast meat or game.

Per portion Energy 204kcal/852kJ; Protein 3.4g; Carbohydrate 24.1g, of which sugars 7.2g; Fat 11.2g, of which saturates 6.8g; Cholesterol 27mg; Calcium 78mg; Fibre 3.8g; Sodium 111mg.

Skirlie

Oatmeal has been a staple in Scotland for centuries. Skirlie is a simple preparation and can be used for stuffings or as an accompaniment, and is especially good with roast meats. It is traditionally cooked in lard but many people prefer butter.

Serves 4

50g/2oz/¼ cup butter

1 onion, finely chopped

175g/6oz/scant 2 cups medium rolled oats

salt and ground black pepper

Variation
To add a lovely rich flavour to the skirlie, grate in a little nutmeg and add a pinch of cinnamon towards the end.

1 Melt the butter in a pan over a medium heat and add the onion. Fry gently until it is softened and very slightly browned.

2 Stir in the rolled oats and season with salt and ground black pepper. Cook gently for 10 minutes. Taste for seasoning and serve immediately.

Per portion Energy 282kcal/1182kJ; Protein 6g; Carbohydrate 34.9g, of which sugars 2.2g; Fat 14.2g, of which saturates 6.5g; Cholesterol 27mg; Calcium 36mg; Fibre 3.5g; Sodium 91mg.

Kailkenny

This is another mashed potato combination dish, originating from the north-east of Scotland. Normally the cabbage is boiled but it is more nutritious to quickly fry it, keeping in the goodness. Kailkenny makes an excellent accompaniment to any meat dish.

Serves 4

450g/1lb potatoes, peeled and chopped

50g/2oz/¼ cup butter

50ml/2fl oz/¼ cup milk

450g/1lb cabbage, washed and finely shredded

30ml/2 tbsp olive oil

50ml/2fl oz/¼ cup double (heavy) cream

salt and ground black pepper

1 Place the potatoes in boiling water and boil for 15–20 minutes. Drain, replace on the heat for a few minutes then mash. Heat the butter and milk in a small pan and then mix into the mashed potatoes. Season to taste.

2 Heat the olive oil in a large frying pan, add the shredded cabbage and fry for a few minutes. Season to taste with salt and ground black pepper. Add the mashed potato, mix well then stir in the cream. Serve immediately.

Per portion Energy 183kcal/766kJ; Protein 3.9g; Carbohydrate 24g, of which sugars 7.3g; Fat 8.5g, of which saturates 2.4g; Cholesterol 7mg; Calcium 73mg; Fibre 3.5g; Sodium 24mg.

Spiced greens

Here is a really good way to enliven your greens, excellent for crunchy cabbages but also good for kale and other purple sprouting leaves. Even Brussels sprout tops work well cooked like this. It's a very good way of persuading people to try leafy green vegetables.

Serves 4

1 medium cabbage, or the equivalent in quantity of your chosen green vegetable

15ml/1 tbsp groundnut (peanut) oil

5ml/1 tsp grated fresh root ginger

2 garlic cloves, grated

2 shallots, finely chopped

2 red chillies, seeded and finely sliced

salt and ground black pepper

1 Remove any tough outer leaves from the cabbage then quarter it and remove the core. Shred the leaves.

2 Pour the groundnut oil into a large pan and as it heats stir in the ginger and garlic. Add the shallots and as the pan becomes hotter add the chillies.

3 Add the greens and toss to mix thoroughly. Cover the pan and reduce the heat to create some steam. Cook, shaking the pan occasionally, for about 3 minutes. Remove the lid and increase the heat to dry off the steam, season with salt and ground black pepper and serve immediately.

Per portion Energy 77kcal/322kJ; Protein 2.6g; Carbohydrate 9.9g, of which sugars 9.4g; Fat 3.1g, of which saturates 0.5g; Cholesterol 0mg; Calcium 90mg; Fibre 3.9g; Sodium 13mg.

Spiced asparagus kale

Kale is a very important part of Scottish tradition. "Kailyards" was the word used to describe the kitchen garden, and even the midday meal was often referred to as "kail". Use the more widely available curly kale if you find it hard to get the asparagus variety.

Serves 4

175g/6oz asparagus kale

10ml/2 tsp butter

25g/1oz piece fresh root ginger, grated

15ml/1 tbsp soy sauce

salt and ground black pepper

1 Prepare the kale by removing the centre stalk and ripping the leaves into smallish pieces.

2 Heat a pan over a high heat and add the butter. As it melts, quickly add the kale and toss rapidly to allow the heat to cook it.

3 Grate the ginger into the pan and stir in thoroughly. Then add the soy sauce and mix well. When the kale has wilted, it is ready to serve.

Per portion Energy 35kcal/145kJ; Protein 1.6g; Carbohydrate 0.9g, of which sugars 0.9g; Fat 2.8g, of which saturates 1.4g; Cholesterol 5mg; Calcium 58mg; Fibre 1.4g; Sodium 301mg.

Kale with mustard dressing

Traditionally, sea kale is used for this dish, available in Scotland between January and March. Its pale green fronds have a slightly nutty taste. Use curly kale if you can't get sea kale, although you will need to boil it briefly for a few minutes before chilling and serving.

Serves 4

250g/9oz sea kale or curly kale

45ml/3 tbsp light olive oil

5ml/1 tsp wholegrain mustard

15ml/1 tbsp white wine vinegar

pinch of caster (superfine) sugar

salt and ground black pepper

1 Wash the sea kale, drain thoroughly, then trim it and cut in two.

2 Whisk the oil into the mustard in a bowl. When it is blended completely, whisk in the white wine vinegar. It should begin to thicken.

3 Season the mustard dressing to taste with sugar, salt and ground black pepper. Toss the sea kale in the dressing and serve immediately.

Per portion Energy 99kcal/409kJ; Protein 2.1g; Carbohydrate 1.9g, of which sugars 1.9g; Fat 9.3g, of which saturates 1.3g; Cholesterol 0mg; Calcium 82mg; Fibre 2g; Sodium 27mg.

Cabbage with bacon

Bacon, especially if smoked, makes all the difference to the flavour of the cabbage, turning it into a delicious vegetable accompaniment to serve with roast beef, chicken or even a celebration turkey. Try it with people who don't like to eat greens.

Serves 4

30ml/2 tbsp oil

1 onion, finely chopped

115g/4oz smoked bacon, finely chopped

500g/1¼lb cabbage (red, white or Savoy)

salt and ground black pepper

1 Heat the oil in a large pan over a medium heat, add the chopped onion and bacon and cook for about 7 minutes, stirring occasionally.

2 Remove any tough outer leaves and wash the cabbages. Shred them quite finely, discarding the core. Add the cabbage to the pan and season. Stir for a few minutes until the cabbage begins to lose volume.

3 Continue to cook the cabbage, stirring frequently, for 8–10 minutes until it is tender but still crisp. (If you prefer softer cabbage, then cover the pan for part of the cooking time.) Serve immediately.

Variations
• This dish is equally delicious if you use spring greens (collards) instead of cabbage. You could also use curly kale.
• To make a more substantial dish to serve for lunch or supper, add more bacon, some chopped button (white) mushrooms and skinned, seeded and chopped tomatoes.

Per portion Energy 151kcal/623kJ; Protein 6.7g; Carbohydrate 7.4g, of which sugars 7g; Fat 10.5g, of which saturates 2.6g; Cholesterol 15mg; Calcium 67mg; Fibre 2.8g; Sodium 452mg.

Braised red cabbage

Red cabbage is a hardy vegetable that can be grown in a garden plot even in the difficult conditions of the Highlands and Islands. Lightly spiced with a sharp, sweet flavour, braised red cabbage goes well with roast pork, duck and game dishes.

Serves 4–6

1kg/2¼lb red cabbage

2 cooking apples

2 onions, chopped

5ml/1 tsp freshly grated nutmeg

1.5ml/¼ tsp ground cloves

1.5ml/¼ tsp ground cinnamon

15ml/1 tbsp soft dark brown sugar

45ml/3 tbsp red wine vinegar

25g/1oz/2 tbsp butter, diced

salt and ground black pepper

chopped flat leaf parsley, to garnish

2 Layer the shredded cabbage in a large ovenproof dish with the onions, apples, spices, sugar, and salt and ground black pepper. Pour over the vinegar and add the diced butter.

3 Cover the dish with a lid and cook in the preheated oven for about 1½ hours, stirring a couple of times, until the cabbage is very tender. Serve immediately, garnished with the parsley.

1 Preheat the oven to 160°C/325°F/ Gas 3. Cut away and discard the large white ribs from the outer cabbage leaves using a large, sharp knife, then finely shred the cabbage. Peel, core and coarsely grate the apples.

Cook's Tip
This dish can be cooked in advance. Bake the cabbage for 1½ hours, then leave to cool. Store in a cool place covered with clear film (plastic wrap). To complete the cooking, bake it in the oven at 160°C/325°F/Gas 3 for about 30 minutes, stirring occasionally.

Per portion Energy 160kcal/668kJ; Protein 4.3g; Carbohydrate 23.8g, of which sugars 22.4g; Fat 5.8g, of which saturates 3.3g; Cholesterol 13mg; Calcium 140mg; Fibre 6.6g; Sodium 58mg.

Young vegetables with tarragon

This is almost a salad, but the vegetables here are just lightly cooked to bring out their different flavours. The tarragon adds a wonderful depth to this bright, fresh dish. It goes well as a light accompaniment to fish and seafood dishes.

Serves 4

5 spring onions (scallions)

50g/2oz/¼ cup butter

1 garlic clove, crushed

115g/4oz asparagus tips

115g/4oz mangetouts (snowpeas), trimmed

115g/4oz broad (fava) beans

2 Little Gem (Bibb) lettuces

5ml/1 tsp finely chopped fresh tarragon

salt and ground black pepper

1 Cut the spring onions into quarters lengthways and fry gently over a medium-low heat in half the butter with the garlic.

2 Add the asparagus tips, mangetouts and broad beans. Mix in, covering all the pieces with oil.

3 Just cover the base of the pan with water, season, and allow to simmer gently for a few minutes.

4 Cut the lettuce into quarters and add to the pan. Cook for 3 minutes then, off the heat, swirl in the remaining butter and the tarragon, and serve.

Per portion Energy 149kcal/619kJ; Protein 4.7g; Carbohydrate 6.1g, of which sugars 3g; Fat 12g, of which saturates 7.3g; Cholesterol 29mg; Calcium 55mg; Fibre 3.5g; Sodium 89mg.

Celeriac purée

Celeriac is a most delicious vegetable which is ignored too often. This is sad as it is so good grated raw with mayonnaise and served with smoked salmon. Here it is made into a delicious purée that goes very well with game, poultry or roast pork or boar.

Serves 4

1 celeriac bulb, cut into chunks

1 lemon

2 potatoes, cut into chunks

300ml/½ pint/1¼ cups double (heavy) cream

salt and ground black pepper

snipped chives, to garnish

1 Place the celeriac in a pan. Cut the lemon in half and squeeze it into the pan, dropping the two halves in too.

2 Add the potatoes to the pan and just cover with cold water. Place a disc of greaseproof (waxed) paper over the vegetables. Bring to the boil, reduce the heat and simmer until tender, about 20 minutes.

3 Remove the lemon halves and drain through a colander. Return to the pan and allow to steam dry for a few minutes over a low heat.

4 Remove from the heat and purée in a food processor. This mixture can be set aside until you need it and can be kept in the refrigerator for a few days, covered with clear film (plastic wrap).

5 When ready to use, pour the cream into a pan and bring to the boil. Add the celeriac mixture and stir to heat through. Season, garnish wth snipped chives and serve.

Per portion Energy 403kcal/1661kJ; Protein 2.2g; Carbohydrate 7.9g, of which sugars 2.3g; Fat 40.5g, of which saturates 25.1g; Cholesterol 103mg; Calcium 65mg; Fibre 1.1g; Sodium 58mg.

Creamed leeks

This dish is a real Scottish favourite, delicious with a full roast dinner, or even on its own. It is very important to have good firm leeks without a core in the middle. The Scottish Musselburgh variety is excellent, if you can find it.

Serves 4

2 Musselburgh leeks, tops trimmed and roots removed

50g/2oz/½ stick butter

200ml/7fl oz/scant 1 cup double (heavy) cream

salt and ground black pepper

Cook's Tip
When buying leeks, choose smaller and less bendy ones as they are more tender.

1 Split the leeks down the middle then cut across so you make pieces approximately 2cm/¾in square. Wash thoroughly and drain in a colander.

2 Melt the butter in a large pan and when quite hot throw in the leeks, stirring to coat them in the butter, and heat through. They will wilt but should not exude water. Keep the heat high but don't allow them to colour. You need to create a balance between keeping the temperature high so the water steams out of the vegetable, keeping it bright green, whilst not burning the leeks.

3 Keeping the heat high, pour in the cream, mix in thoroughly and allow to bubble and reduce. Season with salt and ground black pepper. When the texture is smooth, thick and creamy the leeks are ready to serve.

Variation
Although these leeks have a wonderful taste themselves, you may like to add extra flavourings, such as a little chopped garlic or some chopped fresh tarragon or thyme.

Per portion Energy 363kcal/1496kJ; Protein 2.5g; Carbohydrate 3.8g, of which sugars 3.1g; Fat 37.6g, of which saturates 23.3g; Cholesterol 95mg; Calcium 51mg; Fibre 2.2g; Sodium 89mg.

Baked tomatoes with mint

This is a dish for the height of the summer when the tomatoes are falling off the vines and are very ripe, juicy and full of flavour. Mint flourishes in Lowland gardens and can also be nurtured in the Highlands. This tomato dish goes especially well with lamb.

Serves 4

6 large ripe tomatoes

300ml/½ pint/1¼ cups double (heavy) cream

2 sprigs of fresh mint

olive oil, for brushing

a few pinches of caster (superfine) sugar

30ml/2 tbsp grated Bonnet cheese

salt and ground black pepper

1 Preheat the oven to 220°C/425°F/ Gas 7. Bring a pan of water to the boil and have a bowl of iced water ready. Cut the cores out of the tomatoes and make a cross at the base. Plunge the tomatoes into the boiling water for 10 seconds and then straight into the iced water. Leave to cool completely.

2 Put the cream and mint in a pan and bring to the boil. Reduce the heat and allow to simmer until it has reduced by about half.

3 Peel the cooled tomatoes and slice them thinly.

Cook's Tip
Bonnet is a hard goat's cheese but any hard, well-flavoured cheese will do.

4 Brush a shallow gratin dish lightly with a little olive oil. Layer the sliced tomatoes in the dish, overlapping slightly, and season with salt and ground black pepper. Sprinkle a little sugar over the top.

5 Strain the reduced cream evenly over the top of the tomatoes. Sprinkle on the cheese and bake in the preheated oven for 15 minutes, or until the top is browned and bubbling. Serve immediately in the gratin dish.

Per portion Energy 443kcal/1831kJ; Protein 5g; Carbohydrate 6.7g, of which sugars 6.7g; Fat 44.1g, of which saturates 27.4g; Cholesterol 113mg; Calcium 123mg; Fibre 1.8g; Sodium 105mg.

Watercress salad with pear and Dunsyre Blue dressing

A refreshing light salad, this dish combines lovely peppery watercress, soft juicy pears and a tart dressing. Dunsyre is on the edge of the Pentland Hills in the Borders, and Dunsyre Blue has a wonderfully sharp flavour with a crumbly texture.

Serves 4

25g/1oz Dunsyre Blue cheese

30ml/2 tbsp walnut oil

15ml/1 tbsp lemon juice

2 bunches of watercress, thoroughly washed and trimmed

2 ripe pears (see Cook's Tips)

salt and ground black pepper

1 Crumble and then mash the Dunsyre Blue into the walnut oil.

2 Whisk in the lemon juice to create a thickish mixture. If you need to thicken it further, add a little more cheese. Season to taste with salt and ground black pepper.

3 Arrange a pile of watercress on the side of four plates.

4 Peel and slice the two pears then place the pear slices to the side of the watercress, allowing half a pear per person. You can also put the pear slices on top of the watercress, if you prefer. Drizzle the dressing over the salad.

Cook's Tips
• Choose Comice or similar pears that are soft and juicy for this salad.
• If you want to get things ready in advance, peel and slice the pears then rub with some lemon juice; this will stop them discolouring so quickly.

Per portion Energy 106kcal/442kJ; Protein 2.3g; Carbohydrate 7.6g, of which sugars 7.6g; Fat 7.6g, of which saturates 1.8g; Cholesterol 5mg; Calcium 81mg; Fibre 2g; Sodium 91mg.

Quail's egg salad with Bishop Kennedy cheese

Bishop Kennedy was originally made in the medieval monasteries of France, but now it is produced in Scotland. It is a full-fat soft cheese, with its rind washed in malt whisky to produce a distinctive orangey red crust and a strong creamy taste. It is runny when ripe.

Serves 4

8 quail's eggs

vinegar, for poaching

½ red onion, finely chopped

½ leek, cut into fine strips and blanched

75g/3oz Bishop Kennedy cheese, finely diced

½ red cabbage, shredded

mixed salad leaves, including Little Gem (Bibb) lettuce and lollo bionda

10ml/2 tsp pine nuts

salad dressing

1 Poach the quail's eggs. You need a shallow pan of simmering water with a dash of vinegar added, an eggcup, a slotted spoon, a pan of iced water. Using a thin knife, carefully break the shell of an egg and open it up into the eggcup. Gently lower the cup into the simmering water, allowing some water to cover and firm up the egg, then let it slide into the water and cook for about 2 minutes. The white should change from opaque to just white. Lift the egg out with a slotted spoon and put it straight into iced water.

2 When all the eggs are cooked lift them out of the water and dry them on kitchen paper. This last bit can be done just before you assemble the salad since the quail's eggs will keep in cold water for up to a couple of days.

3 Combine the salad ingredients, including the pine nuts (which can be lightly toasted if you like). Toss with your chosen dressing. To serve, simply place the diced Bishop Kennedy and the quail's eggs on top of the salad.

Per portion Energy 231kcal/956kJ; Protein 11.7g; Carbohydrate 5.3g, of which sugars 4.8g; Fat 17.7g, of which saturates 5.6g; Cholesterol 132mg; Calcium 203mg; Fibre 2.3g; Sodium 183mg.

Desserts

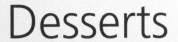

The Scots are well known for their sweet tooth, and there are plenty of delicious traditional desserts to choose from. A recurring theme is fresh berries – especially raspberries – baked in tarts, crumbles and pies or blended with creams and other dairy products. These tasty morsels are available to all to pick wild from the woodlands and hedgerows. The creams and yogurts are a speciality of the Lowlands, although throughout much of Scotland many households would have made their own.

Cranachan

This lovely, nutritious dish is based on a traditional Scottish recipe originally made to celebrate the Harvest Festival. It can be enjoyed, as the original recipe was, as a teatime treat or a dessert, but it is also excellent served for breakfast or brunch. Try fresh blueberries or blackberries in place of the raspberries, too.

Serves 4

75g/3oz crunchy oat cereal

600ml/1 pint/2½ cups Greek (US strained plain) yogurt

250g/9oz/1⅓ cups raspberries

heather honey, to serve

1 Preheat the grill (broiler) to high. Spread the oat cereal on a baking sheet and place under the hot grill for 3–4 minutes, stirring regularly. Set aside on a plate to cool.

2 When the cereal has cooled completely, fold it into the Greek yogurt, then gently fold in 200g/7oz/generous 1 cup of the raspberries, being careful not to crush them.

3 Spoon the yogurt mixture into four serving glasses or dishes, top with the remaining raspberries and serve immediately. Pass around a dish of heather honey to drizzle over the top for extra sweetness and flavour.

Variations
• You can use almost any berries for this recipe. Strawberries and blackberries work very well. If you use strawberries, remove the stalks and cut them into quarters beforehand.
• If you feel especially decadent, you can use clotted cream instead of yogurt.

Per portion Energy 276kcal/1152kJ; Protein 12.4g; Carbohydrate 17.2g, of which sugars 11.1g; Fat 19.7g, of which saturates 8.7g; Cholesterol 0mg; Calcium 255mg; Fibre 2.5g; Sodium 122mg.

Iced cranachan

Here is a twist on the original cranachan idea, where it is made into an ice cream with an oatmeal praline treatment for a luxurious dessert. It is delicious scattered with chocolate shavings and served with a fine Scottish shortbread.

Serves 4

115g/4oz/generous ½ cup caster (superfine) sugar

30ml/2 tbsp water

115g/4oz/1 cup pinhead oatmeal

6 egg whites

250g/9oz/1¼ cups caster (superfine) sugar

200ml/7fl oz/scant 1 cup double (heavy) cream

300ml/½ pint/1¼ cups single (light) cream

Fresh raspberries, to garnish

1 Place the sugar and water in a pan and bring to the boil. When the mixture begins to turn golden brown stir in the oatmeal thoroughly and pour on to an oiled tray. When cool, crush into small pieces using a small rolling pin or a mortar and pestle. The oatmeal praline will keep refrigerated in an airtight jar for a week or more.

2 For the mousse, whisk the egg whites and sugar in a bowl over a pan of hot water until the sugar dissolves. Remove from the heat and whisk until cold, preferably using an electric whisk. Mix the creams together then whisk until they thicken slightly. Fold into the egg mixture and add the praline.

3 Pour into a loaf tin (pan) lined with clear film (plastic wrap), and freeze overnight.

4 To serve, turn out of the tin and peel off the clear film. Using a knife dipped in hot water, cut into slices. Garnish with fresh raspberries.

Per portion Energy 855kcal/3588kJ; Protein 11.1g; Carbohydrate 112.2g, of which sugars 94g; Fat 43.4g, of which saturates 25.8g; Cholesterol 110mg; Calcium 154mg; Fibre 1.7g; Sodium 138mg.

Rhubarb fool

Here is a quick and simple dessert that makes the most of field-grown rhubarb when it is in season. You could use hothouse rhubarb, but the flavour is inferior. Serve with Scottish shortbread and pass around a dish of heather honey for those with a sweet tooth.

1 Cut the rhubarb into pieces and wash thoroughly. Stew over a low heat with just the water clinging to it and the sugar. This takes about 10 minutes. Set aside to cool.

2 Pass the rhubarb through a fine sieve so you have a thick purée.

Serves 4

450g/1lb rhubarb, trimmed

75g/3oz/scant ½ cup soft light brown sugar

whipped double (heavy) cream and ready-made thick custard (see Step 3)

Variations
• You can use another fruit if you like for this dessert – try bramble fruits or apples. Other stewed fruits also work well, such as prunes or peaches. For something a little more exotic, you can use mangoes.
• For a low-fat option, substitute natural (plain) yogurt for the cream.

3 Use equal parts of the purée, the whipped double cream and thick custard. Combine the purée and custard first then fold in the cream. Chill in the refrigerator before serving. Serve with heather honey.

Per portion Energy 439kcal/1828kJ; Protein 4.6g; Carbohydrate 34.1g, of which sugars 31.8g; Fat 31.7g, of which saturates 18.9g; Cholesterol 80mg; Calcium 233mg; Fibre 1.6g; Sodium 74mg.

Strawberry cream shortbreads

These pretty treats are always popular, especially served with afternoon tea or as a quick and easy dessert. Serve them as soon as they are ready because the shortbread cookies will lose their lovely crisp texture if left to stand.

Serves 3

150g/5oz/1¼ cups strawberries

450ml/¾ pint/scant 2 cups double (heavy) cream

6 round shortbread biscuits (cookies)

1 Reserve three attractive strawberries for decoration. Hull the remaining strawberries and cut them in half, discarding any bad parts.

2 Put the halved strawberries in a bowl and gently crush them using the back of a fork. Only crush the berries lightly; they should not be reduced to a purée. A few larger chunks should still be left whole to add to the texture.

3 Put the cream in a large, clean bowl and whip until softly peaking. Add the crushed strawberries and gently fold in to combine. (Do not overmix.)

4 Halve the reserved strawberries – you can choose whether to leave the stalks intact or to remove them.

5 Spoon the strawberry and cream mixture on top of the shortbread cookies. Decorate each one with half a strawberry and serve immediately.

Variations
• You can use any other berry you like for this dessert – try raspberries or blueberries.
• Two ripe, peeled peaches will also give great results.
• Instead of shortbread, you can use freshly baked scones.

Per portion Energy 976kcal/4035kJ; Protein 5.7g; Carbohydrate 34.6g, of which sugars 16.8g; Fat 90.8g, of which saturates 50.1g; Cholesterol 206mg; Calcium 122mg; Fibre 1.3g; Sodium 204mg.

Summer pudding

This traditional pudding is wonderfully easy to make, traditionally made with leftover breads and bannocks and a few handfuls of garden and hedgerow berries.

Serves 4–6

8 x 1cm/½in thick slices of day-old white bread, crusts removed

800g/1¾lb/6–7 cups mixed berries, such as strawberries, raspberries, blackcurrants, redcurrants and blueberries

50g/2oz/¼ cup golden caster (superfine) sugar

lightly whipped double (heavy) cream or crème fraîche, to serve

1 Trim a slice of bread to fit in the base of a 1.2 litre/2 pint/5 cup bowl, then trim another 5–6 slices to line the sides of the bowl, making sure the bread comes up above the rim.

2 Place all the fruit in a pan with the sugar. Do not add any water. Cook gently for 4–5 minutes until the juices begin to run.

3 Allow the mixture to cool then spoon the berries, and enough of their juices to moisten, into the bread-lined bowl. Reserve any remaining juice to serve with the pudding.

4 Fold over the excess bread from the side of the bowl, then cover the fruit with the remaining bread, trimming to fit. Place a small plate or saucer that fits inside the bowl directly on top of the pudding. Weight it down with a 900g/2lb weight, if you have one, or use a couple of full cans.

5 Chill the pudding in the refrigerator for at least 8 hours or overnight. To serve, run a knife between the pudding and the bowl and turn out on to a serving plate. Spoon any reserved juices over the top.

Per portion Energy 230kcal/977kJ; Protein 6.2g; Carbohydrate 51.7g, of which sugars 26.5g; Fat 1.2g, of which saturates 0g; Cholesterol 0mg; Calcium 98mg; Fibre 3g; Sodium 294mg.

Dunfillan bramble pudding

This warming pudding comes from Dunfillan in Perthshire. It is easy to make, if you have a
little time, and is perfect with fresh cream as a tasty dessert or teatime indulgence.

Serves 4

For the Dunfillan pastry

50g/2oz/¼ cup butter

50g/2oz/¼ cup caster
(superfine) sugar

1 large egg, well beaten

115g/4oz/1 cup plain (all-purpose)
flour, sifted

pinch of baking powder

30ml/2 tbsp milk

grated rind of 2 lemons

For the filling

450g/1lb/4 cups blackberries

75g/3oz/scant ½ cup caster
(superfine) sugar

squeeze of lemon juice

sprinkling of cornflour (cornstarch)

1 Preheat the oven to 180°C/350°F/
Gas 4. Put the blackberries in a pan and
barely cover with water, then add the
sugar and lemon juice. Cook until soft,
about 5 minutes.

2 Transfer the blackberries to an
ovenproof dish in layers, sprinkling each
layer with a little cornflour.

3 To make the pastry, cream the butter
and sugar then add the beaten egg.
Mix the flour and baking powder then
add it alternately with the milk to the
butter mixture, mixing well after each
addition. Finally stir in the lemon rind.

4 Spread the pastry evenly over the
fruit, taking small batches from the
bowl and spreading carefully. Cook
in the preheated oven for 20–
30 minutes, or until the top is
golden brown. Serve hot or cold.

Per portion Energy 366kcal/1539kJ; Protein 6.2g; Carbohydrate 60.2g, of which sugars 39.2g; Fat 12.8g, of which saturates 7.2g; Cholesterol 90mg; Calcium 122mg; Fibre 4.4g; Sodium 107mg.

Rhubarb frushie

A frushie is the old Scots word for a crumble. In this instance the topping is made with coarse rolled oats. Other fruits, such as apple, apple and blackberry combined, or gooseberries, can be used according to preference and availability.

Serves 4

450g/1lb rhubarb or other fruit

50g/2oz/¼ cup caster (superfine) sugar or 30ml/2 tbsp redcurrant jelly

45–60ml/3–4 tbsp water

squeeze of lemon juice

For the crumble

50g/2oz/½ cup plain (all-purpose) flour

25g/1oz/scant ⅓ cup coarse rolled oats

50g/2oz/¼ cup soft light brown sugar

50g/2oz/¼ cup butter, softened

1 Preheat the oven to 200°C/400°F/ Gas 6. Cook the rhubarb or other fruit with the sugar or redcurrant jelly, water and lemon juice until soft but not mushy. Transfer to a deep pie dish.

2 Combine all the ingredients for the crumble with your fingers until the mixture has a crumb-like texture.

3 Sprinkle the crumble topping evenly over the fruit.

4 Bake at the top of the preheated oven for 20 minutes, or until the top is crunchy and slightly brown. Serve immediately with hot custard, fresh whipped cream or vanilla ice cream, if you like.

Per portion Energy 267kcal/1126kJ; Protein 3.2g; Carbohydrate 41.4g, of which sugars 27.3g; Fat 11.1g, of which saturates 6.5g; Cholesterol 27mg; Calcium 141mg; Fibre 2.4g; Sodium 83mg.

Plum crumble

The crumble is a perennially popular dessert. Plums can be divided into three categories – dessert, dual and cooking. Choose whichever dual or cooking plum is available locally, although Victoria plums would commonly be used in Scotland.

Serves 4

450g/1lb stoned (pitted) plums

50g/2oz/¼ cup soft light brown sugar

15ml/1 tbsp water

juice of 1 lemon

For the crumble topping

50g/2oz/½ cup plain (all-purpose) flour

25g/1oz/generous ¼ cup coarse rolled oats

50g/2oz/¼ cup soft light brown sugar

50g/2oz/¼ cup butter, softened

1 Preheat the oven to 200°C/400°F/ Gas 6. Place a large pan over a medium heat. Put the plums in the pan and add the sugar, water and lemon juice. Mix thoroughly and bring to the boil, stirring continuously until the sugar dissolves. Cook the plums until they are just beginning to soften. Place the fruit with the juices in a deep pie dish.

2 Place the crumble ingredients in a bowl and mix with your fingers until the mixture resembles breadcrumbs.

3 Sprinkle the crumble topping evenly over the fruit so that it is a good thickness. Bake in the preheated oven for 20 minutes, or until the top is crunchy and brown.

Per portion Energy 304kcal/1284kJ; Protein 2.9g; Carbohydrate 51.5g, of which sugars 37.4g; Fat 11.1g, of which saturates 6.5g; Cholesterol 27mg; Calcium 53mg; Fibre 2.8g; Sodium 82mg.

Scone and fresh fruit pudding

This luscious dessert incorporates good Scottish ingredients – sweet, juicy strawberries and raspberries in season, cream crowdie (a curd cheese) and a scone topping. Served with fresh cream or custard, it is perfect to finish a dinner party or hearty Sunday lunch.

3 Dot spoonfuls of the crowdie over the fruit. If you can't get crowdie, use a good thick Greek (US strained plain) yogurt instead.

4 Place a scoop of the scone dough on top of each spoon of crowdie. Bake for about 20 minutes. The crowdie or yogurt should be oozing out of the scone topping. Serve immediately, and pass around a dish of crowdie (or yogurt) for those who want more.

Serves 4

450g/1lb/4 cups strawberries

250g/9oz/1½ cups raspberries

50g/2oz/¼ cup soft light brown sugar

For the scone topping

175g/6oz/1½ cups self-raising (self-rising) flour

5ml/1 tsp baking powder

50g/2oz/¼ cup soft light brown sugar

grated rind of 1 lemon

50g/2oz/¼ cup butter, melted

1 egg, beaten

250g/9oz cream crowdie

1 Preheat the oven to 220°C/425°F/ Gas 7. Gently mix the fruit with the sugar then place in a bowl in an ovenproof dish.

2 For the scone topping, combine the flour, baking powder and sugar in a bowl with the grated lemon rind then add the melted butter and beaten egg and mix thoroughly.

Variations

• Many other fruits can be used for this wonderful and easy dessert. If you prefer, try orchard fruits such as apples, pears, apricots and peaches. Plums work particularly well, and the flavour can be enhanced with the juice of an orange or lemon.

• If you prefer, you can prepare the recipe without the crowdie (or yogurt) baked into the pie. Serve it on the side, or use custard or thick cream instead.

Per portion Energy 474kcal/1996kJ; Protein 11.6g; Carbohydrate 70.2g, of which sugars 37.7g; Fat 19g, of which saturates 10.4g; Cholesterol 79mg; Calcium 304mg; Fibre 4.2g; Sodium 307mg.

Scone and butter pudding

The word scone originated in 16th-century Scotland. Scones are extremely easy to make but when you're short of time you can usually buy them from a bakery. Another good Scottish ingredient in this dessert is, of course, the whisky.

Serves 4

50g/2oz/scant ½ cup sultanas (golden raisins)

50g/2oz/¼ cup dried apricots, cut into small pieces

50ml/2fl oz/¼ cup whisky

300ml/½ pint/1¼ cups milk

300ml/½ pint/1¼ cups double (heavy) cream

5 egg yolks

50g/2oz/¼ cup caster (superfine) sugar

2 drops vanilla extract

6 scones

75g/3oz/6 tbsp butter

60ml/4 tbsp apricot jam, warmed

1 Place the dried fruit and whisky in a small bowl, cover and leave to soak overnight or for at least 2 hours. Preheat the oven to 200°C/400°F/Gas 6.

Cook's Tip
A bain-marie is a water bath used for cooking delicate dishes, such as custards. Place the ramekin dishes in a large, shallow pan of hot water before putting in the oven.

2 Whisk the milk, cream, egg yolks, sugar and vanilla extract. Slice the tops off the scones and then slice each into three rounds. Butter each round and then layer with the fruit and custard in buttered ramekins. Set aside for 1 hour.

3 Bake in a bain-marie (see Cook's Tip) in the preheated oven for 40 minutes until risen slightly and golden-brown in colour.

4 Remove from the oven and brush with the warmed apricot jam. Serve immediately in the ramekins, or carefully pass a small sharp knife around the inside of each and gently ease the puddings out into bowls or on to individual plates.

Variation
If you prefer, you can use Drambuie or brandy in place of the whisky.

Per portion Energy 796kcal/3305kJ; Protein 8.1g; Carbohydrate 43.2g, of which sugars 43.2g; Fat 63.9g, of which saturates 37.6g; Cholesterol 399mg; Calcium 178mg; Fibre 0.5g; Sodium 187mg.

Clootie dumpling

A rich, dense pudding, traditionally made in a "cloot", a cloth, then boiled in water over the fire. Clootie dumplings are traditionally made for the festive season.

Serves 8

225g/8oz/2 cups plain (all-purpose) flour, plus 15ml/1 tbsp for the cloot

115g/4oz/scant 1 cup suet (US chilled, grated shortening)

115g/4oz/generous 1 cup rolled oats

75g/3oz/scant ½ cup caster (superfine) sugar

5ml/1 tsp baking powder

225g/8oz/generous 1½ cups mixed sultanas (golden raisins) and currants

5ml/1 tsp each ground cinnamon and ground ginger

15ml/1 tbsp golden (light corn) syrup

2 eggs, lightly beaten

45–60ml/3–4 tbsp milk

1 Sift the flour into a dry bowl then add the suet to the flour. Using your fingertips, rub the fat into the flour until it is the texture of breadcrumbs. Add the rolled oats, sugar, baking powder, fruit and spices. Mix in well then add the syrup and eggs. Stir thoroughly, using enough milk to form a firm batter.

If using an ovenproof bowl

2 Lightly grease the inside of the bowl and put the mixture in, allowing at least 2.5cm/1in space at the top. Cover with baking parchment and tie down well.

3 Put an inverted plate or saucer in the base of a deep pan, place the dumpling on top and cover with boiling water. Cook for 2½–3 hours over a low heat.

If using a cloot

2 The cloot – or cloth – should be either cotton or linen, about 52cm/21in square. Plunge it into boiling water, remove it carefully from the pan, wring it out and lay it out on a flat surface.

3 Sprinkle 15ml/1 tbsp flour evenly over the cloot. Place the pudding mixture in the middle of the floured cloth then bring each of the four corners into the middle above the mixture and tie them up with a piece of strong, clean string, leaving plenty of space for the pudding to expand.

4 Either place in a bain-marie (a roasting pan filled with water and placed in the oven) or steam over a double boiler. Cook over a low heat for 2½–3 hours.

5 When the dumpling is cooked, turn out on to a large warmed plate. Serve in slices with hot jam and cream. It can also be eaten cold and will keep in an airtight container for a month.

Per portion Energy 902kcal/3798kJ; Protein 15.1g; Carbohydrate 143.3g, of which sugars 69.2g; Fat 35g, of which saturates 16.6g; Cholesterol 121mg; Calcium 183mg; Fibre 5.5g; Sodium 81mg.

Border tart

The Borders are particularly associated with sweet tarts that make tasty mid-morning snacks, as well as satisfying desserts. This one is delicious served hot or cold with cream.

Serves 4

250g/9oz sweet pastry (see Auld Alliance Apple Tart)

1 egg

75g/3oz/scant ½ cup soft light brown sugar

50g/2oz/¼ cup butter, melted

10ml/2 tsp white wine vinegar

115g/4oz/½ cup currants

25g/1oz/¼ cup chopped walnuts

double (heavy) cream, to serve (optional)

1 Line a 20cm/8in flan tin (tart pan) with sweet pastry. Preheat the oven to 190°C/375°F/Gas 5. Mix the egg, sugar and melted butter together.

2 Stir the vinegar, currants and walnuts into the egg mixture.

3 Pour the mixture into the pastry case and bake in the preheated oven for 30 minutes. Remove from the oven when thoroughly cooked, take out of the flan tin and leave to cool on a wire rack for at least 30 minutes. Serve on its own or with a dollop of fresh cream.

Per portion Energy 312kcal/1307kJ; Protein 3.4g; Carbohydrate 41.1g, of which sugars 41g; Fat 16.1g, of which saturates 7.3g; Cholesterol 74mg; Calcium 54mg; Fibre 0.8g; Sodium 99mg.

Raspberry and almond tart

Raspberries grow best in a cool, damp climate, making them a natural choice for Scottish gardeners. Juicy ripe raspberries and almonds go very well together. This is a rich tart, ideal for serving at the end of a special lunch or at a dinner party.

Serves 4

200g/7oz sweet pastry (see Auld Alliance Apple Tart)

2 large (US extra large) eggs

75ml/2½fl oz/⅓ cup double (heavy) cream

50g/2oz/¼ cup caster (superfine) sugar

50g/2oz/½ cup ground almonds

20g/¾oz/4 tsp butter

350g/12oz/2 cups raspberries

1 Line a 20cm/8in flan tin (tart pan) with the pastry. Prick the base all over and leave to rest for at least 30 minutes. Preheat the oven to 200°C/400°F/Gas 6.

2 Put the eggs, cream, sugar and ground almonds in a bowl and whisk together briskly. Melt the butter and pour into the mixture, stirring to combine thoroughly.

3 Sprinkle the raspberries evenly over the pastry case. The ones at the top will appear through the surface, so keep them evenly spaced. You can also create a pattern with them.

4 Pour the egg and almond mixture over the top. Once again ensure that it is spread evenly throughout the tart.

5 Bake in the preheated oven for 25 minutes. Serve warm or cold.

Variation
Peaches make a very attractive and tasty tart. Use 6 large, ripe peaches and remove the skin and stone (pit). Cut into slices and use in the same way as the raspberries above.

Per portion Energy 548kcal/2284kJ; Protein 10.9g; Carbohydrate 41.7g, of which sugars 18.4g; Fat 38.8g, of which saturates 14.8g; Cholesterol 158mg; Calcium 128mg; Fibre 4.1g; Sodium 282mg.

Auld alliance apple tart

The Auld Alliance is a friendship that has existed between France and Scotland for some
600 years and as well as sharing friendship the two countries have also shared ideas on
food. This is a classic French pudding that has been adapted by the Scots.

Serves 4

200g/7oz/1¾ sticks butter

200g/7oz/1 cup caster
(superfine) sugar

6 large eating apples

For the sweet pastry

150g/5oz/10 tbsp butter

50g/2oz/¼ cup caster
(superfine) sugar

225g/8oz/2 cups plain
(all-purpose) flour

1 egg

1 Make the sweet pastry. Cream the
butter with the caster sugar together in
a food processor. Add the plain flour
and egg. Mix until just combined, being
careful not to overprocess. Leave in a
cool place for an hour before use.

2 Preheat the oven to 200°C/400°F/
Gas 6. Make the filling. Cut the butter
into small pieces. Using a shallow,
30cm/12in ovenproof frying pan, heat
the sugar and butter and allow to
caramelize over a low heat, stirring
gently continuously. This will take
about 10 minutes.

3 Meanwhile peel and core the apples
then cut them into eighths. When the
butter and sugar are caramelized, place
the apples in the pan in a circular fan,
one layer around the outside then one
in the centre. The pan should be full.
Reduce the heat and cook the apples
for 5 minutes then remove from heat.

4 Roll out the pastry to a circle big
enough to fit the pan completely with
generous edgings.

5 Spread the pastry over the fruit and
tuck in the edges. Bake in the oven for
about 30 minutes, or until the pastry is
browned and set.

6 When cooked remove the tart from
the oven and leave to rest. When ready
to serve, gently reheat on the stove for
a few minutes then invert on to a
warmed serving plate, with the pastry
on the base and the apples caramelized
on the top.

Per portion Energy 904kcal/3774kJ; Protein 4.6g; Carbohydrate 95.2g, of which sugars 66.5g; Fat 58.8g, of which saturates 31.5g; Cholesterol 116mg; Calcium 95mg; Fibre 3.6g; Sodium 559mg.

Walnut and honey tart

Some of the best honey in the world comes from Scotland. Especially delicious is the heather honey made by bees that feed on wild heather, which is often found growing on the well-managed grouse moors. Serve this tart with plenty of whipped cream.

Serves 4

90g/3½oz sweet pastry (see Auld Alliance Apple Tart)

6 sugar cubes

200g/7oz/1¾ cups walnuts

75ml/5 tbsp good honey

45ml/3 tbsp double (heavy) cream

1 Preheat the oven to 200°C/400°F/ Gas 6. Roll the pastry out to a disc measuring about 25cm/10in across and allow to rest for 15 minutes. Place on a baking sheet then bake in the preheated oven for about 15 minutes.

2 Put the sugar and 60ml/4 tbsp water in a pan and heat until it caramelizes, stirring continuously. Add the walnuts and coat with caramel, toasting them lightly in the pan for a few minutes. Remove from the heat and allow to cool slightly.

3 Add the honey and cream, mixing thoroughly until the mixture has cooled completely.

4 Spread the walnut mixture over the pastry disc and rest for 10 minutes before serving.

Per portion Energy 563kcal/2338kJ; Protein 9.1g; Carbohydrate 35.9g, of which sugars 30.8g; Fat 43.5g, of which saturates 6.6g; Cholesterol 15mg; Calcium 70mg; Fibre 2g; Sodium 67mg.

Blackcurrant tart

Blackcurrants grow in the wild, are cultivated throughout Europe, and are widely available in North America. This tart makes the most of these exquisite summer fruits, and is quick and easy to prepare using ready-made puff pastry. Serve with whipped cream.

Serves 4

500g/1¼lb/5 cups blackcurrants

115g/4oz/generous ½ cup caster (superfine) sugar

250g/9oz ready-made puff pastry

50g/2oz/½ cup icing (confectioners') sugar

whipped cream, to serve

1 Preheat the oven to 220°C/425°F/ Gas 7. Trim the blackcurrants, making sure you remove all the stalks and any hard parts in the middle. Add the caster sugar and mix well.

2 Roll out the pastry to about 3mm/ ⅛in thick and cut out four discs roughly the size of a side plate or a large cereal bowl. Then using a smaller plate (or bowl) lightly mark with the point of a knife a circle about 2cm/¾in inside each disc.

3 Spread the blackcurrants over the discs, keeping them within the marked inner circle. Bake in the oven for 15 minutes. Dust generously with the icing sugar before serving. Serve hot with a large dollop of whipped cream, or serve cold as a teatime snack.

Per portion Energy 426kcal/1798kJ; Protein 4.9g; Carbohydrate 73.2g, of which sugars 50.9g; Fat 15.3g, of which saturates 0g; Cholesterol 0mg; Calcium 133mg; Fibre 4.5g; Sodium 200mg.

Whisky mac cream

The warming tipple whisky mac is a combination of whisky and ginger wine. This recipe turns the drink into a rich, smooth, creamy dessert – very decadent.

Serves 4

4 egg yolks

15ml/1 tbsp caster (superfine) sugar, plus 50g/2oz/¼ cup

600ml/1 pint/2½ cups double (heavy) cream

15ml/1 tbsp whisky

green ginger wine, to serve

1 Whisk the egg yolks thoroughly with the first, smaller amount of caster sugar. Whisk briskly until they are light and pale.

2 Pour the cream into a pan with the whisky and the rest of the caster sugar. Bring to scalding point but do not boil, then pour on to the egg yolks, whisking continually. Return to the pan and, over a low heat, stir until the custard thickens slightly.

3 Pour into individual ramekin dishes, cover each with clear film (plastic wrap) and leave overnight to set.

4 To serve, pour just enough green ginger wine over the top of each ramekin to cover the cream.

Per portion Energy 892kcal/3682kJ; Protein 5.4g; Carbohydrate 19.7g, of which sugars 19.7g; Fat 86.1g, of which saturates 51.7g; Cholesterol 407mg; Calcium 107mg; Fibre 0g; Sodium 44mg.

Malt whisky truffles

Malt whisky has long been used to flavour Scottish dishes. Here is a new speciality, blending rich chocolate with cool cream and potent whisky for a mouthwatering end to any meal.

Makes 25–30

200g/7oz dark (bittersweet) chocolate, chopped into small pieces

150ml/¼ pint/⅔ cup double (heavy) cream

45ml/3 tbsp malt whisky

115g/4oz/1 cup icing (confectioners') sugar

cocoa powder, for coating

1 Melt the chocolate in a heatproof bowl over a pan of simmering water, stirring continuously until smooth. Allow to cool slightly.

2 Using a wire whisk, whip the cream with the whisky in a bowl until thick enough to hold its shape.

Variation
You can also make Drambuie truffles by using Drambuie instead of whisky.

3 Stir in the melted chocolate and icing sugar and leave until firm enough to handle. Dust your hands with cocoa powder and shape the mixture into bite-sized balls. Coat in cocoa powder and pack into pretty cases or boxes. Store in the refrigerator for 3–4 days.

Per portion Energy 93kcal/387kJ; Protein 0.5g; Carbohydrate 10g, of which sugars 9.9g; Fat 5.5g, of which saturates 3.3g; Cholesterol 9mg; Calcium 8mg; Fibre 0.2g; Sodium 2mg.

Breads and baking

Teatime in Scotland is the occasion for a great spread of breads, sandwiches with jams and jellies, and the inevitable sweets and cakes. There is a great Scottish tradition of cake making, partly a result of the French influences from the Auld Alliance, and partly due to the large quantities of sugar imported into Glasgow from the Caribbean. Dried fruit and nuts are favourite ingredients for cakes, including the famous moist Dundee cake with almonds baked decoratively around the top.

Traditional bannock

This is a great all-purpose bread that makes an excellent breakfast with fresh butter and jams and jellies, a light lunch eaten with cheese and ham, a teatime staple toasted with butter and heather honey, or an accompaniment for dunking into thick soups and stews. The raisins add a slight sweetness with every other bite.

Makes 2 loaves

175g/6oz/generous ¾ cup soft light brown sugar

450ml/¾ pint/scant 2 cups milk

25g/1oz fresh yeast or 10ml/ 2 tsp dried

1kg/2¼lb/9 cups strong white bread flour

pinch of salt

115g/4oz/½ cup butter

115g/4oz/½ cup lard or white cooking fat

450g/1lb/generous 3 cups raisins

1 Preheat the oven to 220°C/425°F/ Gas 7. Dissolve 10ml/2 tsp of the sugar in a little of the milk for the glaze.

2 Warm a little milk, add the yeast with 5ml/1 tsp of sugar, mix to dissolve the sugar and yeast then leave to activate.

3 Put the flour with the salt in a warm place. Melt the butter and lard or white cooking fat with the remaining milk and keep warm. Mix the yeast mixture with the flour then add the milk and fat mixture. Mix together until a stiff dough forms. Knead for a few minutes, cover with a clean dish towel and leave in a warm place until it doubles in size.

4 Knock back (punch down) the dough then knead in the raisins and the remaining sugar. Shape into two rounds. Place on an oiled baking sheet, cover with a clean dish towel and leave to rise again in a warm place, until about twice the size.

5 Bake in the preheated oven for 10 minutes, then reduce the heat to 190°C/375°F/Gas 5 for about 30 minutes. Fifteen minutes before they are cooked, glaze the bannocks with the reserved milk and sugar mixture.

Per portion Energy 1924kcal/8114kJ; Protein 30.6g; Carbohydrate 330.5g, of which sugars 140g; Fat 62.5g, of which saturates 30.7g; Cholesterol 103mg; Calcium 584mg; Fibre 10g; Sodium 322mg.

Bere bannocks

Beremeal is a northern barley that grows well on Orkney, and you can still buy bannocks there made from it. If you can't get beremeal, ordinary barley flour will do instead. Bannocks were traditionally made on a girdle – a griddle – but baking them in the oven works very well. They make an excellent accompaniment to cheese.

Serves 6

225g/8oz/2 cups beremeal flour

50g/2oz/½ cup plain (all-purpose) flour

5ml/1 tsp cream of tartar

2.5ml/½ tsp salt

5ml/1 tsp bicarbonate of soda (baking soda)

250ml/8fl oz/1 cup buttermilk or natural (plain) yogurt

1 Preheat the oven to 180°C/350°F/ Gas 4. Mix the beremeal flour, plain flour, cream of tartar and salt together in a bowl.

2 Mix the bicarbonate of soda with the buttermilk or yogurt then pour this mixture into the dry ingredients. Mix to a soft dough like a scone mix.

Variation
Bere bannocks are delicious if baked with a little cheese on top. Use a harder type of cheese, such as a good mature cheddar or Bishop Kennedy, and grate about 50g/2oz/½ cup over the surface before you put it into the oven to bake. The result is very tasty hot or cold for breakfast or lunch.

3 Turn the dough out on to a floured surface and press down with your hands to make the whole dough about 1cm/½in thick.

4 Cut the dough into six segments and place on an oiled baking sheet. Bake in the oven for about 15 minutes, or until lightly browned.

Per bannock Energy 280kcal/1192kJ; Protein 8.8g; Carbohydrate 61.4g, of which sugars 4.9g; Fat 1.8g, of which saturates 0.4g; Cholesterol 1mg; Calcium 148mg; Fibre 0.4g; Sodium 54mg.

Scottish morning rolls

These rolls are best served warm, as soon as they are baked. In Scotland they are a firm favourite for breakfast with a fried egg and bacon. They also go very well with a pat of fresh butter and homemade jams and jellies.

Makes 10

450g/1lb/4 cups unbleached plain (all-purpose) white flour, plus extra for dusting

10ml/2 tsp salt

20g/¾oz fresh yeast

150ml/¼ pint/⅔ cup lukewarm milk, plus extra for glazing

150ml/¼ pint/⅔ cup lukewarm water

1 Grease two baking sheets. Sift the flour and salt together into a large bowl and make a well in the centre. Mix the yeast with the milk, then mix in the water. Stir to dissolve. Add the yeast mixture to the centre of the flour and mix together to form a soft dough.

2 Knead the dough lightly then cover with lightly oiled clear film (plastic wrap) and leave to rise in a warm place for 1 hour, or until doubled in size. Turn the dough out on to a floured surface and knock back (punch down).

3 Divide the dough into 10 equal pieces. Knead each roll lightly and, using a rolling pin, shape each piece to a flat 10 x 7.5cm/4 x 3in oval or a flat 9cm/3½in round.

4 Transfer the rolls to the prepared baking sheets and cover with oiled clear film. Leave to rise in a warm place for about 30 minutes. Meanwhile, preheat the oven to 200°C/400°F/Gas 6.

5 Remove the clear film – the rolls should have risen slightly. Press each roll in the centre with your three middle fingers to equalize the air bubbles and to help prevent blistering.

6 Brush with milk and dust with flour. Bake for 15–20 minutes, or until lightly browned. As soon as you have taken the rolls out of the oven, dust with more flour and cool slightly on a wire rack. Serve warm.

Per roll Energy 160kcal/682kJ; Protein 4.7g; Carbohydrate 35.7g, of which sugars 1.4g; Fat 0.8g, of which saturates 0.3g; Cholesterol 1mg; Calcium 81mg; Fibre 1.4g; Sodium 401mg.

Oatmeal biscuits

Although not as neat as bought ones, these home-made oatmeal crackers make up in flavour and interest anything they might lose in presentation – and they make the ideal partner for most Scottish cheeses with some fresh fruit to accompany.

Makes about 18

75g/3oz/⅔ cup plain
(all-purpose) flour

2.5ml/½ tsp salt

1.5ml/¼ tsp baking powder

115g/4oz/1 cup fine pinhead
oatmeal, plus extra for sprinkling

65g/2½oz/generous ¼ cup white
vegetable fat (shortening)

1 Preheat the oven to 200°C/400°F/
Gas 6 and grease a baking sheet.

2 Sift the flour, salt and baking powder
into a mixing bowl. Add the oatmeal
and mix well. Rub in the fat to make a
crumbly mixture.

3 Blend in enough water to work the
mxture into a stiff dough.

Cook's Tip
Store the biscuits when absolutely cold
in an airtight container lined with
baking parchment. Check for crispness
before serving; reheat for 4–5 minutes
in a preheated oven at 200°C/400°F/
Gas 6 to crisp up if necessary.

4 Turn on to a worktop sprinkled with
fine oatmeal and knead until smooth
and manageable. Roll out to about
3mm/⅛in thick and cut into rounds,
squares or triangles. Place on the
baking sheet.

5 Bake in the preheated oven for about
15 minutes, until crisp. Cool the biscuits
on a wire rack.

Per biscuit Energy 72kcal/301kJ; Protein 1.2g; Carbohydrate 7.9g, of which sugars 0.1g; Fat 4.2g, of which saturates 1.8g; Cholesterol 3mg; Calcium 9mg; Fibre 0.6g; Sodium 57mg.

Scones with jam and cream

Scones, often known as biscuits in the US, are thought to originate from Scotland where they are still a popular part of afternoon tea with jams, jellies and thick clotted cream.

Makes about 12

450g/1lb/4 cups self-raising (self-rising) flour, or 450g/1lb/4 cups plain (all-purpose) flour and 10ml/2 tsp baking powder

5ml/1 tsp salt

50g/2oz/¼ cup butter, chilled and diced

15ml/1 tbsp lemon juice

about 400ml/14fl oz/1⅔ cups milk, plus extra to glaze

fruit jam and clotted cream or whipped double (heavy) cream, to serve

1 Preheat the oven to 230°C/450°F/ Gas 8. Sift the flour, baking powder, if using, and salt into a clean, dry mixing bowl. Add the diced butter and rub it into the flour with your fingertips until the mixture resembles fine, evenly textured breadcrumbs.

2 Whisk the lemon juice into the milk and leave for about 1 minute to thicken slightly, then pour into the flour mixture and mix quickly to form a soft but pliable dough. The wetter the mixture, the lighter the resulting scone will be, but if they are too wet they will spread during baking and lose their shape.

3 Knead the dough lightly to form a ball, then roll it out on a floured surface to a thickness of at least 2.5cm/1in. Using a 5cm/2in pastry (cookie) cutter, and dipping it into flour each time, stamp out 12 scones. Place them on a well-floured baking sheet. Re-roll any trimmings and cut out more scones if you can.

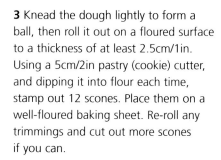

4 Brush the tops of the scones lightly with a little milk then bake in the preheated oven for about 20 minutes, or until risen and golden brown. Remove the baking sheet from the oven and wrap the scones in a clean dish towel to keep them warm and soft until ready to serve. Eat with your favourite fruit jam and a generous dollop of cream.

Variation
To make cheese scones, add 115g/4oz/1 cup of grated cheese (preferably Cheddar or another strong hard cheese) to the dough and knead it in thoroughly before rolling out.

Per scone Energy 170kcal/720kJ; Protein 4.5g; Carbohydrate 29.9g, of which sugars 2.1g; Fat 4.4g, of which saturates 2.6g; Cholesterol 11mg; Calcium 172mg; Fibre 1.2g; Sodium 338mg.

Drop scones

Variously known as girdlecakes, griddlecakes and Scotch pancakes, these make a quick and easy breakfast, elevensies or teatime snacks served with butter and drizzled with honey.

Makes 8–10

115g/4oz/1 cup plain
(all-purpose) flour

5ml/1 tsp bicarbonate of soda
(baking soda)

5ml/1 tsp cream of tartar

25g/1oz/2 tbsp butter, diced

1 egg, beaten

about 150ml/¼ pint/⅔ cup milk

a knob (pat) of butter and heather
honey, to serve

1 Lightly grease a griddle pan or heavy frying pan, then preheat it. Sift the flour, bicarbonate of soda and cream of tartar together into a mixing bowl. Add the diced butter and rub it into the flour with your fingertips until the mixture resembles fine, evenly textured breadcrumbs.

2 Make a well in the centre of the flour mixture, then stir in the egg. Add the milk a little at a time, stirring it in to check consistency. Add enough milk to give a lovely thick creamy consistency.

Cook's Tip
Placing the cooked scones in a clean folded dish towel keeps them soft and moist. Bring to the table like this and ask your guests to pull them out.

3 Cook in batches. Drop 3 or 4 evenly sized spoonfuls of the mixture, spaced slightly apart, on the griddle or frying pan. Cook over a medium heat for 2–3 minutes, until bubbles rise to the surface and burst.

4 Turn the scones over and cook for a further 2–3 minutes, until golden underneath. Place the cooked scones between the folds of a clean dish towel while cooking the remaining batter. Serve warm, with butter and honey.

Per portion Energy 90kcal/379kJ; Protein 2.8g; Carbohydrate 12.1g, of which sugars 1.1g; Fat 3.8g, of which saturates 2.1g; Cholesterol 32mg; Calcium 47mg; Fibre 0.5g; Sodium 36mg.

Black bun

This is a very traditional Scottish sweetmeat, eaten with a nip or two of whisky at the Hogmanay New Year festivities, and often given to visitors on New Year's Day. It is different from most fruit cakes because it is baked in a pastry case. It should be made several weeks in advance to give it time to mature properly.

Makes 1 cake

For the pastry

225g/8oz/2 cups plain (all-purpose) flour

115g/4oz/½ cup butter

5ml/1 tsp baking powder

cold water

For the filling

500g/1¼lb/4 cups raisins

675g/1½lb/3 cups currants

115g/4oz/1 cup chopped almonds

175g/6oz/1½ cups plain (all-purpose) flour

115g/4oz/generous ½ cup soft light brown sugar

5ml/1 tsp ground allspice

2.5ml/½ tsp each ground ginger, ground cinnamon and ground black pepper

2.5ml/½ tsp baking powder

5ml/1 tsp cream of tartar

15ml/1 tbsp brandy

1 egg, beaten, plus extra for glazing

about 75ml/5 tbsp milk

1 First make the pastry. Sift the plain flour into a mixing bowl. Remove the butter from the refrigerator ahead of time and dice it into small cubes. Leave it out of the refrigerator to soften well.

2 Add the cubes of butter to the flour. Rub the butter into the flour with your fingertips until it is the consistency of breadcrumbs. Add the baking powder and mix well. Then add small amounts of cold water, blending it in with a fork, until you can handle the mixture and knead it into a stiff dough.

3 On a floured surface, roll out the dough to a thin sheet. Grease a 20cm/8in loaf tin (pan) and line with the thin sheet of dough. Leave enough to cover the top of the cake.

4 Preheat the oven to 110°C/225°F/ Gas ¼. For the filling, put all the dry ingredients together in a dry warm bowl, including the ground spices and cream of tartar. Mix them together with a spoon until they are thoroughly blended.

5 Stir the brandy and egg into the dry filling mixture and add enough milk to moisten the mixture.

6 Put the filling into the prepared tin and cover with the remaining pastry.

7 Prick all over with a fork and brush with egg. Bake in the preheated oven for about 3 hours. Remove from the oven and leave to cool on a wire rack. Store in an airtight container.

Per cake Energy 1752kcal/7403kJ; Protein 25.8g; Carbohydrate 323.7g, of which sugars 241.9g; Fat 47.4g, of which saturates 18.5g; Cholesterol 115mg; Calcium 496mg; Fibre 11.4g; Sodium 324mg.

Shortbread

The quintessential Scottish snack, shortbread is a great speciality and favourite with the Scots. It is wonderfully satisfying at any time of the day or night.

Makes about 48 fingers

oil, for greasing

275g/10oz/2½ cups plain (all-purpose) flour

25g/1oz/¼ cup ground almonds

225g/8oz/1 cup butter, softened

75g/3oz/scant ½ cup caster (superfine) sugar

grated rind of ½ lemon

1 Preheat the oven to 180°C/350°F/ Gas 4 and oil a large Swiss roll tin (jelly roll pan) or baking tray.

2 Put the remaining ingredients into a blender or food processor and pulse until the mixture comes together.

3 Place the mixture on the oiled tray and flatten it out with a palette knife or metal spatula until evenly spread. Bake in the preheated oven for 20 minutes, or until pale golden brown.

Variation
You can replace the lemon rind with the grated rind of two oranges for a tangy orange flavour, if you prefer.

4 Remove from the oven and immediately mark the shortbread into fingers or squares while the mixture is soft. Allow to cool a little, and then transfer to a wire rack and leave until cold. If stored in an airtight container, the shortbread should keep for up to two weeks.

Cook's Tip
To make by hand, sift the flour and almonds on to a pastry board or work surface. Cream together the butter and sugar in a mixing bowl and then turn the creamed mixture on to the pastry board with the flour and almonds. Work the mixture together using your fingertips. It should come together to make a smooth dough. Continue as above from Step 3.

Per finger Energy 64kcal/266kJ; Protein 0.7g; Carbohydrate 6.1g, of which sugars 1.8g; Fat 4.2g, of which saturates 2.5g; Cholesterol 10mg; Calcium 11mg; Fibre 0.2g; Sodium 29mg.

Dundee cake

A classic Scottish fruit cake, this is made with mixed peel, dried fruit, almonds and spices. It is decorated in the traditional way, covered completely with whole blanched almonds.

Serves 16–20

175g/6oz/¾ cup butter

175g/6oz/¾ cup soft light brown sugar

3 eggs

225g/8oz/2 cups plain (all-purpose) flour

10ml/2 tsp baking powder

5ml/1 tsp ground cinnamon

2.5ml/½ tsp ground cloves

1.5ml/¼ tsp freshly grated nutmeg

225g/8oz/generous 1½ cups sultanas (golden raisins)

175g/6oz/¾ cup glacé (candied) cherries

115g/4oz/⅔ cup mixed chopped (candied) peel

50g/2oz/½ cup blanched almonds, roughly chopped

grated rind of 1 lemon

30ml/2 tbsp brandy

75g/3oz/¾ cup whole blanched almonds, to decorate

1 Preheat the oven to 160°C/325°F/ Gas 3. Grease and line a 20cm/8in round, deep cake tin (pan).

2 Cream the butter and sugar together in a large mixing bowl. Add the eggs, one at a time, beating thoroughly after each addition.

Cook's Tip
All rich fruit cakes improve in flavour if left in a cool place for up to 3 months. Wrap the cake in baking parchment and a double layer of foil.

3 Sift the flour, baking powder and spices together. Fold into the creamed mixture alternately with the remaining ingredients, apart from the whole almonds. Mix until evenly blended. Transfer the mixture to the prepared tin and smooth the surface, making a dip in the centre.

4 Decorate the top by pressing the almonds in decreasing circles over the entire surface. Bake in the preheated oven for 2–2¼ hours, until a skewer inserted in the centre comes out clean.

5 Cool in the tin for 30 minutes then transfer to a wire rack to cool fully.

Per portion Energy 321kcal/1347kJ; Protein 4.7g; Carbohydrate 44.2g, of which sugars 33.3g; Fat 14.7g, of which saturates 6.4g; Cholesterol 59mg; Calcium 76mg; Fibre 1.7g; Sodium 107mg.

Tea loaf

It is always good to have a cake in the home, and fruit cakes are something of a tradition in Scotland. This is a simple fruit cake made by soaking dried fruits in cold tea.

Makes 1 cake

450g/1lb/2⅔ cups mixed dried fruit

250g/9oz/generous 1 cup soft light brown sugar

200ml/7fl oz/scant 1 cup cold tea

400g/1lb/4 cups self-raising (self-rising) flour

5ml/1 tsp mixed (apple pie) spice

1 egg, beaten

1 Mix the dried fruit and sugar together, pour the cold tea over and leave to soak overnight.

2 The next day, preheat the oven to 190°C/375°F/Gas 5. Line a loaf tin (pan) with baking parchment. Add the flour and spice to the soaked fruit, stirring to combine well, then add the beaten egg and mix thoroughly.

3 Put the cake mixture in the prepared loaf tin and bake in the preheated oven for 45–50 minutes. Test with a skewer, which should come out clean. If there is any cake mixture sticking to the skewer, return the cake to the oven for a few more minutes.

Variation
For something a little more special, add 10ml/2 tsp whisky to the tea to give the loaf an aromatic and sumptuous flavour. Add more if you want a really strong flavour – some people replace the tea entirely with whisky blended with a little water.

Per portion Energy 1012kcal/4316kJ; Protein 15.9g; Carbohydrate 245g, of which sugars 152.1g; Fat 3.4g, of which saturates 0.6g; Cholesterol 48mg; Calcium 569mg; Fibre 6.6g; Sodium 531mg.

Glamis walnut and date cake

This is a wonderfully rich and moist cake perfect for afternoon tea. The dates are first soaked before being added to the cake mixture. This gives the cake a lovely texture.

Makes 1 cake

225g/8oz/1⅓ cups chopped dates

250ml/8fl oz/1 cup boiling water

5ml/1 tsp bicarbonate of soda (baking soda)

225g/8oz/generous 1 cup caster (superfine) sugar

1 egg, beaten

275g/10oz/2¼ cups plain (all-purpose) flour

2.5ml/½ tsp salt

75g/3oz/6 tbsp butter, softened

5ml/1 tsp vanilla extract

5ml/1 tsp baking powder

50g/2oz/½ cup chopped walnuts

1 Put the chopped dates into a warm, dry bowl and pour the boiling water over the top; it should just cover the dates. Add the bicarbonate of soda and mix in thoroughly. Leave to stand for 5–10 minutes.

2 Preheat the oven to 180°C/350°F/ Gas 4. Lightly grease a 23 x 30cm/ 9 x 12in cake tin (pan) and line with baking parchment.

3 In a separate mixing bowl, combine all the remaining ingredients for the cake. Then mix in the dates, along with the soaking water until you have a thick batter. You may find it necessary to add a little more boiling water to help the consistency.

4 Pour or spoon the batter into the tin and bake in the oven for 45 minutes. Cut into thick wedges when cool.

Per portion Energy 749kcal/3155kJ; Protein 10.5g; Carbohydrate 125.5g, of which sugars 77.8g; Fat 26.2g, of which saturates 11g; Cholesterol 88mg; Calcium 153mg; Fibre 3.4g; Sodium 141mg.

Preserves, relishes and sauces

Jam and preserve making have been part of the Scottish heritage for thousands of years, mastered so that the flavours and nutrients of summer fruits could be captured for the long winter months. The classic hedgerow and woodland berry jams and jellies are made throughout the country, although orchard fruits are more available in the Lowlands. Sauces and relishes are a popular accompaniment to a snack or basic meal in Scotland, particularly to go with game meats and flavoursome local cheeses.

Bramble jam

Blackberrying is a pleasant recreation and leads to a range of culinary delights too, including this jam. Serve with hot buttered toast, or scones hot from the oven and a dollop of thick clotted cream for a delicious teatime treat.

Makes 3.6kg/8lb

2.75kg/6lb/13¾ cups granulated white sugar

2.75kg/6lb/16 cups blackberries

juice of 2 lemons

150ml/¼ pint/⅔ cup water

Cook's Tip
The heating of the sugar in advance helps speed up the actual jam-making process and gives a brighter, more intense flavour.

1 Put the sugar to warm either in a low oven or in a pan over a low heat.

2 Wash the blackberries and place in a large pan with the lemon juice and water. Bring to the boil and simmer for about 5 minutes.

3 Stir in the sugar and bring back to the boil then boil rapidly. You will know when setting point is achieved as a spoonful of jam put on a plate and allowed to cool slightly will wrinkle when pressed. Ladle into warmed sterilized jam jars and seal immediately.

Per batch Energy 12570kcal/53550kJ; Protein 42g; Carbohydrate 3288g, of which sugars 3288g; Fat 6g, of which saturates 0g; Cholesterol 0mg; Calcium 2820mg; Fibre 93g; Sodium 240mg.

Damson jam

Dark, plump damsons used only to be found growing in the wild, but today they are available commercially. They produce a deeply coloured and richly flavoured jam that makes a delicious treat spread on toasted Scotch pancakes or warm crumpets at teatime.

Makes about 2kg/4½lb

1kg/2¼lb damsons or wild plums

1.4 litres/2¼ pints/6 cups water

1kg/2¼lb/5 cups preserving
or granulated white
sugar, warmed

Cook's Tip
It is important to seal the jars as soon as you have filled them to ensure the jam remains sterile. However, you should then leave the jars to cool completely before labelling and storing them, to avoid the risk of burns.

1 Put the damsons in a preserving pan and pour in the water. Bring to the boil then reduce the heat and simmer gently until the damsons are soft. Add the sugar and stir it in thoroughly. Bring the mixture to the boil.

2 Skim off the stones (pits) as they rise to the surface. Boil to setting point (105°C/220°F). Remove from the heat, leave to cool for 10 minutes, then transfer to warmed sterilized jam jars. Seal immediately.

Per batch Energy 4300kcal/18360kJ; Protein 11g; Carbohydrate 1133g, of which sugars 1133g; Fat 1g, of which saturates 0g; Cholesterol 0mg; Calcium 660mg; Fibre 16g; Sodium 80mg.

Raspberry jam

For many this is the best of all jams: it is delicious with scones and cream. Raspberries are low in pectin and acid, so they will not set firmly – but a soft set is perfect for this jam. Enjoy it lavishly smothered on scones or toasted tealoaf.

Makes about 3.1kg/7lb

1.8kg/4lb/10⅔ cups
firm raspberries

juice of 1 large lemon

1.8kg/4lb/9 cups sugar, warmed

Cook's Tip
To test if jam or jelly will set, put a spoonful of jam or jelly on to a cold saucer. Allow it to cool slightly and then push the surface of the jam with your finger. Setting point has been reached if a skin has formed and it wrinkles. If not, boil for a little longer and keep testing regularly until it sets; the flavour will be better if the boiling time is short.

1 Put 175g/6oz/1 cup of the raspberries into a preserving pan and crush them. Add the rest of the fruit and the lemon juice, and simmer until soft and pulpy. Add the sugar and stir until dissolved, then bring back to the boil and boil hard until setting point is reached, testing after 3–4 minutes.

2 Pour into warmed, sterilized jars. When cold, cover, seal and store in a cool, dark place for up to 6 months.

Variation
For a slightly stronger flavour, 150ml/ ¼ pint/⅔ cup redcurrant juice can be used instead of the lemon juice.

Per batch Energy 7542kcal/32,220kJ; Protein 34.2g; Carbohydrate 1963.8g, of which sugars 1963.8g; Fat 5.4g, of which saturates 1.8g; Cholesterol 0mg; Calcium 1.40g; Fibre 45g; Sodium 162mg

Whisky marmalade

Real home-made marmalade tastes delicious, and flavouring it with whisky makes it a special treat. This is an adaptation of the commercial method, in which marmalade is matured in old whisky barrels and takes the flavour from the wood.

Makes 3.6–4.5kg/8–10lb

1.3kg/3lb Seville oranges

juice of 2 large lemons

2.75kg/6lb/13½ cups sugar, warmed

about 300ml/½ pint/1¼ cups whisky

1 Scrub the oranges thoroughly using a nylon brush and pick off the disc at the stalk end. Cut the oranges in half widthways and squeeze the juice, retaining the pips (seeds). Quarter the peel, cut away and reserve any thick white pith, and shred the peel – thickly or thinly depending on how you prefer the finished marmalade.

2 Cut up the reserved pith roughly and tie it up with the pips in a square of muslin (cheesecloth) using a long piece of string. Tie the bag loosely, so that water can circulate during cooking and will extract the pectin from the pith and pips. Hang the bag from the handle of the preserving pan.

3 Add the cut peel, strained juices and 3.5 litres/6 pints/15 cups water to the pan. Bring to the boil and simmer for 1½–2 hours, or until the peel is very tender (it will not soften further once the sugar has been added).

4 Lift up the bag of pith and pips and squeeze it out well between two plates over the pan to extract as much of the juices as possible as these contain valuable pectin. Add the sugar to the pan and stir over a low heat until it has completely dissolved.

5 Bring to the boil and boil hard for 15–20 minutes or until setting point is reached. To test, allow a spoon of the mixture to cool slightly, and then push the surface to see if a skin has formed. If not, boil a little longer.

6 Skim, if necessary, and leave to cool for about 15 minutes, then stir to redistribute the peel. Divide the whisky among 8–10 warmed, sterilized jars and swill it around. Using a small heatproof jug (pitcher), pour in the marmalade.

7 Cover and seal while still hot. Label when cold, and store in a cool, dark place for up to 6 months.

Per batch Energy 10,736kcal/45,734kJ; Protein 22.8g; Carbohydrate 2657.8g, of which sugars 2657.8g; Fat 1.3g, of which saturates 0g; Cholesterol 0mg; Calcium 1.74g; Fibre 15.6g; Sodium 187mg.

Garden jam

Soft fruit is widely grown in Scottish gardens and, after the first flush of early fruit is over, much of it is used for preserves, such as this useful mixed fruit jam.

Makes about 3.6kg/8lb

450g/1lb/4 cups blackcurrants
(stalks removed)

450g/1lb/4 cups blackberries,
(or whitecurrants or redcurrants)

450g/1lb/2⅔ cups raspberries
(or loganberries)

450g/1lb/4 cups strawberries

1.8kg/4lb/9 cups granulated
sugar, warmed

Cook's Tip
To reduce the risk of mould forming, cover and seal preserves while they are either very hot or when absolutely cold as this prevents condensation.

1 Put the blackcurrants into a large preserving pan and add 150ml/¼ pint/⅔ cup water. Bring to the boil and simmer until the berries are almost cooked. Add the rest of the fruit and simmer gently, stirring occasionally, for about 10 minutes, or until the fruit is just turning soft.

2 Add the warm sugar to the pan and stir over a gentle heat until it is completely dissolved.

3 Bring to the boil and boil hard until setting point is reached. To test, put a spoonful of jam on to a cold saucer. Cool slightly, then push the surface. It is ready if a skin has formed and it wrinkles to the touch. If not, boil for longer and keep testing until it sets.

4 Remove any scum from the jam and pour into sterilized, warm jars. Cover and seal. Store in a cool, dark place for up to 6 months.

Per batch Energy 7583kcal/32,328kJ; Protein 23.9g; Carbohydrate 1991.7g, of which sugars 1991.7g; Fat 1.4g, of which saturates 0g; Cholesterol 0mg; Calcium 1.44g; Fibre 31.1g; Sodium 203mg.

Rowan jelly

This astringent jelly is made from the orange fruit of mountain ash trees, which flourish in areas where deer run wild. It is a traditional accompaniment to game, especially venison.

Makes about 2.25kg/5lb

1.3kg/3lb/12 cups rowanberries

450g/1lb crab apples, or windfall cooking apples

450g/1lb/2¼ cups granulated sugar per 600ml/1 pint/2½ cups juice, warmed

1 Cut the rowanberries off their stalks, rinse them in a colander and put them into a preserving pan.

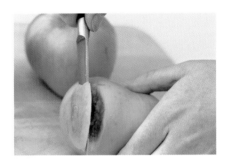

2 Remove any badly damaged parts from the apples before weighing them, then cut them up roughly without peeling or coring them. Add the apples to the pan, with 1.2 litres/2 pints/ 5 cups water, which should just about cover the fruit.

3 Bring to the boil and simmer for about 45 minutes, until the fruit is soft, stirring occasionally and crushing the fruit with a wooden spoon to help extract the pectin. Strain the fruit through a jelly bag or fine sieve into a bowl overnight. Discard the fruit.

4 Measure the juice and allow 450g/1lb/2¼ cups sugar per 600ml/ 1 pint/2½ cups juice. Return the juice to the rinsed preserving pan and add the measured amount of sugar. Stir the mixture thoroughly

5 Stir over a low heat until the sugar has dissolved, and then bring to the boil and boil hard for about 10 minutes until setting point is reached. To test, put a spoonful of jam on to a cold saucer. Allow to cool slightly, and then push the surface with your finger to see if a skin has formed. If not, boil longer.

6 Skim, if necessary, and pour into warmed, sterilized jars. Cover, seal and store in a cool, dark place until needed. The jelly will store well for 6 months.

Variations
• The thinly peeled rind and juice of a lemon can be included for a firmer set; reduce the amount of water slightly to allow for the lemon juice.
• For sloe jelly, substitute 1.3kg/3lb sloes (black plums) for the rowan berries and use 675g/1½lb apples.

Cook's Tip
For a less astringent jelly, an equal quantity of apples and berries may be used, such as 900g/2lb of each.

Per batch Energy 2340kcal/9993kJ; Protein 15.8g; Carbohydrate 606.4g, of which sugars 606.4g; Fat 0.5g, of which saturates 0g; Cholesterol 0mg; Calcium 1.03g; Fibre 54g; Sodium 80mg.

Cranberry and red onion relish

This wine-enriched relish is perfect for serving with hot roast game at a celebratory meal. It is also good served with cold meats or stirred into a beef or game casserole for a touch of sweetness. It can be made several months in advance of any festive season.

Makes about 900g/2lb

450g/1lb small red onions

30ml/2 tbsp olive oil

225g/8oz/generous 1 cup soft light brown sugar

450g/1lb/4 cups cranberries

120ml/4fl oz/½ cup red wine vinegar

120ml/4fl oz/½ cup red wine

15ml/1 tbsp yellow mustard seeds

2.5ml/½ tsp ground ginger

30ml/2 tbsp orange liqueur or port

salt and ground black pepper

1 Halve the red onions and slice them very thinly. Heat the oil in a large pan, add the onions and cook over a very low heat for about 15 minutes, stirring occasionally, until softened. Add 30ml/ 2 tbsp of the sugar and cook for a further 5 minutes, or until the onions are brown and caramelized.

2 Meanwhile, put the cranberries in a pan with the remaining sugar, and add the vinegar, red wine, mustard seeds and ginger. Stir in thoroughly and heat gently, stirring continuously, until the sugar has dissolved, then cover and bring to the boil.

3 Simmer the relish for 12–15 minutes then add the caramelized onions. Stir them into the mixture. Increase the heat slightly and cook uncovered for a further 10 minutes, stirring the mixture frequently, until well reduced and nicely thickened.

4 Remove the pan from the heat then season to taste with salt and ground black pepper. Allow to cool completely in the pan before pouring.

5 Transfer the relish to warmed sterilized jars. Spoon a little of the orange liqueur or port over the top of each, then cover and seal. This relish can be stored for up to 6 months. Store in the refrigerator once opened and use within 1 month.

Variation
Redcurrants make a very good substitute for cranberries in this recipe. They produce a relish with a lovely flavour and pretty colour.

Per batch Energy 1532kcal/6486kJ; Protein 8g; Carbohydrate 314.6g, of which sugars 304.2g; Fat 23.3g, of which saturates 3.1g; Cholesterol 0mg; Calcium 259mg; Fibre 13.5g; Sodium 46mg.

Chunky pear and walnut chutney

This chutney recipe is ideal for using up hard windfall pears. Its mellow flavour is well suited to being brought out after dinner with a lovely selection of strong Scottish cheeses served with freshly made oatcakes or a warm traditional bannock.

Makes about 1.8kg/4lb

1.2kg/2½lb firm pears

225g/8oz cooking apples

225g/8oz onions

450ml/¾ pint/scant 2 cups cider vinegar

175g/6oz/generous 1 cup sultanas (golden raisins)

finely grated rind and juice of 1 orange

400g/14oz/2 cups granulated white sugar

115g/4oz/1 cup walnuts, roughly chopped

2.5ml/½ tsp ground cinnamon

1 Peel and core the fruit, then chop into 2.5cm/1in chunks. Peel and quarter the onions, then chop into pieces the same size as the fruit chunks. Place in a large preserving pan with the vinegar.

2 Slowly bring to the boil, then reduce the heat and simmer for 40 minutes, until the apples, pears and onions are tender, stirring the mixture occasionally.

3 Meanwhile, put the sultanas in a small bowl, pour over the orange juice and leave to soak.

4 Add the orange rind, sultanas and orange juice, and the sugar to the pan. Heat gently, stirring continuously, until the sugar has completely dissolved, then leave to simmer for 30–40 minutes, or until the chutney is thick and no excess liquid remains. Stir frequently towards the end of cooking to prevent the chutney from sticking to the base of the pan.

5 Gently toast the walnuts in a non-stick pan over a low heat for 5 minutes, stirring frequently, until lightly coloured. Stir the nuts into the chutney with the ground cinnamon.

6 Spoon the chutney into warmed sterilized jars, cover and seal. Store in a cool, dark place and leave to mature for at least 1 month. Use within 1 year.

Per batch Energy 3506kcal/14818kJ; Protein 30.9g; Carbohydrate 705.4g, of which sugars 699.5g; Fat 81.4g, of which saturates 6.4g; Cholesterol 0mg; Calcium 634mg; Fibre 40.7g; Sodium 118mg.

Tomato chutney

This spicy and dark, sweet-sour chutney is delicious served with a selection of well-flavoured cheeses and crackers, oatcakes or bread. It is also popular in sandwiches and chunky lunchtime rolls packed with cold roast meats such as ham, turkey, tongue or lamb. Use it also as a condiment or table sauce for meats.

Makes about 1.8kg/4lb

900g/2lb tomatoes, skinned

225g/8oz/1½ cups raisins

225g/8oz onions, chopped

225g/8oz/generous 1 cup caster (superfine) sugar

600ml/1 pint/2½ cups malt vinegar

Variations
• Dried dates may be used in place of the raisins. Stone (pit) and chop them into small pieces. You can also buy stoned cooking dates that have been compressed in a block and these will need chopping finely.
• Red wine vinegar or sherry vinegar may be used in place of the malt vinegar, making a more delicate flavour.

1 Chop the tomatoes roughly and place in a preserving pan. Add the raisins, onions and caster sugar.

2 Pour the vinegar into the pan and bring the mixture to the boil over a medium heat. Reduce the heat and simmer for 2 hours, uncovered, until soft and thickened.

3 Transfer the chutney to warmed sterilized jars. Top with waxed discs to prevent moulds from growing. Use good airtight lids, especially if you mean to store for a long period. Store in a cool, dark place and leave to mature for at least 1 month before use.

Cook's Tip
The chutney will keep unopened for up to 1 year if properly airtight and stored in a cool place. Once the jars have been opened, store in the refrigerator and use within 1 month.

Per batch Energy 1733kcal/7385kJ; Protein 14.9g; Carbohydrate 436.7g, of which sugars 431.6g; Fat 4.1g, of which saturates 0.9g; Cholesterol 0mg; Calcium 342mg; Fibre 16.6g; Sodium 236mg.

Mushroom sauce

This sauce is ideal as an addition to soups and stews and can be added to meat and game sauces for an extra boost of woodland flavour. You can use either wild or cultivated mushrooms for this recipe. Traditionally it would have been made in large quantities when the wild mushrooms were available, and then stored.

Makes 150ml/¼ pint/¾ cup

mushrooms and salt (see Step 1)

For the spice mix

3 garlic cloves, chopped

2 red chillies, seeded and chopped

5ml/1 tsp ground allspice

2.5ml/½ tsp freshly grated nutmeg

2.5ml/½ tsp ground ginger

300ml/½ pint/1¼ cups red wine

1 You will need 15ml/1 tbsp salt for every 450g/1lb mushrooms used. Roughly chop the mushrooms and place in a large ovenproof pan, sprinkling the salt on as you go.

2 Leave, covered in clear film (plastic wrap), for 3 days to exude the juices, giving them a press occasionally.

3 Preheat the oven to 110°C/225°F/ Gas 2. Heat the pan of mushrooms in the oven for 3 hours to get the last of the moisture out.

Cook's Tip
The sauce will keep for a few months unopened. Once opened keep in the refrigerator and use within 1 month.

4 Strain the mushrooms. Measure the quantity of strained mushroom liquid: for every 1 litre/1¾ pints/4 cups of liquid, allow one batch of the spice mix listed in the ingredients including the wine.

5 Add the spices and wine to the mushroom liquid and bring to the boil. Return to the oven for 2–3 hours. Strain the sauce and pour into warmed sterilized jars or bottles. Use as required to flavour sauces and stews.

Per batch Energy 321kcal/1344kJ; Protein 16.5g; Carbohydrate 4.2g, of which sugars 2.4g; Fat 4.5g, of which saturates 0.9g; Cholesterol 0mg; Calcium 75mg; Fibre 9.9g; Sodium 66mg.

Drinks

Whisky is the quintessential Scottish drink, its history going back centuries to a time when it was distilled by clans to enjoy with feasts. Each clan's whisky had a unique flavour, its quality a sign of the clan's prestige and power. Today it is produced in a number of distilleries around the country. Scotland has some delicious drinks using whisky as the base both for everyday enjoyment and also for special occasions.

Sparkling elderflower drink

The elder tree not only produces berries for wine but the fragrant flowers have a very pungent aroma and flavour. Unfortunately the elderflower season is short, just before the berries appear, so take advantage of them while they last.

Makes 9.5 litres/2 gallons/2.4 US gallons

24 elderflower heads

2 lemons

1.3kg/3lb/scant 7 cups granulated white sugar

30ml/2 tbsp white wine vinegar

9 litres/2 gallons/2.4 US gallons water

Cook's Tips
• Collect the elderflowers in full sunshine as this means the flavour will be at its most intense.
• This drink will keep in airtight bottles for a month or so.
• If you can't find elderflowers, or it isn't the right season for them, you can use elderflower cordial, which is available in some health food stores and other specialist outlets.

1 Find a clean bucket that you can cover with a clean cloth. Put all the ingredients into it.

2 Cover the bucket with a plastic sheet and leave overnight.

3 Strain the elderflower drink then pour into bottles, leaving a space of about 2.5cm/1in at the top.

4 Leave sealed for about 2 weeks in a cool place. A fermentation takes place and the result is a delightful, sparkling, refreshing, non-alcoholic drink.

Per batch Energy 1282kcal/5467kJ; Protein 1.7g; Carbohydrate 339.8g, of which sugars 339.8g; Fat 0g, of which saturates 0g; Cholesterol 0mg; Calcium 173mg; Fibre 0g; Sodium 20mg.

Cranachan smoothie

Although a steaming bowl of porridge can't be beaten as a winter warmer, this sumptuous smoothie makes a great, light alternative in warmer months. Just a spoonful or so of oatmeal gives substance to this tangy, invigorating drink.

Makes 1 large glass

25ml/1½ tbsp medium rolled oats

150g/5oz/scant 1 cup raspberries

5–10ml/1–2 tsp clear honey

45ml/3 tbsp natural (plain) yogurt

1 Put the oatmeal in a heatproof bowl. Pour in 120ml/4fl oz/½ cup boiling water and leave to stand in a warm place for about 10 minutes.

2 Put the soaked oats in a food processor or blender and add all but two or three of the raspberries. Reserve the raspberries for decoration.

3 Add the honey and about 30ml/ 2 tbsp of the yogurt to the food processor or blender. Purée the ingredients until smooth, scraping down the side of the bowl halfway through if necessary.

4 Pour the raspberry and oatmeal smoothie into a large glass, swirl in the remaining yogurt and top with the reserved raspberries.

Cook's Tips
• If you don't like raspberry pips (seeds) in your smoothies, press the fruit through a sieve to make a smooth purée, then process with the oatmeal and yogurt as above.
• If you can, prepare it ahead of time because soaking the raw oats helps to break down the starch into natural sugars that are easy to digest. The smoothie will thicken up in the refrigerator so you might need to stir in a little extra juice or mineral water just before serving.

Per portion Energy 186kcal/793kJ; Protein 7.5g; Carbohydrate 34.6g, of which sugars 16.4g; Fat 3.1g, of which saturates 0.4g; Cholesterol 1mg; Calcium 137mg; Fibre 5.5g; Sodium 51mg.

Highland coffee

A good Highland coffee should be served in a tall wine glass with a 300ml/½ pint/1¼ cup capacity. The coffee should be freshly made and very hot. The whisky needs to be a Highland or Island malt, such as Dalwhinnie or Laphroaig.

1 Pour the whisky into the glass and add the sugar. Stir thoroughly.

2 Make a pot of fresh coffee and whilst it is still piping hot pour it into the glass with the whisky and sugar. Stand a spoon in the glass to stop it from cracking. Leave about 2cm/¾in at the top, and stir to dissolve the sugar.

3 Using a teaspoon with its tip just touching the coffee gently pour the lightly whipped cream over the coffee until it reaches the top of the glass. Serve immediately.

Serves 1

30ml/2 tbsp malt whisky

5ml/1 tsp soft light brown sugar

hot black coffee

50ml/2fl oz/¼ cup double (heavy) cream, lightly whipped

Cook's Tips
• If the cream doesn't float well on top of the coffee, then the balance of coffee and sugar is not correct. Add a little bit more sugar, which will make the coffee more dense and the cream more likely to float.
• Use filter coffee or coffee made in a cafetière (press pot) for the best results.

Per portion Energy 83kcal/341kJ; Protein 0.2g; Carbohydrate 1.3g, of which sugars 1.3g; Fat 6.7g, of which saturates 4.2g; Cholesterol 17mg; Calcium 7mg; Fibre 0g; Sodium 3mg.

Het pint

Meaning "hot pint" this is traditionally drunk at Hogmanay, with vendors in the street calling out to punters to try some. It is ideal for the night-long festivities, being both warming and sustaining with the addition of eggs which also provides a rich texture.

Makes about 3 litres/5 pints

1.2 litres/2 pints/5 cups lemonade

1.2 litres/2 pints/5 cups dark beer

5ml/1 tsp ground nutmeg

75g/3oz/⅓ cup caster (superfine) sugar

3 eggs

300ml/½ pint/1¼ cups whisky

3 Whisk the eggs in a bowl and very slowly, while still beating, pour in a couple of ladlefuls of the hot mixture.

4 Gently return the egg mixture to the main pan, whisking to make sure it does not form lumps or curdle by getting too hot around the edges.

5 Add the whisky slowly, stirring continuously, and heat though to just below boiling point. Serve immediately by ladling the liquid into pint glasses (or tall glasses if you prefer) until it reaches the top. Hand it round to all the company and drink a hearty toast to Hogmanay.

1 Put the lemonade and beer into a large heavy pan over a low heat.

2 Add the nutmeg and heat gently to just below boiling point. Add the sugar and stir to dissolve.

Cook's Tip
This drink will only keep for a day or so, and it is better to drink it piping hot as soon as it's made. If you do want to store it, keep it in an airtight bottle.

Per portion Energy 425kcal/1888kJ; Protein 5.7g; Carbohydrate 43.6g, of which sugars 43.6g; Fat 4.2g, of which saturates 1.2g; Cholesterol 143mg; Calcium 70mg; Fibre 0g; Sodium 93mg.

Prince Charlie's coffee

Bonnie Prince Charlie gave the recipe for Drambuie to the MacKinnon family, and it is now used to make this luxurious after-dinner coffee.

Serves 1

30ml/2 tbsp Drambuie

5ml/1 tsp soft light brown sugar

hot black coffee

50ml/2fl oz/¼ cup double (heavy) cream, lightly whipped

1 Pour the Drambuie into a tall wine glass with a 300ml/½ pint/1¼ cup capacity (as for the Highland Coffee). Add the sugar and stir thoroughly until completely dissolved.

2 Make a fresh pot of piping hot coffee – it is preferable to use either filter coffee or coffee made in a cafetière (press pot). It is also best to use a good, smooth coffee. Make it quite strong, although you don't want to smother the taste of the Drambuie completely.

3 Pour the hot coffee into the glass, leaving 2cm/¾in at the top, and stir.

4 Using a teaspoon with its tip just touching the coffee pour the lightly whipped cream over the coffee until it reaches the top of the glass.

Per portion Energy 90kcal/371kJ; Protein 0.2g; Carbohydrate 3.1g, of which sugars 3.1g; Fat 6.7g, of which saturates 4.2g; Cholesterol 17mg; Calcium 7mg; Fibre 0g; Sodium 3mg.

Glasgow punch

Over the last few centuries, the Glaswegians enjoyed the rum that came over from the Caribbean with the sugar shipments. A number of drinks and cocktails were invented using rum as the base, the Glasgow punch being a favourite.

Makes 1.5 litres/3 pints

900ml/1½ pints/3¾ cups water

200g/6oz/scant 1 cup dark brown muscovado (molasses) sugar

1 orange

1 lemon

300ml/½ pint/1¼ cups rum

1 Put the water into a pan over a medium heat. Add the sugar and stir in thoroughly, then allow the water to come to a boil. Boil rapidly to reduce the quantity by about half. Set aside to cool completely.

2 Remove the rinds from the orange and lemon with a zester or a fine grater, avoiding the pith.

3 Pour the rum into a mixing bowl and add the rinds of the lemon and orange, reserving the fruit. Cover and leave to infuse overnight.

4 Squeeze the juice from the orange and lemon, then strain. Add to the bowl with the rum. Stir to mix, then strain the mixture to remove the rind.

5 Add the boiled water and sugar to taste and then bottle the punch. Drink the punch hot.

Per batch Energy 1474kcal/6206kJ; Protein 1.4g; Carbohydrate 214g, of which sugars 214g; Fat 0.1g, of which saturates 0g; Cholesterol 0mg; Calcium 113mg; Fibre 0.1g; Sodium 17mg.

Atholl brose

This is the perfect celebratory drink, with plenty of alcohol and enough "sustenance" to keep you going through a long night of drinking and dancing.

Serves 4

200g/7oz/2 cups medium rolled oats

150ml/¼ pint/⅔ cup water

115g/4oz/½ cup heather honey

900ml/1½ pints/3¾ cups Highland or Island whisky

1 Place the rolled oats in a small bowl with the water and leave for 1 hour, then stir to make a paste.

2 Press the rolled oats complete with the soaking water through a sieve into a large mixing bowl. Add the heather honey and mix thoroughly until completely combined.

3 Pour in the whisky a little at a time, stirring it in completely before adding more. Finally, stir well then pour into small whisky glasses. Keep the drink in bottles and shake well before use.

Per batch Energy 3006kcal/12559kJ; Protein 25.2g; Carbohydrate 229.6g, of which sugars 84g; Fat 17.4g, of which saturates 0g; Cholesterol 0mg; Calcium 116mg; Fibre 13.6g; Sodium 78mg.

Brammle kir

The French Kir and Kir Royale are made with Burgundian Chardonnay and sparkling wine respectively, mixed with cassis. This delicious Scottish version uses either white or sparkling wine mixed with Brammle, a whisky liqueur made with blackberries. Serve as an aperitif.

Serves 1

30ml/2 tbsp Brammle liqueur

dry white wine, such as
Chardonnay or Sauvignon
Blanc, chilled

Variation
For a special occasion, make a Brammle Royale by replacing the white wine with chilled Champagne or fizzy wine.

1 Pour the liqueur into the bottom of a large wine glass.

2 Top up to within 2cm/¾in of the top with the chilled white wine. Enjoy!

Per portion Energy 244kcal/1017kJ; Protein 0.3g; Carbohydrate 11.3g, of which sugars 11.3g; Fat 0g, of which saturates 0g; Cholesterol 0mg; Calcium 24mg; Fibre 0g; Sodium 14mg.

Index

A

Aberdeen 26, 34
Aberdeen Angus 7
    Angus pasties 143
Aberdeen crullas 13
Aboyne Highland Games 31
Act of Proscription 10–11
Agricultural Revolution 15
agriculture 18, 19, 20
Albert, Prince 17
ale 16, 33
    beef stew with oysters and
        Belhaven beer 150–1
Alexander, Duke of Gordon 24
all-in-the-pot beef stew 152
almonds 217
    Dundee cake 62, 227
    raspberry and almond
        tart 210
Angus fruit cake 63
Angus pasties 143
ankerstoek 61
apples 8, 53
    Auld Alliance apple
        tart 211
    black pudding with potato
        and apple 76
    haggis, potato and apple
        tart 142
apricots
    rabbit with apricots 176
Arbroath smokies 6, 7, 26
    smoked haddock pâté 105
asparagus
    asparagus with lime butter
        dip 94
    dressed crab with
        asparagus 100
    saddle of rabbit with
        asparagus 175
Atholl brose 31, 250
Auld Alliance 6, 12, 213
    Auld Alliance apple
        tart 211
Auld Man's Milk 10
Auld Reekie plum cake 63
avocado, spinach and sorrel
    soup 85

B

Ba' game 30
bacon 67
    cabbage with bacon 188
    king scallops with bacon 114
    laver bread and bacon
        omelette 77
    queenies with smoked
        Ayrshire bacon 115
    smoked haddock and
        bacon 74
bagpipes 11
baked salmon with watercress
    sauce 122–3
baked tomatoes with mint 193
bakers 12

Balmoral 16, 17
Balmoral cake 63
bannocks 10, 15, 30, 60
    bere bannocks 19, 219
    Selkirk bannock 7, 61
    traditional bannock 218
baps 60–1
    Scottish morning rolls 220
barley 6, 8, 59
    grilled loin of lamb with
        barley risotto 154
    Scotch broth 91
Beaker People 8
beans 8
beef 6, 7, 10, 48, 139
    all-in-the pot beef stew 152
    Angus pasties 143
    beef stew with oysters and
        Belhaven beer 150–1
    beef with chanterelle
        mushrooms 148
    collops of beef with
        shallots 145
    Dundee beef stew 149
    fillet steak with pickled
        walnut sauce 144
    Lorn sausage with red onion
        relish 79
    roast fillet of beef with wild
        garlic hollandaise 146–7
beetroot and crowdie with roast
    hare 177
Benbecula 20
bere bannocks 19, 217
berries 6, 7, 8, 14, 16, 52–3,
    197, 231
    bramble jam 232
    cranberry and red onion
        relish 238
    Dunfillan bramble
        pudding 203
    summer pudding 202
Bishop Kennedy 51
    quail's egg salad with Bishop
        Kennedy cheese 195
black bun 30, 62, 224–5
black pudding 49, 67
    black pudding with potato
        and apple 76
Black Watch 11
blackberries 52
    bramble jam 232

Dunfillan bramble
    pudding 203
blackcurrant tart 211
blackhouses 15
blewits 54
boar 6, 45
    loin of wild boar with
        bog myrtle 178–9
bog butter 14
bog myrtle 133
    loin of wild boar with
        bog myrtle 178–9
Bonnie Prince Charlie 11, 12
Borders 6
    Border tart 209
Braemar Highland Games 31
braised farm pigeon with
    elderberry wine 170
braised red cabbage 189
braised shoulder of lamb with
    dulse 155
bramble jam 232
Bramble kir 251
breads 6, 60–1, 215
    rowies 67, 70
    Scottish morning rolls 220
Bridge of Allan 33
Bronze Age 8
broonie 19
Burns, Robert 24
    Burns Night 30–1, 33
butter 14, 15, 50
    asparagus with lime butter
        dip 94
    langoustines with garlic
        butter 98
    plaice fillets with sorrel and
        lemon butter 130
    salmon with herb butter 124
    scone and butter
        pudding 207
buttermilk 16, 19
buttermilk bread 61
button mushrooms 54

C

cabbage 8, 9, 56, 181
    braised red cabbage 189
    cabbage and potato soup
        with caraway 84
    cabbage with bacon 188
    kailkenny 184
    spiced greens 185
caboc 51
Caesar's mushrooms 54
cafés 13
Cairnsmore 51
cakes 62–3, 215
    Dundee cake 7, 62,
        215, 227
    Glamis walnut and date
        cake 63, 229
    Hogmanay cake 62, 224–5
Campbells 10
caraway 19, 63

cabbage and potato soup
    with caraway 84
carrots 57, 181
celeriac purée 191
Celts 8–9, 18, 20, 30–1
ceps 54, 55
chanterelles 54, 55
    beef with chanterelle
        mushrooms 148
chard 181
    rabbit salad with ruby
        chard 174
cheese 7, 14, 15, 19, 21,
    50–1, 93
    grilled squid with tomato and
        Strathdon Blue salsa 120
    Lanark Blue and walnut
        salad 95
    quail's egg salad with Bishop
        Kennedy cheese 195
    roast hare with beetroot and
        crowdie 177
    smoked haddock and cheese
        omelette 73
    watercress salad with pear and
        Dunsyre Blue dressing 194
cherries 8
chicken 163
    chicken and mushroom
        pie 166–7
    chicken with summer
        vegetables and tarragon 168
    hunter's chicken 165
    stoved chicken 164
chocolate
    malt whisky truffles 215
Christmas 18, 31
chutney
    chunky pear and walnut
        chutney 239
    tomato chutney 240
Ciao Italia 13
clams 43, 111
    clam stovies 112
clan system 10–11, 14
clapshot 182
    haggis with clapshot
        cake 140–1
clootie dumpling 30, 62,
    63, 226
cockles 43, 111
cod 18, 37

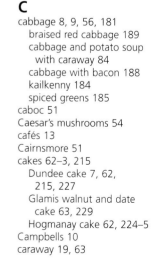

gratin of cod with wholegrain
mustard 134
coffee
Highland coffee 246
Prince Charlie's coffee 248–9
collops of beef with shallots 145
collops of venison with rowan
sauce 156
cookies 13
coulibiac 126–7
crabs 42, 111
dressed crab with
asparagus 100
hot crab soufflés 101
shore crab soup 90
cranachan 30, 198, 199
cranachan smoothie 245
cranberry and red onion relish 238
crayfish 42
cream 14, 15, 16, 19, 50, 193
creamed leeks 192
creamy scrambled eggs with
smoked salmon 75
East Neuk lobster with
wholegrain mustard and
cream 116–17
grilled lobster with tarragon
cream 118–19
iced cranachan 199
pan-fried pheasant with
oatmeal and cream
sauce 172
rhubarb fool 200
scones with jam and
cream 222
spiced creamed parsnip soup
with sherry 82
strawberry cream
shortbreads 201
whisky mac cream 214
crofting 15–16
crowdie 50–1
roast hare with beetroot and
crowdie 177
crustaceans 42
crusted garlic and wild thyme
monkfish 133
Cullen skink 87
Culloden 10, 11, 12, 14
Cumming, Helen 24
cured foods 8–9, 19, 26–7

D
dairy products 14, 15,
50–1, 197
damson jam 233
date and walnut cake 229
deer horns 63
Denmark 9, 18
desserts 12, 197
Dewar, Tommy 25
Donalds 10
Douglas, Robbie 61
Drambuie 12
Prince Charlie's coffee 248–9
dressed crab with
asparagus 100
dried fruit 6, 215
black bun 62, 224
Border tart 209
clootie dumpling 30, 62,
63, 208
Dundee cake 227
rabbit with apricots 176
tea loaf 228
traditional bannock 218
dried mushrooms 55
drop scones 223
Druids 8
Drumloch 51
Dublin Bay prawns 35, 42, 111
duck 46, 163
mallard pâté 108
dulse 155
Dundee beef stew 149
Dundee cake 7, 62, 217, 227
Dunfillan bramble pudding 203
Dunsyre Blue 51
watercress salad with pear
and Dunsyre Blue
dressing 194
Dutch East India Company 13

E
East Neuk lobster with
wholegrain mustard and
cream 116–17
Edinburgh 7, 14
Edinburgh Festival Fringe 30, 31
Edinburgh International
Festival 30, 31
Edinburgh Rock 7, 23
eggedosis 9

eggs 10, 67, 163
coulibiac 126–7
creamy scrambled eggs with
smoked salmon 75
het pint 30, 247
iced cranachan 199
kedgeree 71
laver bread and bacon
omelette 77
pale smoked haddock
flan 136–7
quail's egg salad
with Bishop Kennedy
cheese 195
smoked haddock and cheese
omelette 73
smoked haddock with
spinach and poached
eggs 72
whisky mac cream 212
Eigg 18
elderberries 53
elderberry wine 170
elderflower drink 244
emigration 11
Errington, Humphrey 95

F
fadge 61
Fair Isle 18
Fair Maid of Perth 10
feasts and festivals 30–1
fennel and mussel bree 88
Ferguson, Sandy 23
field mushrooms 54
Fife 7
fillet steak with pickled
walnut sauce 144
fish 6, 7, 8, 9, 13, 18,
38–9, 93, 111
baked salmon with
watercress sauce 122–3
coulibiac 126–7
creamy scrambled eggs
with smoked salmon 75
crusted garlic and wild
thyme monkfish 133
Cullen skink 87
fish and chips 13
flaky smoked salmon with
warm new potatoes 121
gratin of cod with
wholegrain mustard 134
haddock and smoked salmon
terrine 106–7
halibut with leek and
ginger 132
herrings in oatmeal 128
kedgeree 71
mackerel with gooseberry
relish 129
marinated smoked haddock
fillets 104
pale smoked haddock
flan 136–7

plaice fillets with sorrel and
lemon butter 130
quenelles of soles 131
rocket soup with kiln smoked
salmon 86
salmon fish cakes 125
salmon with herb butter 124
sea trout mousse 103
smoked fish 40–1, 67
smoked haddock and
bacon 74
smoked haddock and
cheese omelette 73
smoked haddock pâté 105
smoked haddock with
spinach and poached eggs 72
west coast fisherman's
stew 135
fishing 17, 18–19, 22, 23
flaky smoked salmon with
warm new potatoes 121
Flockhart, Mrs 23
Forfar Bridies 7

France 6, 12, 211, 215
Francis II 12
fricadellans 9
fruit 6, 8, 14, 15, 16, 52–3,
217, 231
scone and fresh fruit
pudding 206
summer pudding 202

G
Gaelic 18, 19, 20, 21
Galloway 7
game 6, 7, 14, 44–7, 93, 163
gaming estates 16–17
garden jam 236
garlic 57
crusted garlic and wild thyme
monkfish 133
langoustines with garlic
butter 98
roast fillet of beef with wild
garlic hollandaise 146–7
smoked venison with garlic
mashed potatoes 160
Gigha 51
Gigha Pear and Gigha
Orange 51

ginger and leek with
   halibut 132
gingerbread 19
Gladstone, William 60–1
Glamis walnut and date
   cake 63, 229
Glasgow punch 248–9
Glorious Twelfth 17
goats 6
goose 26, 46, 163
gooseberries 53
   mackerel with gooseberry
      relish 129

gratin of cod with wholegrain
   mustard 134
Greeks 8
Green Stenton 12
grey partridge with lentils and
   sausage 171
griddles 69
grilled lobster with tarragon
   cream 118–19
grilled loin of lamb with barley
   risotto 154
grilled oysters with highland
   heather honey 99
grilled squid with tomato and
   Strathdon Blue salsa 120
grouse 6, 47
   roast young grouse 169
guga 21

H
haddock 6, 37, 38, 40, 111
   Cullen skink 87
   haddock and smoked salmon
      terrine 106–7
   kedgeree 71
   marinated smoked haddock
      fillets 104
   pale smoked haddock
      flan 136–7
   smoked haddock and
      bacon 74
   smoked haddock and
      cheese omelette 73
   smoked haddock pâté 105
   smoked haddock with
      spinach and poached eggs 72
haggis 7, 49
   Burns Night 30–1, 33
   haggis, potato and apple
      tart 142
   haggis with clapshot cake
      140–1
halibut 41

halibut with leek and
   ginger 132
Hallowe'en 30–1
hare 6, 45
   roast hare with beetroot and
      crowdie 177
Harris 18, 21
Harvest Festival 30, 199
Hebrides 9, 18, 20–1
herbs 6, 8, 15
   baked tomatoes with
      mint 193
   chicken with summer
      vegetables and tarragon 168
   crusted garlic and wild thyme
      monkfish 133
   grilled lobster with tarragon
      cream 118–19
   salmon with herb butter 124
herring 9, 38–9, 41
   herrings in oatmeal 128
het pint 30, 247
highland coffee 246
Highlands 14–15
   clan system 10–11
   Highland Clearances 11, 15
   Highland Games 11, 30–1
Hlodvisson, Sigurd 31
Hogmanay 30
honey 9, 14, 16, 63
   cranachan smoothie 245
   grilled oysters with highland
      heather honey 99
   walnut and honey tart 210
hospitality 10
hot crab soufflés 101
hotch potch 12
hunter's chicken 165
hunting 16–17

I
ice creams 6, 7, 13, 19
iced cranachan 199
Inverloch 51
Iona 20
Ireland 8
Iron Age 8
Islands 18–21
Islay 7, 18, 20
Isle of Mull cheese 51
Italy 13

J
Jacobite Rebellions 10, 11
James V 12
jams 6, 53, 67, 217, 231
   bramble jam 232
   damson jam 233
   garden jam 236
   raspberry jam 234
   scones with jam and
      cream 222
jellies 53, 217, 231
Jerusalem artichoke broth with
   king scallops 89
Jura 18

K
kailkenny 184
kale 14, 19, 56, 77, 181

kale with mustard dressing 187
   spiced asparagus kale 186
kedgeree 71
king scallops in Jerusalem
   artichoke broth 89
king scallops with bacon 114
Kintyre 20
kippers 6, 41
kir 251
Kirrie loaf 63

L
lamb 6, 48–9, 139
   braised shoulder of lamb with
      dulse 155
   grilled loin of lamb with
      barley risotto 154
   lamb's kidneys with a devil
      sauce 78
   mutton hotpot 153
   Scotch broth 91
Lanark Blue and walnut salad 95
langoustines 42, 93
   langoustines with garlic
      butter 98
   langoustines with saffron and
      tomato 96–7
laver bread and bacon
   omelette 77
leeks 14, 56
   creamed leeks 192
   halibut with leek and
      ginger 132
   leek and potato soup 83
   mussels with Musselburgh
      leeks 102
lemon butter 130
lentils and sausage with
   grey partridge 171
Lewis 18, 20, 21
ling 18–19
liver muggies 9
lobster 42, 111
   East Neuk lobster with
      wholegrain mustard and
      cream 116–17
   grilled lobster with tarragon
      cream 118–19
Loch Fyne 27, 35
   kippers 7
   shellfish 34, 42
loganberries 52
loin of wild boar with bog
   myrtle 178–9
Lorn sausage with red onion
   relish 79
Lowlands 6, 22–3, 50

M
Macdonald, Flora 11
MacGregor, Rob Roy 11
mackerel 37, 41
   mackerel with gooseberry
      relish 129
MacKinnons 12
mallard pâté 108
malt whisky truffles 215
marinated smoked haddock
   fillets 104
Marischal, Fifth Earl 26
marmalade 7, 35, 53, 67
   whisky marmalade 235
Mary of Guise 12
Mary Queen of Scots 12
mead 9
meat 8, 14–15, 19, 48–9,
   81, 139
meatballs 9
Mendelssohn, Felix 20
milk 14, 16, 50
   Auld Man's Milk 10
mint with baked tomatoes 193
Moffat toffee 7, 23
molluscs 43
monkfish 37
   crusted garlic and wild thyme
      monkfish 133
Montrose cake 63
morels 54
morning rolls 7
   Scottish morning rolls 220
mulberries 52
Mull 7, 20
Museum of Scotland,
   Edinburgh 14
mushrooms 6, 54–5
   beef with chanterelle
      mushrooms 148
   chicken and mushroom
      pie 166–7
   coulibiac 126–7
   mushroom sauce 241
   pheasant and wild mushroom
      ragoût 173
mussels 43, 111
   mussel and fennel bree 88
   mussels with Musselburgh
      leeks 102
   steamed mussels with spinach
      salsa 113
mustard
   East Neuk lobster with
      wholegrain mustard and
      cream 116–17

gratin of cod with wholegrain
mustard 134
sea kale with mustard
dressing 187
mutton 9, 16, 48–9
mutton hotpot 153

N

Netherlands 13
nettles 14, 56
New Year 30, 31
Northern Isles 9
Norway 9
Norway lobsters 42
nuts
chunky pear and walnut
chutney 239
Dundee cake 62, 227
fillet steak with pickled
walnut sauce 144
Glamis walnut and date
cake 63, 229
Lanark Blue and walnut
salad 95
raspberry and almond
tart 210
walnut and honey
tart 212

O

oats 6, 8, 15, 16, 19,
58–9, 67
Atholl brose 31, 250
clootie dumpling 30, 62,
63, 208
cranachan 30, 198
cranachan smoothie 245
herrings in
oatmeal 128
iced cranachan 199
oatmeal biscuits 219
pan-fried pheasant with
oatmeal and cream
sauce 172
plum crumble 205
rhubarb frushie 204
skirlie 183
onions 9, 14
collops of beef with
shallots 145
cranberry and red onion
relish 238
Lorn sausage with red onion
relish 79
organic food 7, 34, 35
Orkney 7, 8, 9, 18–19, 30

Orkney Farmhouse
cheese 51
oysters 43, 93, 111
beef stew with oysters and
Belhaven beer 150–1
grilled oysters with highland
heather honey 99

P

pale smoked haddock
flan 136–7
pampurdy 12
parsnips 181
spiced creamed parsnip soup
with sherry 82
partridge 47
grey partridge with lentils and
sausage 171
pears 8, 53
chunky pear and walnut
chutney 239
watercress salad with pear
and Dunsyre Blue
dressing 194
peas 8, 13
Peat Inn, Fife 115
pheasant 17, 46–7, 163
pan-fried pheasant with
oatmeal and cream
sauce 172
pheasant and wild mushroom
ragoût 173
Picts 8
pigeons 16, 47
braised farm pigeon with
elderberry wine 170
plaice fillets with sorrel and
lemon butter 130
Plockton 15
plum cake 62
plums 53
plum crumble 205
pollack 19
pork 9, 15, 139
porridge 10, 15, 67, 68
Portree plum cake 63
potatoes 7, 19, 57, 181
black pudding with potato
and apple 76
cabbage and potato soup
with caraway 84
clapshot 182
Cullen skink 87
flaky smoked salmon with
warm new potatoes 121
haggis, potato and apple
tart 142
haggis with clapshot
cake 140–1
kailkenny 184
leek and potato soup 83
pale smoked haddock
flan 136–7
potato cakes 69
smoked venison with garlic
mashed potatoes 160
poultry 163
preserves 53
Prince Charlie's coffee 248–9
puffballs 54–5

Q

quail's egg salad with Bishop
Kennedy cheese 195
queenies with smoked Ayrshire
bacon 115
quenelles of sole 131

R

rabbit 6, 45
rabbit salad with ruby
chard 174
rabbit with apricots 176
saddle of rabbit with
asparagus 175
raspberries 7, 197
cranachan 30, 198
cranachan smoothie 245
raspberry and almond
tart 210
raspberry jam 234
reested mutton 9
religion 20, 31
restaurants 6, 7, 13, 17
rhubarb fool 200
rhubarb frushie 204
Rhum 18
rice
kedgeree 71
roast fillet of beef with wild
garlic hollandaise 146–7
roast hare with beetroot and
crowdie 177
roast venison 157
roast young grouse 169
rocket 56–7
rocket soup with kiln-smoked
salmon 86
Romans 8
rosehips 53
Ross, John 12
rowanberries 53
rowan jelly 237
collops of venison with rowan
sauce 156
rowies 67, 70
Royal Highland Gathering 31
rum 248
Glasgow punch 248–9

S

saddle of rabbit with
asparagus 175
saffron
langoustines with saffron and
tomato 96–7
St George's mushrooms 54
St Kilda 20, 21
salmon 6, 7, 17, 19, 20, 21,
28–9, 93, 111
baked salmon with watercress
sauce 122–3
coulibiac 126–7
creamy scrambled eggs with
smoked salmon 75
flaky smoked salmon with
warm new potatoes 121
haddock and smoked salmon
terrine 106–7
rocket soup with kiln-smoked
salmon 86

salmon fish cakes 125
salmon with herb butter 124
sassermaet 19
sausage and lentils with grey
partridge 171
scallops 43
king scallops in Jerusalem
artichoke broth 89
king scallops with bacon 114
queenies with smoked
Ayrshire bacon 115
Scandinavia 6, 9
scones
scone and butter
pudding 207
scone and fresh fruit
pudding 206
scones with jam and
cream 222
Scotch broth 91
Scotland 34–3
Bronze Age 8
clan system 10–11
feasts and festivals 30–1
France 6, 12
Highlands 14–17
Iron Age 8
Islands 18–21
Italy 13
Lowlands 6, 22–3, 50
Netherlands 13
Stone Age 8
Vikings 6, 9, 18, 20, 33
whisky distilleries 24–5, 64–5
Scott, Sir Walter 10, 61
Scottish Cheddar 51
Scottish morning rolls 220
sea bass 37
sea trout mousse 103
seaweed 18, 21
braised shoulder of lamb with
dulse 155
laver bread and bacon
omelette 77
Selkirk bannock 7, 61
shellfish 7, 8, 18, 21, 42–3,
93, 111
beef stew with oysters and
Belhaven beer 150–1
clam stovies 112
dressed crab with
asparagus 100
East Neuk lobster with
wholegrain mustard and
cream 116–17

grilled lobster with tarragon
cream 118–19
grilled oysters with highland
heather honey 99
hot crab soufflés 101
Jerusalem artichoke broth
with king scallops 89
king scallops with bacon 114
langoustines with garlic
butter 98
langoustines with saffron and
tomato 96–7
mussel and fennel bree 88
mussels with Musselburgh
leeks 102
queenies with smoked
Ayrshire bacon 115
shore crab soup 90
steamed mussels with spinach
salsa 113
sherry
spiced creamed parsnip soup
with sherry 82
Shetlands 9, 18–19, 31
shore crab soup 90
shortbread 33, 226
strawberry cream
shortbreads 201
Sigurd the Stout 31
Skara Brae, Orkney 8
skirlie 183
Skye 12, 18, 20
Smith, George 24
smoked foods 26–7
smoked fish 40–1, 67
smoked haddock and bacon 74
smoked haddock and cheese
omelette 73
smoked haddock pâté 105
smoked haddock with spinach
and poached eggs 72
smoked venison with garlic
mashed potatoes 160
Solan goose (gannet) 21
sole quenelles 131
sorrel
avocado, spinach and sorrel
soup 85
plaice fillets with sorrel and
lemon butter 130
Spanish Armada 18
sparkling elderflower drink 244
speciality foods 7
spices 6
spiced asparagus kale 186
spiced creamed parsnip soup
with sherry 82
spiced greens 185

spinach 77, 181
avocado, spinach and sorrel
soup 85
smoked haddock with
spinach and poached
eggs 72
steamed mussels with spinach
salsa 113
sponge cakes 62–3
squid with tomato and
Strathdon Blue salsa 120
Staffa 20
steamed mussels with spinach
salsa 113
Stewart kings 11
Stone Age 8
stoved chicken 164
Strathdon Blue 51
grilled squid with tomato and
Strathdon Blue salsa 120
strawberries 53
strawberry and smoked
venison salad 109
strawberry cream
shortbreads 201
sugar 6, 22–3, 217
summer pudding 202
swedes 181
clapshot 182
sweeties 22–3, 217

T
take-aways 13
Talisker 20
tarragon
chicken with summer
vegetables and tarragon 168
grilled lobster with tarragon
cream 118–19
young vegetables with
tarragon 190
tartan 10, 11
Tayside 7
tea loaf 228
thyme 133
Tobermory cheese 51
Tobermory Mornish 51
Tobermory, Mull 7, 20
tomatoes
baked tomatoes with
mint 193
grilled squid with tomato and
Strathdon Blue salsa 120
langoustines with saffron and
tomato 96–7
tomato chutney 240
Torry Research Station,
Aberdeen 26

tourism 17, 34
traditional bannock 218
trout 6, 17, 37, 41, 111
sea trout mousse 103
turnips 7, 57, 181
clapshot 182
haggis with clapshot
cake 140–1
tweeds 21

U
Up-Helly-Aa 9, 31

V
vegetables 8, 14, 15, 56–7,
81, 181
spiced greens 185
venison 6, 9, 16, 17, 44, 139
collops of venison with rowan
sauce 156
roast venison 157
smoked venison with garlic
mashed potatoes 160
strawberry and smoked
venison salad 109
venison pie 158–9
venison stew 161
Victoria, Queen 11, 17, 31, 61
Vikings 6, 9, 18, 20, 33
vivda 9, 19

W
walnuts
chunky pear and walnut
chutney 239
fillet steak with pickled
walnut sauce 144
Glamis walnut and date
cake 63, 229
Lanark Blue and walnut
salad 95

walnut and honey
tart 212
watercress
baked salmon with
watercress sauce 122–3
watercress salad with pear
and Dunsyre Blue
dressing 194
west coast fisherman's
stew 139
Western Isles 19–20
whig 61
whipkull 9, 31
whisky 7, 10, 16, 20, 243
Atholl brose 31, 250
distilleries 24–5, 64–5
het pint 30, 247
Highland coffee 246
malt whisky
truffles 215
scone and butter
pudding 207
whisky mac cream 214
whisky marmalade 235
Wilson, David 115
wine 6, 33
braised farm pigeon with
elderberry wine 170
bramble kir 251
woodcock 17, 47

Y
yogurt 193
cranachan 30, 198
cranachan smoothie 245
Young Pretender 11
Young vegetables with
tarragon 190
Yule 9, 18, 311

Publisher's Acknowledgements
All pictures © Anness Publishing Ltd, except where the
publisher would like to thank the following picture
agencies and photographers for use of their images:
Alamy Images: jacket. Arbroath Fisheries: p26 (bottom).
Balvenie Distillery: p7 (bottom), p24 (bottom), p25 (top).
Glenfiddich: p10 (bottom), p20 (top), p24 (top), p64
(top), and p65 (bottom). Glenmorangie: p25 (bottom).
Loch Fyne Fisheries: p14 (top), p18 (top), p21, p23
(bottom), p27 (bottom), p34 (top and bottom), p35 (top),
p40 (top), p42 (bottom). MacSween of Edinburgh:
p11 (top), p31 (top), p49 (bottom). Rannock Smokeries:
p27 (top right). Scottish Viewpoint: p7 (top), p8 (top and
bottom), p9 (bottom), p12 (top and bottom), p13 (top
and bottom), p15 (top and bottom), p16 (top and
bottom), p17, p19, p22 (bottom), p28 (bottom), p27 (top
and bottom) p31 (bottom), p32 (bottom), p33 (top and
bottom), p35 (bottom), and p38 (bottom). Uig Lodge
Smoked Salmon, murdojohnsmith@gmail.com: p26 (top).
VisitScotland.com: p11 (bottom), p30, p32 (top).